OCEAN

Barents Sea

FINLAND

U.S.S.R.

Bering Sea

E. GERMANY
W. GERMANY
POLAND
CZECHOSLOVAKIA
AUSTRIA
HUNGARY
YUGOSLAVIA
ROMANIA — BULGARIA

Sea of Okhotsk

Aral Sea

MONGOLIA

N. KOREA

Black Sea

Caspian Sea

AFGHANISTAN

Sea of Japan

JAPAN

TURKEY
SYRIA
CYPRUS
LEBANON

CHINA
PEOPLES REP.

S. KOREA

Sea

IRAQ

IRAN

PAKISTAN

NEPAL   BHUTAN

PACIFIC OCEAN

ISRAEL

JORDAN
KUWAIT
QATAR

The Gulf

BANGLADESH

TAIWAN

EGYPT

SAUDI
ARABIA

U.A.
EMIRATES

OMAN

Arabian Sea

INDIA

LAOS

BURMA

HONG KONG

Red Sea

Bay of Bengal

THAILAND

SUDAN

Gulf of Aden

VIETNAM

PHILIPPINES

CENTRAL
AFRICAN
REP.

S. YEMEN
N. YEMEN

KAMPUCHEA

BRUNEI

ETHIOPIA

DJIBOUTI

MALAYSIA

GANDA

SOMALIA

SRI LANKA

PAPUA
NEW GUINEA

ANDA
RUNDI
ZAIRE

KENYA

INDIAN OCEAN

SINGAPORE

TANZANIA

INDONESIA

MALAWI

FIJI

MOZAMBIQUE

ZAMBIA

MADAGASCAR

AUSTRALIA

SWAZILAND

UTH
RICA

LESOTHO

Tasman Sea

NEW
ZEALAND

T·O·W·A·R·D·S T·O·M·O·R·R·O·W

Canada in a Changing World
Geography

STEWART DUNLOP

HBJ

Harcourt Brace Jovanovich, Canada

TORONTO • ORLANDO • SAN DIEGO • LONDON • SYDNEY

Canadian Cataloguing in Publication Data

Dunlop, Stewart.
    Towards tomorrow: Canada in a changing world—geography

For use in high schools.
Includes index.
ISBN 0-7747-1256-2

1. Anthropo-geography.   2. Geography.   I. Title.

GF41.D86 1987   910   C87-093780-4

    93 94 95   9 8 7 6

Design: Robert Garbutt
Composition: Trigraph Inc.
Printed and bound in Canada by
McLaren Morris & Todd Ltd.

Cover photograph: John de Visser Photographer Ltd.

TABLE OF CONTENTS

ACKNOWLEDGEMENTS

The publishers would be pleased to have any omissions or errors in the following acknowledgements brought to their attention.

Cartoons: Page 14 Geoffrey Dickinson, The Financial Times; page 80 The Toronto Star Syndicate; page 140 Hilary Scannel, Third World First; page 154 East Bay Municipal Utility District, California; the poster on page 16 is reproduced by kind permission of Ducks Unlimited and Canadian Tire Corp.

Figures: Those figures for which a source is not given are based upon information prepared by the author. The following individuals, however, provided help and information with specific figures: Donald MacDonald (Figures 3.6 and 5.12); Ian MacIver (Figures 4.9 and 4.10); and Jean Forbes (Figures 6.16 and 7.11).

Photographs

Introduction: IDRC.

Chapter 1: Canapress Photo Service: 3, 5 (bottom), and 12; Chip and Rosa Peterson: 4, 11, and 13; Image Bank: 5 (top), and 15; Bill Ivy: 6; SSC-Photocentre: 8.

Chapter 2: Birgitte Nielsen: 19; John de Visser: 21, 38, and 46; Dick Hemingway: 22; Image Bank: 24, 41, 43, 44, 48, and 50; UNICEF: 27, 31, and 33; Chip and Rosa Peterson: 34; Canapress Photo Service: 36; Daniel Vanderlugt: 49.

Chapter 3: UNICEF: 55 (left) 69, 70, and 72; Stewart Dunlop: 55 (right); Chip and Rosa Peterson: 59 (top), and 66; Dick Hemingway: 59 (bottom); Image Bank: 61, 65, 67, and 70; John de Visser: 62 (left); Stewart Dunlop: 62 (right); Canapress Photo Service: 73, and 74.

Chapter 4: UNICEF: 77, 86, 87, and 102; Canapress Photo Service: 82, 89, 90, 91, and 93; Canadian Centre for Remote Sensing: 83; Image Bank: 95, 103, 105, and 106; Chip and Rosa Peterson: pages 96, 99, and 110; John de Visser: 97, and 108; CIDA: 101.

Chapter 5: Dick Hemingway: 113; Image Bank: 114, 115, 117, 125, 127, 135 (top), 138, 139, 141, 143, 147, 155, and 156; SSC-Photocentre: 116, and 131; DRIE: 119; John de Visser: 121, 135 (bottom), and 149; Canapress Photo Service: 123, 136, 144, and 146; Chip and Rosa Peterson: 132, 133, and 137; John de Visser: 149; Stewart Dunlop: 151, and 153.

Chapter 6: DRIE: 159, 191, and 193; Bettmann Archives Inc.: 162; Image Bank: 163, 167, 168, 169, 171, 195, and 199; Alcan Aluminium Limited: 165; General Motors Corp.: 172; Canapress Photo Service: 174, 177, and 201; Daniel Vanderlugt: 175, and 179; IDRC: 181 (left), and 183; Chip and Rosa Peterson: 181 (right); and 186; Stewart Dunlop: 189, and 194; NASA: 197; John de Visser: 200.

Chapter 7: SSC-Photocentre: 205 (left), and 233; Image Bank: 205 (right); John de Visser: 206, 228, 242, and 243; Stewart Dunlop: 208, 210, 211, 223, 225 (top), 229, 234, and 248; Chip and Rosa Peterson: 212, 213 (left), 214, 216, 217, 218, and 220; Margaret Gwilliam: 213 (right); Dick Hemingway: 225, 238, and 239; Government of B.C.: 231, and 237.

Chapter 8: UNICEF: 251, 256, 259, 261, 262 (top), 267, 269; CIDA: 253, 254, and 271; Fotolex: 262 (bottom); Chip and Rosa Peterson: 264; Canapress Photo Service: 268; Operation Eyesight: 272.

CANADA

WORLD POPULATION
POPULATION MONDIALE

5.000.000.000 PERSONS
PERSONNES

1.568.938.717 HECTARES

TERRE ARABLE DISPONIBLE
REMAINING ARABLE LAND

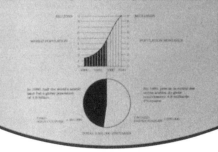

In the lobby of the International Development Research Centre in Ottawa stands a clock—with a difference. This clock does not measure the passing of time. Instead, it keeps track of two things: the growth of the Earth's population, and the loss of crop land worldwide. Every minute, the clock records another 156 people; every hour, over 9000 more; every day, another 225 000—equal to the population of Victoria, British Columbia. It also shows that, every 14 s, another hectare of the world's crop land is lost to urban use or soil erosion.

Population growth is one of the major issues affecting the future of the world. The global population has been rising rapidly and is expected to do so for several decades. The world's people have very different standards of living, whether these standards are measured by income or by some other measure such as health or access to a good water supply. In 1980, 2 thousand million people had no safe water to drink, and 3 thousand million had no sanitation. Food is another major human need. Efforts to increase the food supply and prevent famine have been given wide publicity in recent years.

A growing population brings with it an increased demand for other resources in addition to safe water and food. People have to be housed, clothed, and kept warm, as well as fed. The use people make of resources involves the level of technology of a society—a major theme of this book. Changes in technology are profoundly affecting not only industry but also the way people live. Technology lies behind what is perhaps the most important of today's population trends: the rapid growth of cities. These major global trends produce problems, both economic and environmental, which people must solve. Only a limited number of the problems appear to have simple solutions. Most of them are very complex and must be tackled on a global scale.

To draw valid conclusions about major world issues, it is necessary to be well informed about them. In this book you will find the information you need in order to approach the issues in a sensitive way. During class discussions, many points of view are likely to emerge. Your own views will be influenced by your political, religious, and/or ethical background—but this will be true for everyone else as well. It is important to recognize and consider different points of view. But ultimately you will make up your own mind and form your own opinions about the issues under discussion. At the same time, it is to be hoped that you will be ready to revise these views as you continue to learn and reflect. The world offers new challenges each day, and all of us are faced with finding new solutions to diverse new problems.

The Resource Clock at the IDRC, Ottawa. On July 11, 1987, the world's population reached five billion (based on UN statistics).

CHAPTER 1

The Global Village

The elderly lady was on an Air Canada flight from Winnipeg to Edmonton. She had made the trip west across the prairies often. Her first journey, more than 60 years earlier, had taken several days by train and horse-drawn wagon to the bleak quarter section she and her husband had come from Europe to farm. Exchanging letters with her family in "the old country" took eight weeks in each direction.

During the flight, the pilot announced, "We're experiencing severe headwinds, so we expect to arrive in Edmonton about ten minutes late." The grey-haired lady turned to a fellow passenger and asked, "How in the world can something travelling at 800 km an hour be late?"

In her lifetime, the elderly pioneer had seen the speed of travel increase by a factor of several hundred. She'd lived to see the day when she could communicate instantly with relatives half a world away.

In this chapter, you will look at how these two technological factors—transportation and communication—have affected the way people see the world. You will also consider the idea that more is needed than just technology to form a global community. Finally, you will explore the concept of a single world community further, in light of three elements of the world—the physical world, the biological world, and the economic world. As you read through the chapter, keep the following questions in mind.

- *A common expression is, "It's a small world." In what ways is this becoming increasingly evident?*

- *Why can actions taken in one part of the world affect people living across the globe?*

- *Why are conservation and resource management important to a rapidly growing world population?*

2

Global Attitudes

Canada is an enormous country. If you have ever travelled by land—or even air—from one end of it to the other, you were likely impressed by its size. Yet Canada is only part of a much larger world, most of which is far from you in distance and even farther in experience.

The size of the world produces different reactions in different people. Many Canadians spend their lives close to home, among familiar people and places. It may be difficult for some people to relate to starving families in drought-stricken areas, who may not even seem to be part of the same world. Other people, on the contrary, feel close to and identify with people and events around the globe. This attitude often results from the immediacy of radio and television news which, in combination with other modern communication methods and air travel, has made the world seem a smaller place. People with this attitude feel a sense of responsibility as citizens of this smaller world.

Taking part in public demonstrations such as this Vancouver march for peace is one way for individuals to try to change global attitudes.

Why would some people consider the presence of a McDonald's restaurant in Japan to be an indication that the world is losing its cultural diversity?

Our Shrinking World: Communications

Some years ago, the Canadian writer and educator Marshall McLuhan coined a very apt and descriptive phrase: "the global village". It summed up McLuhan's observation that modern communications have created such a mass of widely available information that the world's many different ways of life are being blended into one. The worldwide popularity of the products of such companies as McDonalds and Coca-Cola supports his viewpoint. The American films and television programs seen in many countries are further evidence for it.

Whether or not you agree with McLuhan's claim, the powerful role of the media in bringing the world closer together can be seen in many aspects of modern life. It certainly affects you personally. Several years ago, a study found that North American teenagers spent an average of 15 000 hours watching television during their high school years. Today the figure may be less, if only because many teenagers spend so much time at computer keyboards. Add to this the time you spend on the telephone, and you will see just how many of your waking hours could well be devoted to communications.

The main agent which has changed our world into a global village is the widespread use of communications satellites. Satellites have made it possible for vast amounts of information to travel around the globe at the speed of light. Today, television can bring live pictures by satellite from almost any part of the world into Canadian homes. Satellites also transmit vast quantities of verbal and numerical information in business applications. In addition, they are used by telephone companies for international calls. All these communication methods contribute to making the world seem a smaller place.

As satellite communications become increasingly widespread, national boundaries may have less and less significance. Goods can be stopped and checked at national borders. Information beamed by satellite recognizes no such barriers (though it is possible to jam signals to prevent them from being received). This disregard of boundaries between countries also helps make the world into a global village.

Our Shrinking World: Modern Transportation

Another factor contributing to the process of shaping the world into a global village is modern transportation. The journey from London, England to Vancouver, B. C. takes about nine hours today (non-stop by jet). At the start of this century, the same journey would have taken two or three weeks by sea and another week by rail. A few years before that, the pioneers took months to cross the continent by horse and wagon and on foot.

A dramatic development in flight is the trans-Atlantic crossing of the Concorde, which takes only about three hours. Since the time difference between London, England and eastern Canada is five hours, the westbound Concorde traveller arrives two hours local time before leaving!

Canadians see such rapid travel as reducing the size of the world. It is a common human tendency to measure distance in terms of travelling time. Also, many Canadians have travelled by air or expect to do so. But

Using animals as beasts of burden is a traditional transportation method throughout the world.

The Concorde's unique profile indicates that it is a supersonic aircraft—the first commercial supersonic jet. How has the emphasis on fast transportation created a smaller world?

Developed and Less Developed Countries

Developed countries are industrialized and have a high or relatively high per capita *income. Less developed countries (sometimes referred to as "developing countries") are highly dependent on agriculture and have a low* per capita *income. The two terms will be discussed more fully in Chapter 3.*

keep in mind that most people do not travel by airplane. About half of the world's population still journey on foot or in wagons drawn by animals. Some may have a bicycle, or use a bus. For people in **less developed countries**, the world has shrunk very little.

It is impossible to predict whether improvements in transportation will be as dramatic in the next half century as in the last. Whatever these improvements turn out to be, it is likely that they will reinforce the concept of the world as a global village.

QUESTIONS

1. What is meant by "the media"? List as many types of media as you can.

2. Explain what is meant by the expression "the global village".

3. Why has the world shrunk less for people living in less developed countries?

One World

Explain why an aquarium is a simple example of a system.

Modern communications and transportation are not by themselves enough to create a sense of the world as a global village. In every age there have been people who have shown a practical concern for the needs of others. This remains true today. From Mother Teresa to the rock stars who organized the Live Aid concert, people have given of their resources to help those in need in their own country and beyond. Such actions are a recognition of the fact that, since people inhabit a single planet, they have responsibilities to each other.

Thus, the world may be regarded as a single, though complex, system. A **system** can be defined as a set of elements which interact with each other in a particular way. An aquarium is a simple example of a system. Oxygen and fish food must be added to the water to maintain life, and, from time to time, waste must be removed. A change in any element of the system—temperature, oxygen, or food—is enough to upset the delicate balance necessary to keep the fish alive.

The World as a System

The concept of a system applies to many elements of the world. In the rest of this chapter, you will be examining three elements in light of this concept: the physical world, the biological world, and the economic world. As you read, keep in mind two important points. First, each of these elements of the global system is also a system in itself. Second, none of these smaller systems is wholly independent. Just as a person interacted with the aquarium, people interact with the physical world and the biological world. The various systems also interact with each other to produce that single, complex system—the Earth.

One Physical World

The physical elements of the world—air, wind, waterways, precipitation, soils, and so on—are just one part of the vast system we call the Earth. In turn, the physical world itself consists of smaller systems. For example, the climate, soils, and drainage patterns of the Canadian tundra form one distinct system. The same elements of the coastal rainforests of British Columbia form another. As in the aquarium system, it is necessary to avoid changing any element in a way that is likely to affect any of the others negatively. For instance, you can see in Figure 1.1 that cutting down trees exposes the soil beneath to rainfall and wind. The unprotected soil erodes easily, and its erosion leads to changes in river flows and **groundwater** levels. This system has been disrupted by human action.

FIGURE 1.1   *After deforestation and extensive erosion, why is it difficult for a forest to regenerate itself?*

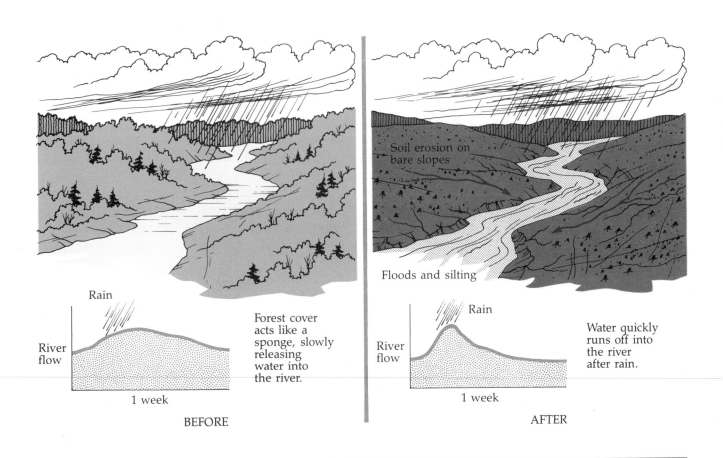

Rain

River flow

1 week

BEFORE

Forest cover acts like a sponge, slowly releasing water into the river.

Soil erosion on bare slopes

Floods and silting

Rain

River flow

1 week

AFTER

Water quickly runs off into the river after rain.

Tall smokestacks such as this one in Sudbury, Ontario were designed to protect local communities from polluted air. Some environmentalists claim, however, that these smokestacks pollute distant communities. How can this occur?

Many examples of environmental problems such as floods, soil erosion, and air and water pollution can be found not only in Canada, but also throughout the world. As you read above, certain elements of the environment can be affected by human beings. However, there are some elements of the physical world over which people have no control. Examples are the cycling of air and water. The wind blows and the rain falls where they will; the physical environment has no boundaries. Consider the scene in the photograph of Sudbury. A tall smokestack such as this one may solve the problem of polluted air in the immediate vicinity. However, the gases emitted remain in the atmosphere and are carried great distances by the wind. Spreading the pollution does not eliminate the problem. Instead, the gases accumulate until whole nations are affected. Much of eastern Canada's **acid rain** is a result of the concentration of power stations and heavy industry across the border in the United States.

Like the wind and rain, the ocean currents cannot be controlled by people. Therefore, any pollutants discharged accidentally or deliberately into the oceans will affect wildlife—and people—far beyond the area originally polluted. Oil spills, for example, can spread for thousands of kilometres along coastlines, and kill sea birds and other marine life. The effects of heavy metals such as mercury are slower but equally deadly. Small ocean creatures absorb the mercury. Larger creatures eat many of the smaller ones, so the degree of contamination in them is greater. Eventually, people who eat contaminated fish and shellfish take in a very high concentration of the mercury, which damages the brain and the nervous system.

Perhaps the worst case of environmental pollution would be a major nuclear disaster anywhere on the planet. It would not be long—a matter of days—before air and water circulation carried the fallout around the globe. The accident that occurred at Chernobyl in the U.S.S.R. in April, 1986 created serious radioactive contamination in parts of Europe and Asia (Figure 1.2). Crops, milk, and other agricultural products had to be destroyed and food imported. The longer-term effects of the disaster will not be known for years.

In short, harm experienced by any element of the physical world will have either local or widespread consequences. The other elements of the system will be affected—as will other systems, including the biological world.

FIGURE 1.2 *The areas affected by radioactive dust from the Chernobyl accident of 1986. Wind circulation rapidly carried the dust as far away as Iceland. Scientists are predicting that new effects of the disaster may be surfacing over a period of years.*

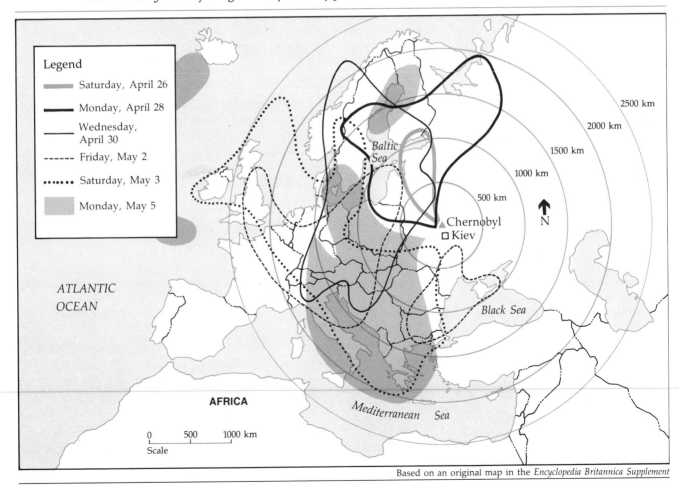

Based on an original map in the *Encyclopedia Britannica Supplement*

CLOSE-UP

Acid Rain

Acid rain (and acid snow) are caused by the emission of certain gases, mainly sulphur dioxide and nitrogen oxides, from vehicle exhausts, homes, factories, and power stations (Figure 1.3). Up to 50 percent of the emissions falls locally in dry form. About 30 percent is contained in the local precipitation, and the rest can travel for hundreds of kilometres to create problems for other areas.

The effects of acid rain are becoming more widespread and alarming. Trees in the maple forests of Quebec are dying, and some people are predicting the end of the maple syrup industry. Germany's Black Forest is also suffering the loss of many trees. Numerous lakes in Scandinavia and Canada have become acidic and cannot support fish and other life. The stonework of many of Europe's historic buildings has been eroded, and the stained glass windows have been damaged by acid rain. It is estimated that acid rain causes 50 percent of all car corrosion in Canada. Canada has been negotiating with the United States to achieve a joint solution to the problem of the industrial emissions which cause acid rain.

FIGURE 1.3   *Acid rain—where it comes from, where it goes. How does the U.S.—Canada acid rain problem show the interdependence of our two nations?*

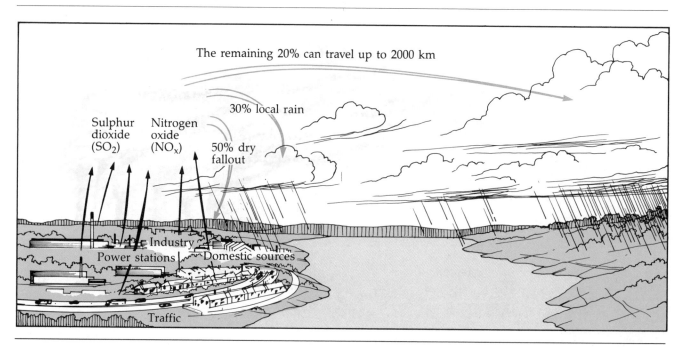

QUESTIONS

1. (a) What is a system?
   (b) Some of the elements of the physical world are air, wind, and water. Name three other elements of this system.

2. (a) What is acid rain? What causes acid rain?
   (b) Why is it a problem?

3. (a) Do you think an agreement between Canada and the United States will solve all of the two nations' acid rain problems?
   (b) Why is it so difficult to solve such environmental problems?

One Biological World

When a certain element of a physical system is altered, other elements of that system experience a change as well. The effects are also felt by trees, birds, fish, and people. These are not considered elements of the physical world, but rather of the biological world. The elements of the biological world, like those of the physical, make up a system. Again like the physical world, the biological world can be seen as many smaller systems.

The biological world contains an enormous variety of plant and animal life. Human beings certainly did not produce this rich variety; indeed, people have done much to reduce the list of species. The Great Auk and the passenger pigeon, for example, are extinct, and only about two dozen California condors, the world's largest birds, survive. It is estimated that at least one species of plant or animal becomes extinct every day somewhere in the world. Some conservation agencies predict that, by the turn of the century, this figure will increase to one species per minute. No nation has a monopoly on plant and animal life. Great efforts are required to ensure the survival of endangered species. For some species, such efforts have been made—and have succeeded. The whooping crane, the Hawaiian goose, and the European and

In the past, farmers all over the globe were encouraged to clear land to grow crops. Why, then, are present-day farmers criticized for clearing the rainforests?

American bison are just four species which have been saved from extinction by wise conservation practices.

One of the worst contemporary examples of human interaction with the biological world is the destruction of the tropical rainforests of Central and South America. The recent increase in the rate at which these forests are being cleared is the result of several factors. One of them is the need of the farmers in these regions for farm land. Another is the growth of fast-food outlets in Canada and the United States. As these chains spread, meat suppliers have increasingly looked for less expensive sources of beef.

To help supply this demand for beef, Central American governments have provided loans for people wishing to start cattle ranches. Rural families have found that they can make more money by producing as few as two calves a year than by growing crops. Thus, large areas of the rainforests have been cleared for the grazing of cattle. This new industry does have benefits. The ranchers gain income; consumers can buy cheaper beef products; and many thousands of people in North America can earn a living in the fast-food industry. But the price to be paid for these gains is the destruction of large areas of tropical forest.

Why is the destruction of the rainforests a cause for concern? First, it is important that the world should not lose the enormous reservoir of plant genes which the tropical forests provide. The danger of losing rare species of plant life is particularly great in these forests, where many species have not yet been studied and classified. Some could prove to be of great benefit as sources of new types of food or medicine, for example.

The second concern raised by the destruction of rainforests is that farm land and overgrazed pastures are easily eroded if the soil is exposed to violent tropical rainstorms and the fierce heat of the Sun.

Gene Pool

Genes are the parts of the cell which transfer the characteristics of plants and animals from one generation to the next. The term "gene pool" refers to the total number of genes within any group of plants or animals. The tropical forests are a valuable reservoir of plant genes, since they contain the greatest diversity of vegetable life on this planet. The protection of gene pools is important not only in forestry but also in agriculture, since plants with new characteristics provided by new genes may be required by plant breeders to protect crops against new forms of disease.

Some environmentalists claim that in taking a bite from a hamburger, you might also be taking a bite from a rainforest. What is the link between hamburgers and rainforests?

What appeared to be rich soil under the canopy of tropical forest may end up as infertile wasteland. Robert Goodland of the World Bank sums up the seriousness of this deforestation as follows: "If a tropical forest is cut, 80 percent of the nutrients are gone for ever. They are washed out to sea. The forest will not come back....I would like to firmly dispel the notion that tropical deforestation is useful. It is not. At most, it gains three harvests for a peasant before he is compelled by declining yields and increasing waste to move on and cut another patch of forest. Even at that level, he can barely survive."

The third concern is less immediately obvious. The Smithsonian Institute in Washington, D.C. has estimated that, since the clearing of the rainforests began, 4 percent fewer migrating birds return annually to the United States after wintering in Central America. This decrease is caused by the steady destruction of their winter habitat. Since a breeding pair of birds can consume 10 000 insects per day, it is easy to see why farmers and gardeners in North America are suffering increased insect damage to their crops.

Finally, the forests of the hot, wet tropics are thought to play an important role in recycling the Earth's oxygen supply. In the process of making food for themselves, plants also produce oxygen. Some experts think that cutting down a substantial number of oxygen-producing trees could reduce the world's oxygen supply, and seriously threaten our atmosphere. Tropical forests are being destroyed at a faster rate than any other type of natural vegetation. An area of rainforest almost half the size of Nova Scotia is being destroyed or badly damaged each year. The destruction of the tropical forests is regarded by environmentalists and other concerned people as one of the most serious threats to the world's environment today.

The rainforest provides many valuable resources, such as latex from rubber trees.

One Economic World

Earlier in this book it was said that the world is a single complex system having various elements. You have seen that two of the elements you have examined, the physical world and the biological world, are interdependent. While reading about the fate of the rainforests, you likely noticed at least one other element of the world which is interdependent with both of these: the economic world. Why are the rainforests being destroyed? Farmers require land for growing crops. Ranchers need land on which to graze cattle. At least some of the crops and the cattle are intended for sale. Thus, they are part of the economic world. In economic terms, the farmers and ranchers are the producers, while the people who buy the crops and cattle are the consumers.

The needs and actions of consumers frequently affect the lives of people who live on the other side of the globe. You have just seen one example of this. Another is the fashion trends of Europe which for decades affected the lives of seal hunters in Newfoundland by creating a demand for seal furs. In the early 1980's, consumer action in the form of a boycott reduced this demand and virtually ended the seal fur industry.

The changing value of a country's currency can also affect the lives of its people. Much of the coal produced in British Columbia is exported to Japan, mainly for use in the Japanese steel industry. Australia also exports coal to Japan. An increase in the value of the Canadian dollar in relation to the Australian dollar makes our coal more expensive than Australian coal. In this case, the Japanese are more likely to buy coal from Australia than from Canada. Employment in British Columbia's coal mining communities would be seriously affected by this situation. A fall in the value of our dollar relative to the other currency could, of course, produce the opposite effect.

Even seemingly trivial matters can have serious unforeseen consequences. Take the example of frogs' legs. The consumption of frogs' legs has rapidly increased in the homes and restaurants of Europe and the United States. Several hundred million frogs' legs a year are exported from Indonesia and Bangladesh to meet the demand. India used to be one of the largest exporters until 1987, when it banned the export of frogs' legs. The popularity of the delicacy has led to some unexpected results in the exporting countries.

Frogs play an important role in the environment, since they eat mosquitoes and other pests which spread malaria or attack crops. Because there is now a shortage of frogs, farmers in the exporting countries are finding it increasingly necessary to use pesticides, including DDT, to control the growing insect population. Pesticides, like heavy metals, tend to build up in the bodies of animals. (DDT is particularly dangerous in this regard and has been banned in Canada.) Thus there is a danger that frog flesh may become increasingly affected by chemical residues. The World Wildlife Fund has mounted a campaign to "let the frogs keep their legs".

Very few of those who dine on frogs' legs in France and other consuming countries have any idea of the effects of their taste for this dish. Perhaps you can think of other examples in which the demand for products affects the lives of people in unexpected ways.

"He told me he was worth $3 a kilo in Europe and I never saw him again"

Resource Conservation and Management

One of the most important economic issues that people must face is the question of how to strike a balance between *consuming* our limited resources now, and *conserving* them for future generations. This question applies particularly to mineral and energy resources, which are in limited supply and cannot be renewed. Petroleum is particularly scarce; some economists and scientists fear that only a 50-year supply may remain. If we consume more than our rightful share of such resources as petroleum, future generations will blame us for squandering the Earth's limited wealth. On the other hand, it is necessary to make some use of the resources at hand, in order to provide the goods and services which the world's present population needs or demands. Governments and companies continually make decisions as to how

How might planned forests such as this one protect the future of the biological world?

resources should be managed. For example, the decision to tax oil, and therefore raise its price, is one way to conserve this limited resource. As the price rises, people will tend to consume less of the product.

The world's forest resources represent an area in which good management is urgently needed. In less developed countries throughout the world, forests have been severely depleted. However, attempts to manage forest resources have been introduced in places such as Nepal. Community groups have been involved in replanting and caring for trees—a practice sometimes referred to as "social forestry". Good forest management in mountainous Nepal could pay off in the form of reduced flooding in Bangladesh. Figure 1.1 should help you to see why.

Here in Canada, the policy is to replant logged areas to achieve what is called **sustained yield management**. When properly carried out, this policy ensures that the volume of timber cut is balanced by new growth. The policy is an excellent one, but some critics of forestry in Canada claim that it has not been adequately carried out.

It is easy to blame governments for failing to solve problems and plan for the future. But the responsibility really lies with all people, as consumers. If people are unmindful of the future, governments are unlikely to devote the necessary time and resources to ensuring sound, thoughtful planning. If, on the other hand, every individual cares about the future of the world, governments will come to reflect that concern.

QUESTIONS

1. In what sense is a forest an example of a system?

2. How does deforestation upset the system of vegetation, soil, and water shown in Figure 1.1?

3. If people are aware of the problems caused by deforestation, as well as of how to solve them, why do these problems continue?

Chapter Summary

In this chapter it has been suggested that modern communications and transportation have made the world seem to be a smaller place. Nevertheless, the world must accommodate ever-larger numbers of people. As a result, it is essential to view the Earth as a single community. Irrespective of their national backgrounds, people are fellow citizens of the global village.

Human beings interact with all the various elements of the world, including the physical and biological environments. Many problems can arise in the delicate systems which make up the Earth. One of them, acid rain, is at the present time a major threat to industrial regions such as eastern North America and western Europe. Other problems may become even more serious in the future; for example, the cutting down of the tropical forests not only causes immediate problems but may also have long-term consequences which are not yet fully clear. Finally, economic systems are easily upset by political events, changes in currency values, or even consumer behaviour. To avoid a disruption of any or all of these systems, good decision-making, wise management, and careful conservation of resources are essential.

IN REVIEW

1. (a) How have improvements in transportation and communications helped to create a global village?
   (b) What are some consequences of this trend toward a smaller, interdependent world?

2. (a) Name some ways in which people pollute the world's oceans.
   (b) Why can these problems not be limited to one area?
   (c) What measures can be taken to control the pollution of bodies of water?

3. Give examples of how demands made by consumers can affect the lives of people in other areas of the world and the environments in which they live.

APPLYING YOUR KNOWLEDGE

1. "People today are not making sufficiently sure that the world of the future will have a safe environment and an adequate supply of resources." Do you agree or disagree with this statement? Give your reasons.

2. (a) What could an individual do to reduce pollution?
   (b) What pollution control measures could a community undertake?
   (c) What types of pollution control measures would require national action?

3. With which of the media do you spend the most time? Has your usage of the media changed over the past five years? Do you anticipate any changes in your usage patterns in the next five years?

FURTHER INVESTIGATION

1. Calculate how long it would take you to cross Canada (a) on foot; (b) by bicycle; and (c) by car. Compare your answers with the time for travelling by jet.

2. Do research to find as many examples as possible of the effects of acid rain.

3. Find out what restrictions are placed on industries in your area to reduce pollution.

CHAPTER 2

World Population

At some point in 1987, the world's population reached 5 thousand million. It has continued to grow at an annual rate of 82 million—over three times the entire population of Canada! The fact that countries with a high rate of population growth inevitably have a large number of young people normally leads to even more population growth in the future. The breaking of this upward spiral is a major challenge facing the human race. Today— perhaps for the first time—there are signs that population stability might be achieved late in the 21st century. However, this goal can be reached only if the present trend in western countries in favour of smaller families spreads to all parts of the world. By the time the goal is achieved, world population will have at least doubled from present levels.

In this chapter, you will examine not only the major issue of stabilizing world population growth, but also the details of how a country's population is made up, how long its people are likely to live, and what actions its government might take to influence population trends. Finally, you will look at the overall distribution of the world's people, noting the tendency of people to favour urban rather than rural living. Here are a few of the questions which you will explore in this chapter:

* *What measurements are used to study the world's growing population?*

* *Why does the rate of population growth vary from country to country?*

* *Can the world's population be stabilized? If so, at what level?*

* *How is the world's growing population distributed?*

Counting People

It may be a little difficult for Canadians to realize why a rapidly increasing population is widely regarded as a world problem. In this vast country, there are, on average, only two people for every square kilometre. A short visit to Bangladesh or the Republic of Singapore would soon show you how much space Canadians really have. Bangladesh, a country dominated by farming, has a **population density** of 640 persons per square kilometre. Singapore, which is almost entirely urban, has over 4000 people per square kilometre. The population in

How might a high rate of population growth affect living conditions in high density areas, such as this section of Hong Kong?

FIGURE 2.1 *World Population Growth*

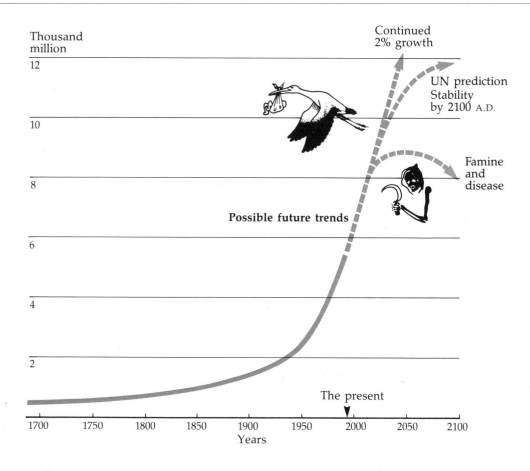

Possible future trends

both these places is growing much more quickly than Canada's. If a rapid population growth rate is indeed a problem, can it be stabilized at a level which the Earth can sustain?

Figure 2.1 shows some projections of world population growth. You may wonder which of these possibilities is most likely to happen, and what this means for the future of the human race.

The study of population numbers is known as **demography.** To quote a former United States representative to the United Nations, Daniel P. Moynihan: "There is simply nothing so important to a people and its government as to know how many of them there are, whether their number is growing or declining, how they are distributed between different ages, sexes and different social classes and racial and ethnic groups, and again, which way these numbers are moving. . . ."

Governments have many reasons for wanting information about

their people. Developing social facilities such as schools, hospitals, and roads takes years, and governments must be able to plan ahead. Information about how many people there are, where they live, what they do for a living, and many other factors helps governments predict the needs of the population. To finance their expenditures, governments raise money by taxation; therefore, they need information about earning and spending habits. Private businesses also use population trends in deciding where to locate, for the sake of both obtaining a labour force and reaching a market. Finally, social scientists use the same information to deal with various social problems. For example, they may analyze the occurrence of poverty in relation to age groups, occupations, and population density. The information they obtain from such studies can be of great help in solving various problems.

How might the percentage of a nation's population under the age of 18 affect government spending?

The Population Census

Most countries undertake a population **census**, a national count of population, at regular intervals. Canada has a major census every ten years (in years ending with the number "1"), and a minor one in the middle of the period (in years ending with a "6"). A population census is an attempt to obtain a complete record of basic facts about a country's people. These may be physical facts determined at birth, such as birthplace, age, and sex. A census may also record social facts, which are not determined at birth. Such information may include language spoken, the ability to read and write, the type of employment, and details about people's dwellings.

A census has its limitations. Despite its expense, it never gives a completely accurate count. The 1986 Canadian census, which recorded 25 675 200 people, probably undercounted the population by about 2 percent, while the 1970 United States population census probably failed to enumerate 5.3 million people (2.6 percent of the total). Many of the latter were poor people living in urban slums which the census enumerators either missed or ignored. One problem directly related to this omission is that the slum areas most needing financial help received less in *per capita* (per person) grants than they were entitled to.

Censuses are much less accurate in countries where poor communications and illiteracy are common. In parts of Africa and Asia, for instance, it is possible that up to one-third of all births and deaths may never be recorded. All statistics on population, including those published by the United Nations, must therefore be viewed with some caution.

Governments need information about what is happening to the population in the years between censuses as well. They get these facts

This button was part of the Canadian government's campaign to notify people of the 1986 census. Why do you think the government felt it was important to print their message in several languages?

by means of a second method of collecting demographic data—the collection of **vital statistics.**

Vital Statistics

In countries like Canada, departments of vital statistics record daily information on births, marriages, and deaths. As well, they keep statistics on **immigration**, the entry of new people into the country. Information on immigration is also available from registrations for Social Insurance Numbers, driver's licence applications, and family allowance payments. Statistics on **emigration**, the departure of people from the country, are much less accurate, since they have to be compiled from other countries' immigration records.

All these sources help in maintaining population estimates for individual years and even months between censuses. However, it is the major censuses that give the government the most accurate picture.

QUESTIONS

1. (a) What was the world population in 1785, 1885, and 1985?
   (b) How many times larger was the world population in 1985 than in 1785?
   (c) What trend is evident in these statistics for population growth?

2. Define the term "demography".

3. What are the limitations of a census?

4. Why might census figures be less accurate in a poor country?

Population Structure

The total number of people, and their ages and sex, are the most obvious facts about a population. Using these basic facts, it is possible to construct a simple but very informative diagram of a country's population commonly known as a **population pyramid.**

If you were to divide the population into age groups and then imagine the different groups lined up in sequence, with the youngest on the bottom and the older groups standing on the shoulders of the younger, you would get a figure which would look something like a pyramid. This figure would reveal at a glance how people of different ages were distributed through the population. If you were to divide the age groups into males and females, you could also see how many people of each sex there were in each age group. This kind of diagram would represent the **age-sex structure** of the population. Demographers frequently construct age-sex pyramids to help them analyze a country's population.

FIGURE 2.2   *Population Pyramid for Canada (1981)*

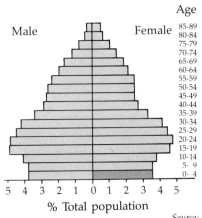

Source: Census of Canada

Figure 2.2 shows the age-sex structure of Canada's population in 1981. In this type of diagram, males are placed on the left, females on the right. Normally, five-year age groups (technically known as **cohorts**) are used, with a top category such as "85 and over". Each horizontal bar shows the percentage in a particular age group in relation to the total population. In Figure 2.2, for example, females aged 0 to 4 account for 3.6 percent of Canada's total population. The "baby boom", which is made up of people born between about 1945 and 1965, shows up clearly in the width of the graph for the 20 to 39 cohorts.

The dependency rate takes account of both young and old members of a nation's population.

The Dependency Ratio

One way to interpret a population pyramid is to calculate the **dependency ratio.** This figure is based on the assumption that neither the youngest nor the oldest people in a society work. They must therefore be supported by people of working age. Remember that senior citizens have put in a full working life and have earned the support they now receive. Nevertheless, a country with a high proportion of workers enjoys an economic advantage, since it has many people to create wealth, and relatively few who must be supported. A country in the opposite position is at a disadvantage, since it contains more dependants who must be supported with the wealth created by relatively fewer people of working age.

To calculate the dependency ratio, you need to find the percentage of total population of so-called "working age", usually taken as 15 to 64 years of age. Those who are younger and older are called "young dependants" and "old dependants" respectively. Note that, in fact, not all persons between 15 and 64 work, nor are all those outside that range dependent.

The dependency ratio is calculated as follows:

$$\frac{\text{Young dependants (\%)} + \text{Old dependants (\%)}}{\text{People of working age (\%)}} \times 100$$

If this is calculated for Canada using 1981 figures, you get $\frac{22.5 + 9.7}{67.8} \times 100 = 47.5$. That is, Canada had the relatively low figure of 47.5 dependants for every 100 people of working age. This is a much lower ratio than in many countries, which have large percentages of either children or old people. Canada's ratio will become less economically favourable as the population ages.

QUESTIONS

1. What is the purpose of a population pyramid?

2. Refer to the population pyramid for Canada (Figure 2.2). Compare the percentages of Canada's population which were females aged 25–29 and females aged 5–9. Comment on the future implications for Canada's population.

3. What does the dependency ratio measure?

Fertility and Mortality

The key factors in understanding population structure are fertility and mortality. **Fertility** deals with factors affecting the rate of reproduction of the human race, while **mortality** has to do with the death rate. The main measures of these two factors are the birth rate and the death rate, respectively.

Birth Rate

The **birth rate** measures the number of live births per thousand of population in one year. The formula can be expressed thus:

$$\frac{\text{Total live births}}{\text{Total population}} \times 1000$$

The multiplier of 1000 is used to avoid having to use decimal points (unless fine detail is required). Thus, Canada, with 377 031 births and a 1984 population of 25 124 100, had a birth rate of 15.0 per thousand.

General Fertility Rate

The birth rate (more properly the crude birth rate) measures births in relation to thousands of total population. The general fertility rate measures births in relation to thousands of women in the 15 to 44 age group. Thus, the formula for calculating the general fertility rate is

$$\frac{\text{Total live births}}{\text{Total women aged 15-44}} \times 1000$$

Canada's general fertility rate in 1981 was 58.4, contrasting with a figure of 136 for India. The general fertility rate will obviously be much higher than the crude birth rate. It is more meaningful, however, in that it eliminates the distortions which arise because of differences in the age-sex characteristics of populations.

Try the calculation yourself, using the following 1984 data:

Country	Births	Total Population
Mexico	*2 395 000*	*67 396 000*
Brazil	*2 770 000*	*118 675 000*
West Germany	*620 000*	*61 638 000*

Canada's birth rate would be less than 15.0 if it were not for the fact that so many Canadians are in the 20 to 39 age brackets. From a world map of birth rates (Figure 2.3), you can see that birth rates in Africa are approximately four times higher than those in Western Europe, where they have fallen steadily throughout this century.

FIGURE 2.3 *World Birth Rates. Are the birth rates of tropical nations generally higher or lower than those of nations in higher latitudes?*

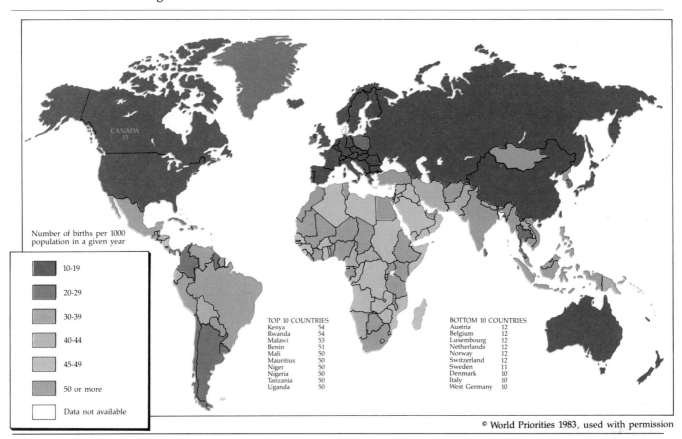

© World Priorities 1983, used with permission

Total Fertility Rate

In order to be more accurate when you talk about stabilizing the world birth rate, you need to consider another population measure. The **total fertility rate** is a measure of how many children the average woman

Organizations such as UNICEF provide medical treatment and childcare information to families throughout the world.

would have in her lifetime. The formula is fairly complicated, but the figure itself is easy to interpret. You might assume that a total fertility rate of 2 would be necessary for a population to replace itself in the long term. This is almost, but not quite, correct, since allowance has to be made for the few children who unfortunately do not survive to the reproductive ages. In North America, a total fertility rate of 2.1 is reckoned to be the level required for the population to replace itself in the long term. The figure would be higher in less developed countries, since more children would fail to survive to a reproductive age.

From Figure 2.4, you will notice that population replacement levels have not been achieved in Canada since 1972. The same is true for the United States and for most developed countries. This fact seems to indicate that Canada's population will decline in the future if the total fertility rate remains below 2.1. The reason that the population is not declining now is the disproportionately large number of Canadians in the 20 to 39 cohorts. The concentration of people in these age groups helps to keep the birth rate well above the death rate. Similar total fertility rates in the populations of Western Europe, which are proportionately older, have led to zero population growth, or even to slow decline, as in the case of West Germany.

By contrast, the total fertility rate is about 6 in many less developed countries. Mexico's has recently fallen from 6.5 to 4.5, indicating a reduction in the rate of population increase in that country.

FIGURE 2.4 *Canada's Total Fertility Rate. The replacement level refers to the total fertility rate necessary for a population to replace itself. In North America the replacement level is 2.1.*

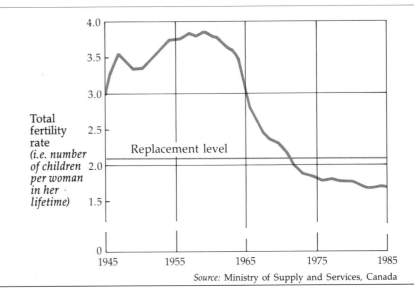

Source: Ministry of Supply and Services, Canada

Death Rate

The **death rate** measures the total number of deaths in a year per thousand of population. The formula can be stated in this form:

$$\frac{\text{Total deaths}}{\text{Total population}} \times 1000$$

Death rates throughout the world have been falling for many years. In less developed countries typical death rates are now around 16 per thousand. The death rate for Canada in 1984 was 7.0 per thousand.

Once again, try the calculation yourself, using the following 1984 data:

Country	Deaths	Total Population
Mexico	377 000	67 396 000
Brazil	809 000	118 675 000
West Germany	714 000	61 638 000

Age-Specific Death Rate

Like the birth rate, the death rate requires some refinement. Some populations have more older people than others. Since the probability of death increases with age, an older population would tend to have a higher death rate. Therefore, to compare the mortality of people in different countries, it is necessary to compare the death rate in a given age group. This figure is the **age-specific death rate.** It is calculated as follows (in this case, for the 60 to 64 cohort):

$$\frac{\text{Total deaths of people aged 60–64}}{\text{Total number of people aged 60–64}} \times 1000$$

FIGURE 2.5   *World Infant Mortality Rates. Compare this map with the map of world birth rates. Do countries of high birth rate usually have a high rate of infant mortality?*

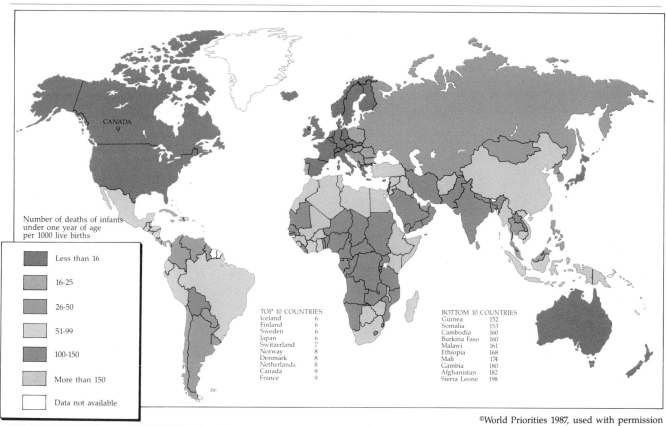

TOP 10 COUNTRIES
Iceland	6
Finland	6
Sweden	6
Japan	6
Switzerland	7
Norway	8
Denmark	8
Netherlands	8
Canada	9
France	9

BOTTOM 10 COUNTRIES
Guinea	152
Somalia	153
Cambodia	160
Burkina Faso	160
Malawi	161
Ethiopia	168
Mali	174
Gambia	180
Afghanistan	182
Sierra Leone	198

Number of deaths of infants under one year of age per 1000 live births

▉	Less than 16
▉	16-25
▉	26-50
▉	51-99
▉	100-150
▉	More than 150
☐	Data not available

CANADA 9

©World Priorities 1987, used with permission

Infant Mortality Rate

The death of a child is always tragic, but it is unfortunately a common event throughout the world. Young children under one year of age are far more vulnerable to disease and death than older children. This is true even in developed countries, but in less developed countries as many as one in five children do not survive the first year of life (Figure 2.5). Think of it like this. If you and your class had been born in a less developed country, at least a fifth of you would not have survived to your present age. The **infant mortality rate** is calculated thus:

$$\frac{\text{Total deaths of infants under 1 year}}{\text{Total live births}} \times 1000$$

Canada's infant mortality rate in 1985 was 8.1 per thousand. Finland had the lowest world figure, 6.5. By contrast, Sierra Leone in West Africa had an infant mortality rate of 180!

Life Expectancy

Life expectancy (the average lifespan of individuals) is much higher in developed countries. Life expectancy may be thought of as a kind of hurdle race in which each year's hurdle measures the probability of death. The course for western countries is a long one with many low hurdles, which gradually rise after the age of 50. Half the population in these countries would clear the hurdles until over 70. In the poorest countries the first hurdle is particularly difficult, but even thereafter the hurdles are higher than for western countries, and few people remain in the race after 50 years of age.

Life expectancy has been increasing in virtually all countries, as you can see in Figure 2.6. In most countries, women achieve three to four years more than the average, while men fall three to four years below it. As though to compensate for their shorter life expectancies, male babies normally outnumber females by about 5 percent throughout the world.

FIGURE 2.6   *Life Expectancies in Selected Countries*

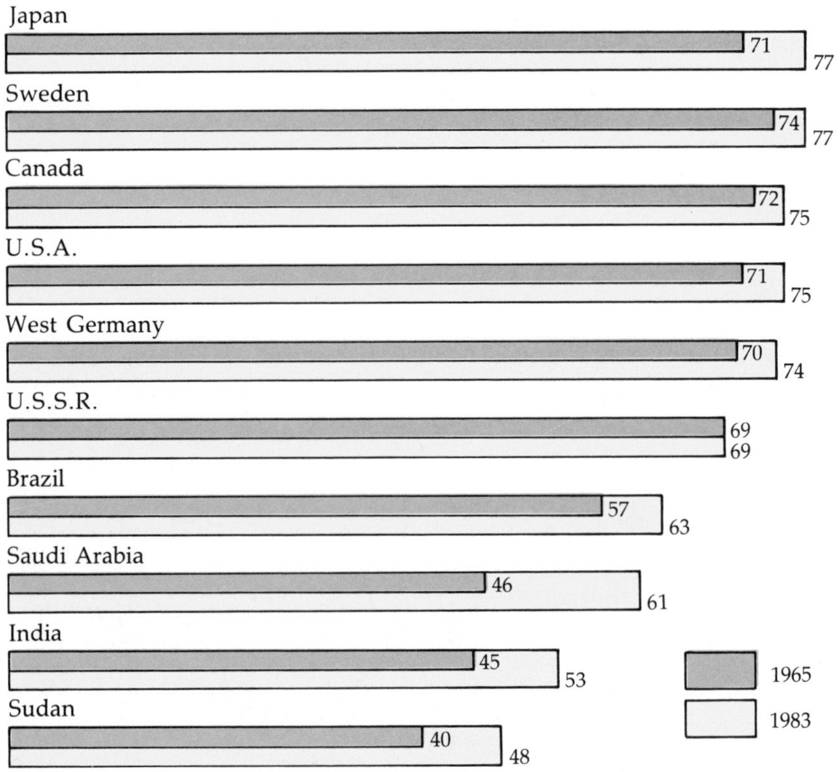

Country	1965	1983
Japan	71	77
Sweden	74	77
Canada	72	75
U.S.A.	71	75
West Germany	70	74
U.S.S.R.	69	69
Brazil	57	63
Saudi Arabia	46	61
India	45	53
Sudan	40	48

Source: World Bank Development Report 1986

QUESTIONS

1. (a) Which continent has the highest birth rate, and which has the lowest?
   (b) Using Figure 2.5, name the two continents which have the highest infant mortality rates.

2. What can you predict about the population of a country which has a total fertility rate of 5?

3. What changes in birth and death rates would have to occur to bring about changes in a country's total fertility rate?

4. Why do age-specific death rates make comparisons between areas or countries more reliable than the death rate by itself?

C L O S E - U P

The Child Survival Revolution

You saw in Figure 2.5 that deaths of infants under one year are all too common in the less developed world. According to the United Nations International Children's Emergency Fund (UNICEF), 15 million children under the age of five die every year throughout the world—40 000 every day.

Most of these deaths occur in poorer countries. The main cause of death is not some exotic tropical disease, but rather the acute **dehydration** (water loss) caused by diarrhea. The bodies of small

Children are especially vulnerable to death through dehydration. These children are being given oral rehydration salts to prevent dehydration caused by diarrhea.

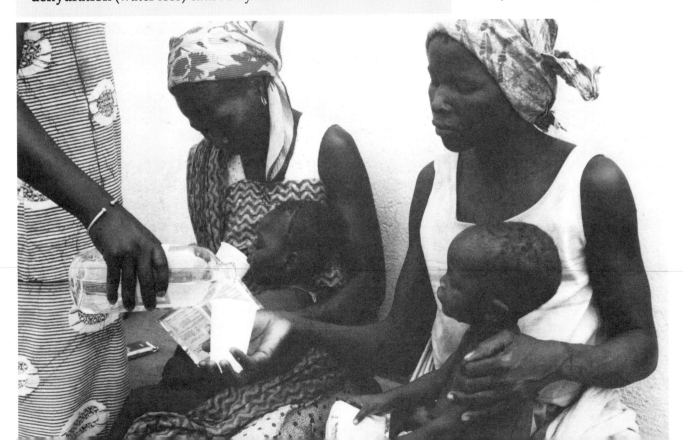

children cannot cope with a serious loss of fluids. In the early 1980's, five million children died each year from this cause alone. Other major causes of death were the common cold, and a group of diseases which can be successfully treated by immunization: measles, tetanus, tuberculosis, polio, diptheria, and whooping cough. Collectively, these diseases accounted for about four million deaths. Another leading cause of death was malnutrition, which can lead directly to death by starvation. You have seen this happening during the recent years of famine in Africa. More commonly, however, malnutrition contributes to death by weakening a child's resistance to the various infectious diseases.

A low-cost, but very effective, cure for diarrhea was first used in Bangladesh in 1971 and has been increasingly adopted throughout the less developed world. Known as **oral rehydration therapy (ORT),** it involves nothing more complicated than feeding a child (or adult) a solution of salt, sugar, and water. This solution prevents the acute dehydration which is the usual cause of death. The diarrhea itself usually goes away in a few days. The infant mortality rate in Bangladesh has been cut dramatically as a result of a nationwide program to educate families about oral rehydration therapy. Many other countries have followed suit, with great success.

Immunization against the other killer diseases is also spreading rapidly. In the early 1980's, UNICEF set the target of immunizing all the world's children by 1990. This is a gigantic task, but one which could be achieved at a cost lower than the sum spent annually on cigarette advertising worldwide. In 1985 the civil war in El Salvador was halted for three days with the agreement of both sides in order to immunize the children of that country.

A question may have occurred to you as you have been reading. If so many more children survive, will the problems associated with population growth not become even greater? This would certainly be the case if an emphasis on family planning did not accompany oral rehydration therapy. In fact, family planning measures have been put in place by many governments, with the encouragement of the United Nations Fund for Population Activities. It appears that the reduced infant mortality rate, coupled with education in family planning methods, is having some effect in reducing fertility rates in less developed countries. Since having a large number of children represents security for parents in their old age, families are likely to limit the number of births only when they see some hope for the future health of their children (Figure 2.7).

Oral Rehydration Therapy and Its Implementation

ORT has been called the "medical miracle of the 20th century." It is being used in many less developed countries, including Brazil, Egypt, Haiti, and El Salvador. In 1983, UNICEF launched a drive for child survival under the code name "GOBI," the initial letters of the following low-cost measures:

Growth monitoring (of the weight and health of infants)
Oral rehydration therapy
Breast feeding (as opposed to the use of formulas)
Immunization

The results of GOBI have been encouraging. By 1986 it was estimated that the world infant mortality rate had dropped by 22 percent since oral rehydration therapy began to be used. Also the total fertility rate is estimated to have fallen from approximately 7 to 5 in the areas of Bangladesh where ORT has been implemented.

FIGURE 2.7 *Effect of Future Family Size on World Population Growth.*

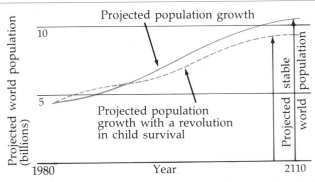

When people are more confident that their children will survive they tend to have only the number of children they actually want—one reason why there has never been a steep fall in birth rates. With a child survival revolution, total world population would eventually stabilize at a lower level and at an earlier date.

Source: UNICEF

Fertility and the Status of Women in Less Developed Countries

Many experts see the answer to the high birth rates in less developed countries as being closely related to the educational levels of women in these countries. Two-thirds of all women in less developed countries

Name two factors which you think influence the size of families in less developed nations.

The level of education is one factor that influences a nation's fertility rate.

are illiterate, almost twice the rate among men. It is claimed that an important factor in population control is to enhance the status of women, particularly through education. Improvements in the educational levels of women have almost always been followed by later marriage, fewer births with longer intervals between them, and better levels of nutrition and hygiene for the family (Figure 2.8).

FIGURE 2.8   *Improved Literacy Among Women. How does the education of women seem to affect the number of children born?*

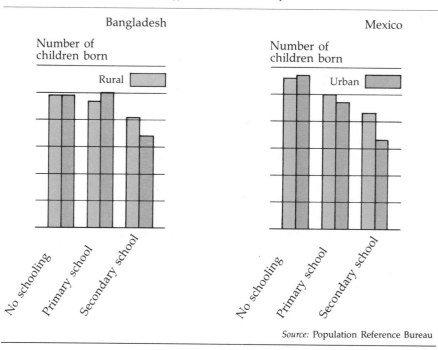

Source: Population Reference Bureau

QUESTIONS

1. List two factors that could (**a**) increase life expectancy and (**b**) reduce life expectancy in a country.

2. Using Figure 2.6, compare life expectancies in western countries, the U.S.S.R., and less developed countries. What might account for the differences?

3. (**a**) Define "ORT".
   (**b**) Explain how a reduction in infant mortality resulting from the use of ORT might help to decrease the world's population growth.

4. How can enhancing the status of women help promote population control?

Population Change

Having studied fertility and mortality, you can now link the two as follows:

Births − Deaths = Natural increase (actual numbers)
Birth rate − Death rate = Rate of natural increase (per thousand)

In Canada, the rate of natural increase is 15 − 7 = 8 per thousand. This rate is more frequently expressed as a percentage, in which case Canada's rate is 0.8 percent. This is much less than Kenya's 4.0 percent (birth rate 53 per thousand and death rate 13 per thousand). If deaths exceed births, the natural increase is of course a negative number; that is, there is a natural decrease.

Natural Increase: Doubling Time

When you see these rates of increase as percentages, they may not seem very alarming. The question you should ask yourself, however, is, "How long does it take the population to double, at a given percentage growth rate?" The following simple but fairly accurate formula enables you to work out the answer to this question.

$$\frac{70}{\% \text{ rate of growth of population}} = \frac{\text{number of years for population}}{\text{to double}}$$

This gives Canada a lengthy 87 years, assuming of course that the rate remains unchanged for the entire period. On the other hand, the population of a country with a 2 percent growth rate would double in 35 years; Kenya, with 4 percent, would double its population in a mere 18 years.

Table 2.1 is a summary of world birth and death rates by continents.

TABLE 2.1   *Population Data by Continent*

	Birth Rate (per 1000)	Death Rate (per 1000)	Natural Increase (percent)	Doubling Time (years)
Africa	45	16	2.9	24
Asia	28	10	1.8	39
North America	16	9	0.7	100
Latin America	31	8	2.3	30
Europe	13	10	0.3	233
U.S.S.R.	20	11	0.9	78
Oceania	21	9	1.2	58
World	28	11	1.7	41

People choosing to migrate to Canada are part of Canada's overall population growth.

Migration

Natural increase is not the only factor to be considered when computing population change. Many countries gain people by migration, and, obviously, other countries lose people. **Net migration** is found by subtracting the number of emigrants (people who leave a country) from the number of immigrants (people who enter a country). Like the natural increase of population, this number may be negative, in which case there is net emigration. **Total population change** in a country is therefore the sum of natural increase and net migration, as shown by this formula:

Population Change = Natural Increase + Net Migration
or (in more detail)
Population Change = (Births − Deaths) + (Immigration − Emigration)

Migration is an important factor in the population growth of many countries. The United States, like Canada, was built on immigration. Between 1830 and 1930, approximately 41 million people entered these countries, mainly from Europe. The migrants brought with them skills, a willingness to work, and in some cases capital (money). Today's **migrants** are usually young, ambitious people whose arrival brings many advantages to their new country. It is a different story for the countries from which the migrants come. Since migrants are usually fairly young, they leave their countries with a population whose age is older than average.

Both Canada and the United States have accepted many refugees. These differ from migrants in that they are normally fleeing from some form of persecution in their country of origin. For example, the unsuccessful Hungarian Revolution in 1956 led numerous refugees to the United States or Canada. Similarly, at the end of the Vietnam War in 1973 many Vietnamese refugees arrived in Western countries. For both political and humanitarian reasons, these communities (and others) have been welcomed into Canada and the United States.

The following Close-Up examines in more detail the outlook for Canada's population in light of these trends in natural increase and migration.

CLOSE-UP

The Prospects for Canada's Population

The trends in Canada's births and deaths in recent years are shown in Figure 2.9. You read above that Canada's rate of natural increase is 8 per thousand, or 0.8 percent per year. Now, with calculator in hand, start with 25 million in 1986, and multiply by 1.008 for each year after 1986. You should reach 30.27 million by

FIGURE 2.9 *The Prospects for Canada's Population*

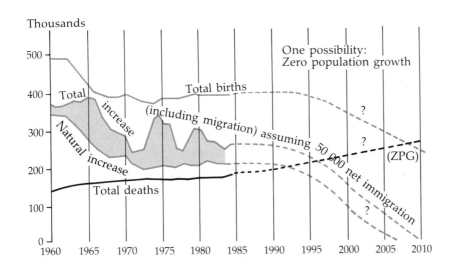

Source: Statistics Canada

the year 2010. Bear in mind that this growth rate does not allow for immigration.

Can it be assumed, however, that our population will go on increasing at the same rate? Look back at Figure 2.2, Canada's population pyramid. The present "bulge" of the people born in the baby boom years (who are now in their twenties and thirties) will by 2001 have moved four bars up the pyramid. The people having children in the year 2001 will be mainly those born in the late 1960's and 1970's—a much smaller group than the one that produced the baby boom. Should the present low fertility trend continue to 2001, the overall number of births in Canada would then fall substantially, as Figure 2.9 forecasts. On the other hand, the overall number of deaths will increase, as the number of Canadians in the older age brackets goes up. Many population forecasters predict that total deaths will overtake total births in Canada sometime around 2010. Canada will then experience a natural decrease of population, as West Germany is doing today.

How does all this affect *you*? After all, as a representative of the "baby bust" (post-baby boom) generation, you are a member of a relatively scarce group. One problem you will have to face as an adult is the rising cost of Canada's social services, especially those concerned with senior citizens. Higher pension contributions will have to be levied on those who are working to pay for the

Today's students are tomorrow's wage earners. It will be their responsibility to meet the cost of caring for an aging population.

increased number of pensioners in the future. Medical plans will also require higher premiums to meet the demands on medical services. There will be higher deductions from paycheques to pay for the costs of an aging population. Remember, however, that you hope to survive to enjoy these benefits yourself someday.

There are some other compensations to look forward to as well. The number of students graduating from high school each year between 1980 and 2000 is likely to be smaller than in the preceding year. This trend should mean reduced competition for jobs, although the job situation also depends on how technology affects the supply of jobs available—a subject dealt with in Chapter 6.

Finally, the decline in Canada's fertility rate raises the question of whether this country should relax control over immigration in order to prevent the population from decreasing in the 21st century. Much depends on whether total fertility rates remain low. Figure 2.9 suggests that more immigration will be required by the turn of the century. Some increase in immigration into Canada began in 1986.

Immigration should not be regarded as simply a matter of jobs. Immigrants create jobs as well as occupy them, since they spend the money they bring with them and earn, and thereby help to expand the economy. More important are the long-term factors of population size and age structure. Unless the fertility rate in Canada increases dramatically in the near future, immigration will certainly have to be encouraged if our country is to avoid an older-than-average age structure in the 21st century.

QUESTIONS

1. How is the rate of natural increase computed?

2. How could the doubling time for a country be lengthened?

3. What is meant by "net migration"?

4. What information would you need to determine the rate of growth of Canada's population?

The Demographic Transition Model

In your study of population so far, you have seen that countries at different levels of social and economic development have different population structures. Figure 2.10 suggests that there is a normal sequence of stages through which most countries pass as their living conditions improve. This graph shows a generalized model of population growth called the **demographic transition model.** A model is a simplified version of the way things work in the real world. Some countries have reached the final stage in the demographic transition model, but many more are part-way through the sequence. Consider the factors which underlie each stage in this model.

FIGURE 2.10   *Demographic Transition Model. Why is population growth greatest during late Stage 2 and early Stage 3?*

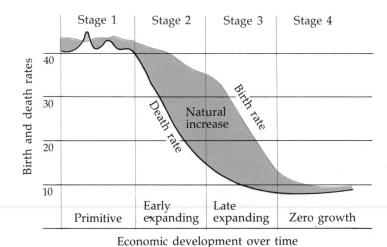

FIGURE 2.11 *Population
Pyramids
Associated with
Stages on Model*

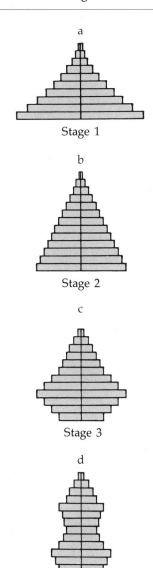

Stage 1: Primitive

Very few, if any, countries remain entirely at this stage today. However, some areas of countries, such as the Amazon Basin, may show the very high birth and death rates which are typical of Stage 1. Life expectancy at this stage is very short, and the population pyramid for such an area has a very wide base. See Figure 2.11.

Stage 2: Early Expanding

The first significant change which leads from Stage 1 to Stage 2 occurs in the death rate. Improved hygiene and medical techniques have an almost immediate effect in reducing mortality. Birth rates remain high, however, since large families are the traditional way of coping with high infant mortality rates and the demand for labour in the fields. A country's culture and religion might also encourage a high birth rate. In economic terms, it is also a means by which parents ensure that they will be looked after in their old age. Moreover, birth control is hampered in poorer countries by poverty and lack of education.

The rate of natural increase, that is, the gap between the birth and death rates, is at its highest in Stage 2. The population diagram remains broadly based and pyramid shaped, but not so extremely as at Stage 1. Countries such as Mexico have Stage 2 population pyramids. Most less developed countries have pyramids of a similar shape.

Stage 3: Late Expanding

Some years, or even generations, after the rapid fall in the death rate which signals Stage 2, the birth rate, too, begins to fall. The result is a declining rate of population increase. The birth rate falls in Stage 3 because of a change in attitude towards family size. This change comes about when living standards rise and the growth of manufacturing reduces the need for farm labour. In modern Canada (which is at late Stage 3), the costs of raising and educating children also keep the average family size down. So do the increasing participation of women in the work force and the widespread availability of birth control methods. The population pyramid for the United States can be used as an example of Stage 3 (Figure 2.11). Notice that it is similar to Canada's (Figure 2.2).

Stage 4: Zero Population Growth

Only in the last 10 or 15 years have any countries in the world reached the point where the birth rate falls to approximately the same level as the death rate. At Stage 4, total population count is at a maximum, but population growth is close to zero. A population such as this shows an

increase in average age; there are more older people and fewer children. Canada (at late Stage 3) will automatically enter Stage 4 as the members of the baby boom generation pass out of their child-bearing years. West Germany is an example of a Stage 4 country (Figure 2.11). In recent years, West Germany's death rate has actually risen (as a result of aging) and has slightly exceeded the birth rate. As countries reach this stage, population decline, rather than population increase, can become a problem.

West Germany has reached zero population growth. Suggest reasons why Canada should or should not aim for zero population growth.

Interpreting the Model

This chapter began by noting the vast increase in world population since the Industrial Revolution. From what you have read about the demographic transition model, you can conclude that this growth was initially caused by developed nations passing through Stage 2. These nations are now in either late Stage 3 or Stage 4, and therefore contribute very little to current world population growth. However, many less developed countries, which are currently at Stage 2, are growing by 2 to 3 percent per year. Like the developed nations, less developed countries are likely to move into Stages 3 and 4 of the model.

Can world population stability be achieved? Population experts conclude that, even if less developed countries are successful in limiting their birth rates, it will take until late in the 21st century before some degree of stability in world population can be achieved. The reason for this is the very high proportion of young people in less developed countries today. By the time overall stability is achieved—if indeed it is—the total world population will have risen to at least 10 thousand million, and possibly to 12 or even 14 thousand million.

QUESTIONS

1. Define the term "model".

2. Refer to the demographic transition model (Figure 2.10).
   (a) At which stage does the greatest population growth take place?
   (b) At which stage is total population at a maximum?
   (c) What would be the effect on total population if the death rate were to rise above the birth rate?

3. Why does the death rate normally fall before the birth rate?

4. Why is it harder to reduce the birth rate in less developed countries than in western countries?

5. What are the main reasons for a declining birth rate during the "late expanding" stage?

CLOSE-UP

Population Control— The Example of China

Many governments see population control as desirable. Few, however, view the matter with such urgency as the government of China, a country which had over one thousand million people in 1984—22 percent of the world's population. Yet China has only 7 percent of the world's **arable** land (land on which crops can be grown). (Canada has 3 percent, but only 0.5 percent of the world's people.) In China, this works out to one-tenth of a hectare per person (roughly one-ninth of the amount in the United States and one-half the amount in India). Much of China consists of mountains and desert. All good arable land has been in cultivation for many years.

China's birth and death rates were similar to those of any less developed nation throughout the 1950's and 1960's. (See Figure 2.12.) Birth control campaigns in these decades were weak and ineffective. The one period when births fell sharply was during the "Great Leap Forward" and its aftermath, in 1958–1959. At this time the government used intense propaganda in an attempt to change the nation into a totally communist and highly productive society. Its hopes proved to be short-lived; indeed, in 1960–1961 there was a two-year famine caused by low farm output. Births fell sharply and deaths rose during this whole period, but soon afterwards the birth rate was once again very high.

FIGURE 2.12 *Birth and Death Rates in China*

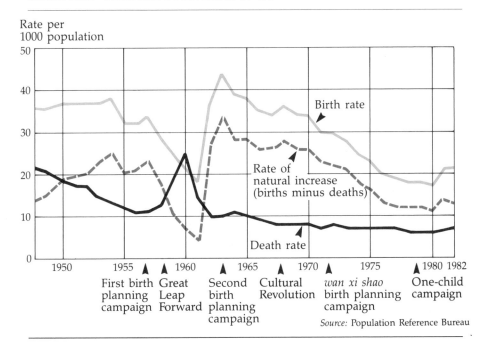

Rate per
1000 population

Birth rate

Rate of
natural increase
(births minus deaths)

Death rate

First birth planning campaign — Great Leap Forward — Second birth planning campaign — Cultural Revolution — *wan xi shao* birth planning campaign — One-child campaign

Source: Population Reference Bureau

Early Birth Control Policy

Since 1971, the Chinese government has been totally committed to reducing the birth rate. Its first campaign, known as *wan xi shao* ("later and fewer") began in 1971, and established a two-child norm: "One is not too few, two are good, three are too many." The campaign was based on three policies:

- later marriage (mid-20's for women, late 20's for men)

- longer intervals between births (three to four years)

- fewer children (a limit of two in urban and three in rural areas)

This campaign met with considerable success, as you can see in Figure 2.12, mainly because of delayed marriage. But the government felt that stricter controls were necessary, because the birth rate would inevitably jump when the baby boom of the 1960's reached marriageable age.

The One-Child Policy

This policy dates from 1979. Publicity through all forms of media extolled the virtues of small families. It was reinforced by the use of group and personal meetings to put strong pressure on families to conform to government policies. "Planned Birth" certificates giving official permission to have a child were issued to couples. Remember, however, that a population whose religion and culture encourage large families does not readily adapt to controls of this nature. Rewards were therefore promised to those who conformed to the policy. Penalties were provided for those who did not.

Chinese couples who adhere to the one-child policy now receive free medical care, monthly wage bonuses, preferential housing, and extra pension income. The one child is promised free tuition and even an eventual job. If a second child is born, the benefits cease, and some repayments may have to be made. A third child may result in a 10 percent reduction in wages for the parents. As a result of the policy, the birth rate fell in 1979 and 1980, but it has risen since then because of difficulties in enforcing the policy.

Problems with the One-Child Policy

Difficulties with the one-child policy have been pointed out by critics both outside and within China. The most highly publicized problem arises from China's traditional preference for male children. There has been some infanticide of female babies, especially

China's youth will be the group most affected by the success or failure of China's one-child policy.

in more remote areas, although this practice is not widespread. The government has therefore relaxed the one-child rule in certain cases when the first child is female. But if this were done regularly it would upset the sex ratio in the country, which is already 106 males for every 100 females. As a means of counteracting the bias against female children, most government posters show a happy couple with a lovely daughter.

A prolonged one-child campaign would distort China's age structure. Most couples would have four dependent parents, but only one child to help with support by earning an income. A future labour shortage is also thought to be possible, though unemployment is high today.

The Outlook for China's Population

Figure 2.13 shows China's population pyramid as it was in 1982. Its shape points out an immediate problem for China as it attempts to keep the birth rate down over the next decade. Can you see why the shape of the pyramid virtually guarantees a continued rise in population into the early 1990's? There are two other reasons as well why the one-child policy may have only limited success. First, marriage laws were amended in 1980 to

FIGURE 2.13   *China's Population Pyramid (1982)*

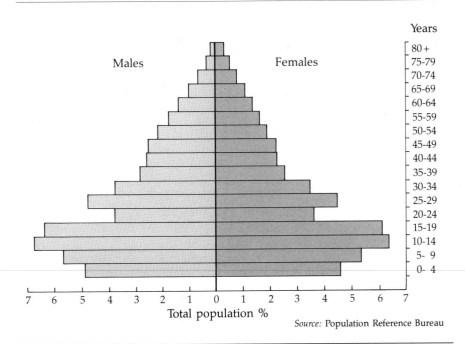

Source: Population Reference Bureau

As of 1983, India's birth control programs had not brought its rate of natural increase below 2 percent. (Jaipur, India.)

allow marriage at 20 for women and 22 for men (three to five years earlier than in the *wan xi shao* campaign). This change recognized the fact that many couples were living together while awaiting marriage. The immediate result was a jump in the number of births in 1981 (refer to Figure 2.12).

The second reason for a continued rise in population in China is less directly related to the one-child policy. The laws relating to the sale of farm produce were relaxed in 1979. This change made it profitable for farmers to increase production on their plots of land. Extra hands make the task easier—another reason why the one-child policy has little chance of total success in rural China, where 80 percent of the population lives.

The government of China has more power to exert pressure on its population than, for example, the government of India, whose political system is more democratic. India's natural increase was 2 percent in 1983 (birth rate 34, death rate 14), as compared with China's 1.2 percent (birth rate 20, death rate 8). If this difference holds good for several decades, India's population will outstrip China's by the year 2040.

QUESTIONS

1. From Figure 2.12, state the approximate rate of natural increase of China's population in 1963, 1971, and 1979.

2. What penalties does China impose on couples who have more than one child?

3. What is the role of persuasion in bringing down the rate of growth of population in China?

4. Why is the one-child policy more difficult to implement in rural areas than in urban areas?

5. On the basis of what you know about the total fertility rate, what do you predict will be the eventual result if the majority of Chinese couples have only one child?

Population Distribution

You might suppose that the growth of the world's population has had the effect of distributing people more evenly across the globe. In fact, the very opposite is true. People are more concentrated into small areas now than they have ever been. Figure 2.14 shows the distribution of world population in the 1980's.

FIGURE 2.14   *World Population Density*

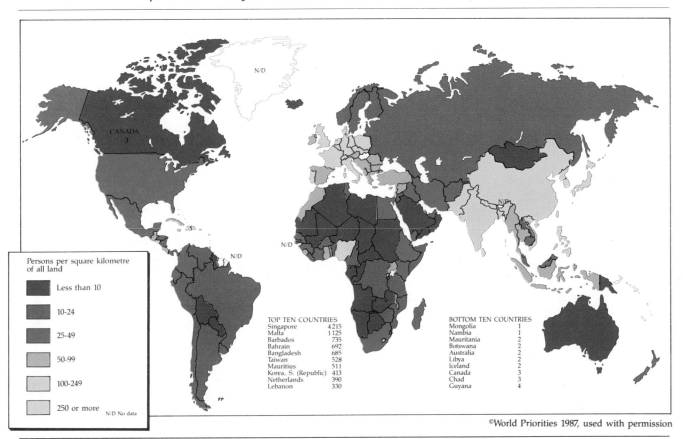

Persons per square kilometre of all land

- Less than 10
- 10-24
- 25-49
- 50-99
- 100-249
- 250 or more   N/D No data

TOP TEN COUNTRIES	
Singapore	4215
Malta	1125
Barbados	735
Bahrain	692
Bangladesh	685
Taiwan	528
Mauritius	511
Korea, S. (Republic)	413
Netherlands	390
Lebanon	330

BOTTOM TEN COUNTRIES	
Mongolia	1
Nambia	1
Mauritania	2
Botswana	2
Australia	2
Libya	2
Iceland	2
Canada	3
Chad	3
Guyana	4

The Empty Lands

Imagine that the Earth's land areas—only 29% of the entire globe—are divided into fifths. Roughly four-fifths of the globe are relatively empty, with little prospect of supporting a high population density.

One-fifth is empty because the climate is very cold. This area includes the northern lands and Antarctica, where temperatures are well below the minimum required for successful farming (approximately five months over 6°C).

Another fifth of the world's land area may be said to be too dry. Irrigation permits some arid areas to support dense farming settlement, as in the Nile Valley in Egypt. Such areas are small, however, compared to the vast expanses of desert and semi-desert around the globe. Moreover, the deserts are expanding faster than they are being reclaimed by irrigation.

A third type of area is empty because the land is either too high or too steep to permit the growing of crops. Steeply sloping land can be used only for grazing. However, soils are very thin and stony on sloping ground and the risk of erosion from grazing is serious. Farming in mountainous areas is also limited by cold temperatures.

The remaining almost-empty fifth of the Earth has limited attractions for settlement for biological reasons. Several types of natural environment have proved hard for people to settle in large numbers. These include the tropical rainforests, the temperate coniferous forests, and the tropical grasslands (savanna).

The rainforests have plenty of heat and moisture, but if the soil is exposed by forest clearing it is quickly **leached** (the plant nutrients are washed out by rainfall). Animal farming is made difficult by the abundance of disease-bearing insects. The coniferous forests, though a valuable source of softwood lumber, grow in poor acid soils in areas

What environmental factor pictured here discourages settlement?

Name the features that would allow this area to support a larger population than that shown on page 48.

where the growing season is too short for large-scale farming. The tropical grasslands face the problem of a highly seasonal rainfall. Also, like the rainforests, the savanna harbours disease-bearing insects such as the tsetse fly. For all these reasons, only limited areas of these three types of natural environment have a high population density.

The Crowded Lands

Approximately 90 percent of all the world's inhabitants live in the remaining one-fifth of the globe (refer to Figure 2.14). This fifth is also where most of the rapid population growth is concentrated. There are, however, two quite different types of economy in the world's crowded lands. One is rural and traditional. The other is urban and technological. A look at the population map (Figure 2.14) will show you where these lands are. South and East Asia contain the bulk of the traditional farming economies; lesser concentrations are found in Africa and Latin America.

Farming is also important in the urbanized and industrialized areas of the world, such as North America and Western Europe. However, in these regions farming is highly commercial; that is, directed toward selling products for cash. It also depends heavily on science and industry, since it makes use of machinery, chemical fertilizers, pesticides, and scientific plant breeding. The farm produce is sold mainly for urban consumption. Farming in the western world is therefore an extension of urban technological society. Very few people in these areas

FIGURE 2.15 *World Urbanization*

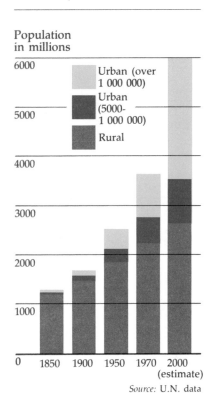

Population in millions

- Urban (over 1 000 000)
- Urban (5000-1 000 000)
- Rural

6000

5000

4000

3000

2000

1000

0

1850 1900 1950 1970 2000 (estimate)

Source: U.N. data

farm for a living—usually less than 5 percent of the population. Industry employs 25 to 35 percent, and no fewer than 60 to 70 percent are employed in services of many kinds. This type of employment pattern is an indication of an advanced economy. Most of the population, often up to 80 percent, live in cities and towns. It is in the lower income residential areas of the large cities that some of the highest densities of population are found. Hong Kong, with an average density of 5000 people per square kilometre, reaches over 20 000 in some districts. What you may not know is that these figures are equalled in parts of Vancouver's West End.

Urbanization

After reading this about Hong Kong and Vancouver, you may be wondering how many of the world's people live in cities. The percentage of urban dwellers has risen from 14 percent in 1920 to 40 percent in 1980, and will probably exceed 50 percent by the year 2000 (see Figure 2.15). By then, there are likely to be at least 60 cities in the world with 5 million inhabitants or more, compared with fewer than 30 in the early 1980's. Figure 2.16 shows the locations of the twelve cities likely to be the world's largest in the year 2000. Urban living is therefore becoming the norm for an increasing number of the world's people in both poorer and richer countries. Urbanization is an important theme which you will look at more fully in Chapter 7.

What factors might encourage people to live in a large urban centre like Rio de Janiero?

FIGURE 2.16 *Estimated Population of World's Largest Cities in 2000 A.D. Which city is forecast to be the largest? Which continent will have the most cities over 12 million?*

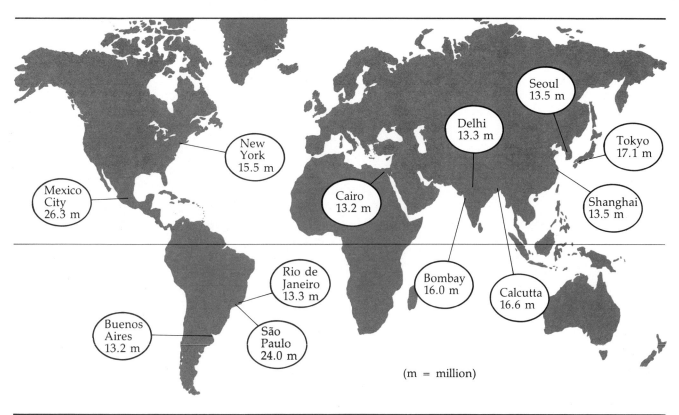

(m = million)

Source: UNFPA

QUESTIONS

1. What four conditions referred to in the previous section account for four-fifths of the world's land area being sparsely peopled?

2. Look at Figure 2.14. List the main parts of the world where very high population densities are found. State whether each area is based mainly on rural or urban living.

3. In which situation is a high density of population more likely to be a problem: a rural area dependent on agriculture or an urban area dependent on manufacturing and services? Why?

4. Give reasons why developed countries are more highly urbanized than countries in the less developed world.

Chapter Summary

In this chapter, you have examined some of the key factors involved in world population growth. In developed countries, birth rates have fallen sharply, creating slow overall population growth, and, in some cases, a decline in population. In less developed countries, falling death rates have led to a very high rate of population growth. The fall in birth rates, which is necessary for population stability, is only now beginning to happen. Not until late in the 21st century can population stability be hoped for. By then, the world population will have more than doubled.

Reductions in infant mortality, and other improvements in health, have helped to raise the life expectancy in poor countries. Nevertheless, average lifespans remain considerably below the levels found in western countries.

Most of the current population growth is taking place in small areas of the world, which are already crowded. The cities of the less developed world are growing particularly rapidly.

IN REVIEW

1. **(a)** List three organizations that might make use of census data. In each case, suggest how the data might be used.
   (b) Why do you think governments keep census data anonymous?
   (c) Name some ways in which you might be affected by government decisions made on the basis of data from a population census.

2. What differences are noticeable in the age structures of the developed and less developed parts of the world?

3. Describe the relationship between world birth rates and infant mortality rates. Suggest reasons for this relationship.

4. What combination of measures is necessary to reduce the deaths of children in developing countries?

5. **(a)** Explain the term "zero population growth".
   (b) Name a country which is currently at this stage of population growth.

6. **(a)** Explain China's one-child policy.
   (b) Why did the government introduce the policy?
   (c) What problems are being encountered in the present implementation?
   (d) What are the future advantages and disadvantages of this measure?

7. Why has the world's population grown so dramatically in the 20th century?

8. (a) Why should Canada avoid an older-than-average age structure in the 21st century?
   (b) Are there any advantages to an older-than-average age structure?

APPLYING YOUR KNOWLEDGE

1. What strains on social services might arise when a population increases rapidly for each of the following reasons?
   (a) The birth rate is rising.
   (b) Life expectancy is increasing.
   (c) Net migration is increasing.

2. Use the following data to calculate dependency ratios for Oak Bay and Esquimalt in Greater Victoria. Suggest some possible reasons why these two communities have different population features.

	Oak Bay	Esquimalt
Young dependants (aged 0–14)	14%	19%
Old dependants (aged 65 and over)	26%	11%
Population of working age (aged 15–64)	60%	70%

3. Calculate **(a)** the rate of natural increase as a percentage, and **(b)** the doubling time for the following countries and for the world as a whole.

Country	Birth Rate	Death Rate	Natural Increase	Doubling Time
Mexico	32	6		
Brazil	31	8		
India	34	14		
United Kingdom	13	12		
WORLD	28	11		

4. Women in the less developed world tend to receive less education than men. Why do you suppose this is so?

5. (a) What policies might be introduced to increase population growth within a country?
   (b) Can you think of countries where they would be appropriate?

6. "Immigration into Canada should rise again before the end of this century." Do you agree with this statement? Give your reasons.

FURTHER INVESTIGATION

1. If you have access to population figures for your community, draw the population pyramid and discuss its shape. What conclusions can you make?

2. Governments are sometimes accused of lack of long-term planning. Find out what measures are being taken in Canada at the federal level to anticipate changing population trends and needs.

CHAPTER 3

Standards of Living

Have you ever considered how different your life would have been if you had been born somewhere else in the world? Only one in every 350 of the 135 million babies born in the world each year will be born in Canada. Eighty-seven percent of all babies will be born in less developed countries. Many of them will face a life of ill health and hunger, because most of these countries have the high birth rates characteristic of Stage 2 of the demographic transition model.

Now visualize the environments in which people at both ends of the standard of living scale might live. Your ideas of very high and very low standards of living may not coincide exactly with the striking contrasts shown in the photographs.

Place yourself into the photographs on the facing page for a moment. In one you sleep in a private, well-furnished bedroom, with the temperature maintained at a steady comfort level. On getting up, you turn a tap, and clean water, hot or cold, is delivered to you from an elaborate system of reservoirs, filtration plants, and pipes. The flick of a switch brings electricity generated in multi-million dollar power stations. Getting dressed involves putting on clothes made from both natural fibres and a whole range of petrochemical products. For breakfast you can choose among foods from several continents. Perhaps you travel to school in a car or bus—assembled from about 3000 separately made components. All this before 9 o'clock in the morning! A vast range of resources and technology which to you seems perfectly ordinary has helped to launch you into another day.

Now look at the other photograph and try to imagine what your life would be like if you lived there. What factors have created a situation where some parts of the world—the developed parts—can make full use of resources and technology, while others—the less developed parts—appear to have missed out?

In this chapter, you will look in detail at what is meant by "developed" and "less developed". Within the less developed world, some countries have improving economies, but there is a group of very poor nations in which serious problems of famine and poverty persist.

Many attempts to classify countries by living standards have been made. The most effective classification systems use levels of nutrition, health, and literacy as keys to understanding global contrasts in living standards. This chapter will answer questions such as these:

- *Which parts of the world are "developed" and "less developed"?*

- *Are there distinctions to be made among less developed nations?*

- *What is meant by the term "standard of living"?*

- *What indicators can be used to measure differences in living standards?*

Living standards vary throughout the world. Contrast the standards of living suggested by these two photographs.

Classifying Countries

Is there any link between the rate of population growth, which you read about in the previous chapter, and a country's standard of living? Figure 3.1 suggests that there may well be. This graph compares the rate of population growth with *per capita* income. This is the total value of the amount of goods and services produced in a country divided by its population. In other words, *per capita* income is a measure of the average annual income of a country. From Figure 3.1, you can see that, in general, countries with a high rate of population growth have a low *per capita* income.

FIGURE 3.1 *Scatter Graph of Population Growth and* Per Capita *Income*

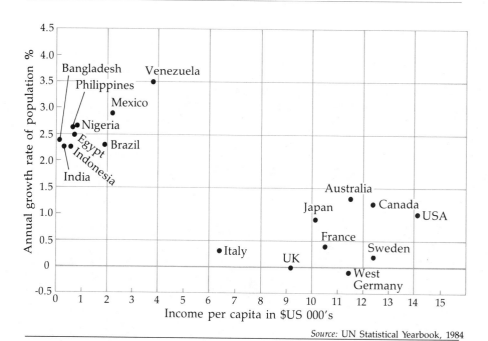

Source: UN Statistical Yearbook, 1984

The First, Second, and Third Worlds

From Figure 3.1 it is clear that there are great contrasts between developed and less developed countries. The latter are commonly referred to as the "Third World". Developed countries are commonly divided into the western democracies or "First World" countries, which include Canada and the United States, and the centrally planned "Second World" countries, which include the U.S.S.R. and associated eastern European nations. Figure 3.2 shows the distribution of the "three worlds". Occasionally the labels "North" and "South" are given to developed and less developed nations respectively. Finally, the less developed nations are sometimes also referred to as "developing" nations.

FIGURE 3.2 *"Three Worlds"*

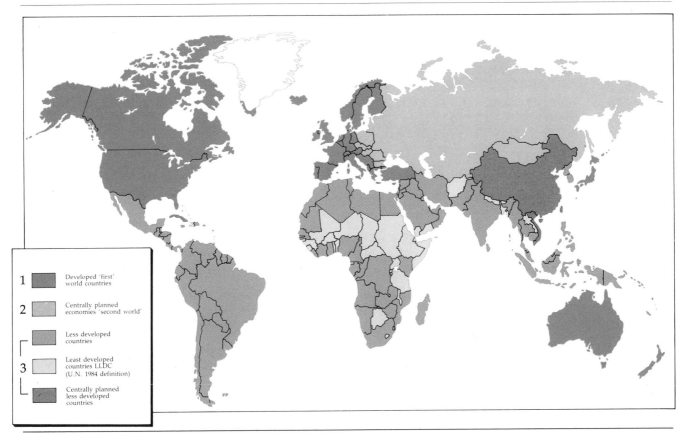

1 — Developed 'first' world countries

2 — Centrally planned economies 'second world'

— Less developed countries

3 — Least developed countries LLDC (U.N. 1984 definition)

— Centrally planned less developed countries

You have encountered the terms "developed" and "less developed" many times already in this book. But what do they mean, exactly? The practice of dividing the world's nations along these lines has its uses, but it can also be quite misleading. It is necessary to make some distinctions within the large numbers of countries in the Third World. A report assembled in 1984 by the United Nations made two subdivisions within the Third World: less developed countries (LDC's) and least developed countries (LLDC's).

The UN report identified 36 very poor countries as least developed countries (see Figure 3.2). They were chosen on the following grounds:

- low *per capita* income ($250 in 1975–1980)

- low literacy rates (less than one-third of the adult population)

- low contribution of manufacturing in relation to the total economy (less than 10 percent)

Examples of LLDC's include Sudan and Afghanistan. The average income in LLDC's in 1981 was only 23 percent of the average in all Third World countries, which in turn was about 7 percent of the average income in the developed world. LLDC's have higher birth and death rates than the Third World average. Life expectancy in LLDC's was only 46 years in the early 1980's, compared with 55 in all developing nations, and the infant mortality rate was 141, compared with 105. Many of the most serious problems described in this book occur in the 36 least developed countries.

To understand better what life is like in the Third World, you need to look more closely at what is meant by "standards of living".

QUESTIONS

1. Which country in Figure 3.1 has (a) the lowest *per capita* income, and (b) the highest *per capita* income?

2. What does Figure 3.1 tell you about the population of West Germany?

3. In your own words, express the relationship between population increase and *per capita* income, as shown on the graph in Figure 3.1.

4. List five countries from the "First World" (outside North America), five from the "Second World", five from the "Third World" (excluding LLDC's), and five from the "least developed countries" (LLDC's). Make your lists representative of as many continents as possible.

5. Why does the United Nations use the contribution (percentage) of manufacturing in relation to the total economy as a measure of development?

Our Needs and Wants

First and foremost, "standard of living" includes the basics which are essential for survival: food, clothing, and shelter. But human beings have other needs which are also basic, such as health and education. Still other needs, such as security from violent crime, are less obvious and are easily taken for granted.

All of these are human needs. But would you be satisfied if all you had was an adequate supply of food, clothing, and shelter, together with basic health and educational facilities and freedom from robbery or violence? You—and many other people in the world—have come to expect more from life than that. It is desirable to have some extra money to spend on recreation and leisure interests. You probably also expect to take holidays, and even to travel while on vacation. Your ideas of what standards of food, clothing, shelter, and other needs are acceptable are likely far above the level required to keep you alive and healthy. In other words, the idea of a satisfactory standard of living includes human wants as well as basic human needs.

Some problems occur, however, when you try to compare the standards of living of groups of people from different cultures and different geographical backgrounds. You will now look at three such problems.

FIGURE 3.3   *Poverty in Canada. Which, if any, items listed here would you consider luxuries rather than necessities? Give reasons to support your answer.*

In 1985, poverty levels of income in Canada were:

$20 800 or less for an urban family of 4
$10 230 for a single person (urban)

Of all poor families in Canada,

15% had a VCR.
87% had a color TV.
48% had a freezer.
24% had a dishwasher.
64% had an automatic washing machine.
61% had a clothes drier.
98% had a radio.
52% had at least one car.

Source: Statistics Canada

Poverty Is Relative

The minimum level of goods and services which are considered acceptable continues to rise. Many articles, from cars to television sets, were considered luxuries a few decades ago. In Canada today, a person who could not afford a second-hand television set or an older car would be considered poor. The level of income below which an urban Canadian family of four is considered poor was set at $20 800 in 1985 by Statistics Canada (Figure 3.3). Over one million Canadian families, or 15 percent of the total, fell below this poverty line. The Statistics Canada poverty line keeps rising, mainly because of inflation—but also because of the increasing expectations within our society.

Problems of Comparing Societies

Ideas about living standards not only change over time, but also vary among different societies. In the first place, needs and wants differ partly because of different climates. The vast majority of the world's people, who inhabit warm climates, would have no use for Canadian winter clothing; nor would they spend much on heating their homes.

In addition, people in different parts of the world have very different ideas as to what is considered desirable. Western countries put a high value on material goods such as dwellings and cars. Certain African peoples measure their wealth by the number of cattle they own. Some North Americans enjoy spending their leisure hours on golf courses, while many Icelanders and Russians enjoy playing chess—but there are many parts of the world where these activities are unheard of. A major problem in comparing the living standards of different cultures is finding areas where genuine comparison is possible.

The contrast in material wealth suggested by these two photographs is misleading; in many non-western countries such possessions as cars and houses, for example, tell very little about actual living standards.

Gross National Product (GNP)

A country's gross national product is the sum total of the value of all goods and services produced in that country in one year. Per capita GNP is the GNP of a country divided by the total population. In comparing countries, all per capita GNP data are normally expressed in U.S. dollars.

Per capita GNP may be regarded as equivalent to per capita income, since income is earned from production of goods and services.

The Problem of Using Income as a Measure

An obvious way of comparing countries is to use the readily available *per capita* income data. The shading on the world map shown in Figure 3.4 indicates the *per capita* GNP (**gross national product**) within each country. In 1983, Canada had an average *per capita* income of about $12 000 (U.S.), while Indonesia's was about $600 (U.S.). Does this mean that Canada's living standard is 20 times higher than Indonesia's, or that its population is 20 times more satisfied? Such a conclusion would almost certainly be wrong. Besides, *per capita* income figures are averages, and averages reveal nothing about the extremes of wealth or poverty which may exist. In less developed countries such as Indonesia, these extremes are more pronounced than they are in most western countries.

FIGURE 3.4 *World Map of GNP. Which continent seems to have the lowest overall GNP?*

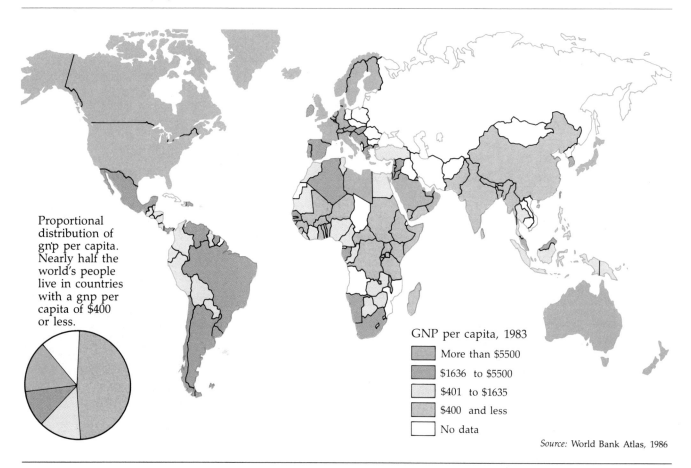

Proportional distribution of gnp per capita. Nearly half the world's people live in countries with a gnp per capita of $400 or less.

GNP per capita, 1983
- More than $5500
- $1636 to $5500
- $401 to $1635
- $400 and less
- No data

Source: World Bank Atlas, 1986

What measure besides money might this subsistence farmer use to determine whether he has an acceptable living standard?

The majority of people in Indonesia, as in the rest of the less developed world, make their living by **subsistence farming.** That is, they consume most of the food they grow. This home-grown food is the main item in the standard of living of most Indonesians. However, because it is not received in the form of cash it is not included in Indonesia's *per capita* income figure.

Finally, to compare incomes it is necessary to use a common currency, such as the U.S. dollar. (Notice that the income figures for Canada and Indonesia were given in U.S. dollars.) But the value of currencies fluctuates on foreign exchange markets. In the early 1980's, the U.S. dollar gained greatly at the expense of most other world currencies. This made it appear that the living standards of these other countries went down when measured in U.S. dollars. They appeared to rise again when the value of the dollar fell in the mid-1980's. These changes created the false impression that living standards had fluctuated a great deal.

For all these reasons, you can see that it is not entirely reliable to use income as a measure of the standard of living.

Foreign Exchange Markets

The currency of most countries may be bought and sold just like goods and services. If you wish to visit the United States, for example, you are likely to buy U.S. dollars before you go, and you may sell any unspent dollars when you return. This happens on a larger scale every time goods or services are imported or exported. Foreign exchange markets are simply the network of connections for buying or selling foreign currencies maintained by banks and other financial institutions throughout the world.

QUESTIONS

1. What five needs are considered basic?

2. Make a list of your spending priorities and divide them into needs and wants. How does your list compare with that of some of your classmates?

3. Explain what is meant by the statement, "Poverty is relative."

4. Figure 3.3 gives information about families below the poverty line in Canada. How do you think this standard of poverty compares with the situation in the least developed countries (LLDC's)?

5. Refer to the world map of GNP (Figure 3.4).
   (a) List six countries with a *per capita* income of below $400, and six (outside North America) with a *per capita* income of over $5500.
   (b) Which countries have a GNP greater than the whole of Latin America?

Indicators of Living Standards

There are many ways of measuring the extent to which the needs and wants of people are being met. For example, the amount and quality of food which people eat and the range of health and educational facilities at their disposal are all part of their standard of living. However, it would be useful to be able to summarize living standards on a single index.

The Physical Quality of Life Index

Many efforts to produce such an index have been made. Perhaps the most successful has been the **physical quality of life index** (PQLI). It was devised in the late 1970's by the economist M.D. Morris and published for the Overseas Development Council, an American non-profit organization set up to study the problems of the Third World.

The index uses three themes, normally called **indicators:** life expectancy, infant mortality, and level of literacy. Each of these has the advantage of being an easily observed sign of well-being. They were also chosen because each relates closely to levels of social and economic development in any country. In addition, each is free from cultural bias, in the sense that the death of an infant, for example, would be regarded as a sad event in any society in any part of the world.

Each of the three indicators is recorded in the form of a percentage (that is, 0 is the lowest possible score and 100 is the highest). Life

What difference in quality of life are indicated by these two photographs?

FIGURE 3.5   *PQLI. Do the people of South America or Africa have a better quality of life?*

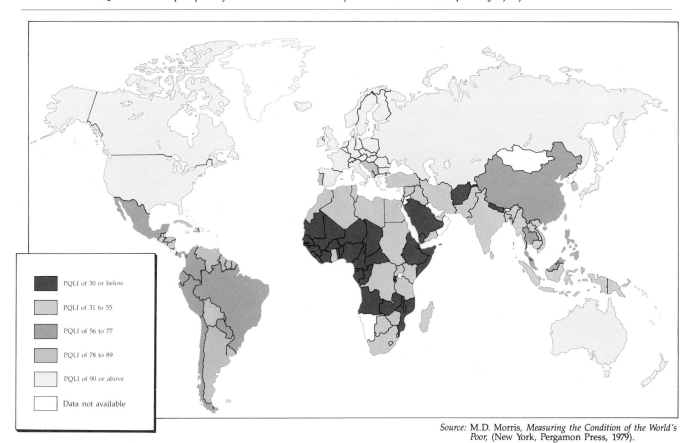

Source: M.D. Morris, *Measuring the Condition of the World's Poor*, (New York, Pergamon Press, 1979).

expectancy figures are taken at the age of one year, to avoid double-counting infant deaths, which are represented in the index by the infant mortality rate. The PQLI, or, more simply, the quality of life for any country, is the average of the three percentages. See Table 3.1.

TABLE 3.1   *Examples of the Physical Quality of Life Index. Based on their PQLI, contrast life in Nigeria with life in Sweden.*

Country	Life Expectancy (years)	(index)	Infant Mortality (I.M.Rate)	(index)	Literacy Rate (percent)	(index)	PQLI
Nigeria	49	28	180	22	25	25	25.0
Saudi Arabia	52	36	152	35	15	15	28.7
India	56	46	122	48	34	34	42.7
Brazil	65	70	82	66	66	66	67.3
Sri Lanka	70	83	45	83	81	81	82.3
U.S.S.R.	70	82	28	91	99	99	90.7
U.S.A.	72	88	16	96	99	99	94.3
Canada	73	90	15	96	98	98	94.7
Sweden	75	94	8	99	99	99	97.3

The quality of life index distinguishes between standard of living and *per capita* income. A country such as the U.S.S.R., for example, has reasonably good medical facilities and adequate nutrition, even though life expectancy has been falling slightly. It also has a very high literacy rate. Thus, even if the population at large does not share in an affluent living standard, the quality of life figure can be as high as 90. Sri Lanka is another case where the quality of life is higher than the *per capita* income would indicate.

The opposite is true of some oil exporting countries, such as Saudi Arabia. This country has recently attained great wealth, but the wealth is owned by a select few. Its benefits were initially slow to improve the quality of life for the average Saudi Arabian. Thus, *per capita* income may be high, but the quality of life figure remains low.

The physical quality of life index has the advantage of combining indicators to give each country a single score which summarizes its living standards. To find out in more detail why countries vary so much in well-being, you must look at each indicator separately. In the remainder of this chapter you will focus on health, literacy, and nutrition, each of which the United Nations considers very important in the measurement of living standards.

QUESTIONS

1. What is the purpose of the physical quality of life index?

2. What three indicators are used to determine quality of life?

3. Using the map in Figure 3.5, name three countries, outside of Africa, where the physical quality of life index is 30 or less.

4. Why do some countries have such high quality of life scores?

5. Compare the information in Figure 3.5 with that in Figure 3.4.
   (**a**) Name two countries which have a high quality of life and a low *per capita* income.
   (**b**) Name two countries which have a low quality of life and a high *per capita* income.
   (**c**) Can you make any suggestions as to why the quality of life and *per capita* income can differ like this?

6. Suggest four ways in which your life might be different if you lived in a country with a quality of life figure of 30.

Health and Disease

The World Health Organization has defined "health" as having social, emotional, and physical aspects. "Disease" is more difficult to define, since many diseases can be latent for a long time, so a person may not be obviously ill or disabled. Many diseases are infectious, which means that they can be transmitted from person to person, either by direct contact or by some **vector** (carrier). Examples of vectors are malaria-carrying mosquitoes or the rats which carried bubonic plague throughout medieval Europe. Common infectious diseases include typhus, cholera, and measles. Non-infectious diseases include strokes, heart disease, and the various forms of cancer.

Physical Factors Related to Disease

The physical factors related to disease range from the temperatures and humidity of the climate to dust and fumes breathed in the workplace. The nature of the water supply is yet another physical factor. For example, soft water—water which contains few or no dissolved minerals—is commonly linked to high rates of dental decay as well as to possible heart disease.

Contaminated drinking water is one of the foremost causes of health problems. In many countries, people dispose of all forms of waste in the rivers, then bathe in the same waters. Imagine how easily infection can be transmitted from person to person in such a situation.

Human Factors Related to Disease

These factors include an individual's diet, whether inadequate or excessive, and such social habits as smoking and drinking alcohol. A sedentary life-style, and/or the emotional stress caused by personal or financial problems, may contribute to such physical conditions as malfunctions of the circulatory system or the heart. Unsanitary conditions such as crowded living quarters, inadequate ventilation, and a lack of fresh, clean water all encourage the rapid spreading of infectious diseases. They may also contribute to mental and emotional stress which may lead to physical breakdown. It is not yet known just how

A community's health can be affected by the cleanliness of its environment. How might the human actions pictured here affect the health of the people in the community? in the neighbouring communities?

Suggest how protecting the health of these children in Lima could improve Peru's future living standards.

such physical elements as industrial pollutants interact with human factors such as diet and stress. It is known, however, that all these factors have an effect on health.

Infant Mortality

Infant mortality is often taken as one of the clearest indicators of the level of health in a country. In Chapter 2 you read about the enormous differences in infant mortality rates among different parts of the world. A lower rate can be achieved in a number of ways. One is a reduction of the number of children a woman gives birth to in her lifetime. Another is an increase in the spacing of births. Both of these factors greatly improve the health of women and children. Other priorities include adequate nutrition and pre-natal and post-natal care for mothers and infants.

The Special Problems of the Tropics

Disease is more widespread in the tropics than in the temperate zones. In the tropics, the combination of high temperature and high humidity creates the ideal environment for an enormous variety of insects, which are potential vectors. The tropics suffer from all of the developed world's ailments, such as influenza and measles. In addition to these, tropical countries have their own range of diseases. One of the most widespread is sleeping sickness, carried by the tsetse fly. Another is

FIGURE 3.6 *Malaria Cycle. Why are draining swamp areas and spraying standing water effective in malaria control programs.*

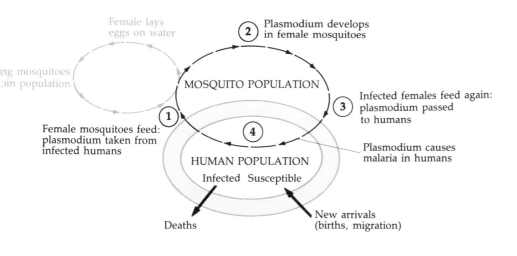

Female lays
eggs on water

(2) Plasmodium develops
in female mosquitoes

ng mosquitoes
oin population

MOSQUITO POPULATION

(1)

(3) Infected females feed again:
plasmodium passed
to humans

Female mosquitoes feed:
plasmodium taken from
infected humans

(4)

Plasmodium causes
malaria in humans

HUMAN POPULATION

Infected Susceptible

Deaths

New arrivals
(births, migration)

malaria. Disease-carrying parasites can enter the body under the toenails or through the skin of the feet where people go barefoot in the fields. The low productivity of millions of Third World farmers is, at least in part, the result of poor general health and the weakening effect of body parasites.

Figure 3.6 shows how malaria is transmitted from person to person by mosquitoes. One way to eliminate malaria is to drain the swampy areas in which mosquitoes breed. Doing this not only involves much expense but also results in a loss of plant and animal life. Another method of reducing malaria is spraying the mosquitoes' breeding areas. This, too, causes various ecological problems. Can you suggest what some of them might be? Perhaps the most effective method of combatting malaria is inoculating people against the disease. Unfortunately, many tropical countries are unable to afford the doctors and health facilities needed to control these and other diseases.

Sometimes improving one aspect of a community's living standards can have negative results on another aspect. For instance, the walk taken through an irrigated field by this man in Egypt could infect him with a water-transmitted disease.

Literacy

Literacy may be defined as the percentage of the adult population (15 years and over) who can read and write to a basic standard. Figure 3.7 indicates that there are many countries in which the literacy rate is still below the 20 percent level. The choice of literacy as part of the quality of life index shows how vital it is to any society.

FIGURE 3.7   *World Literacy. How do literacy and quality of life appear to be related?*

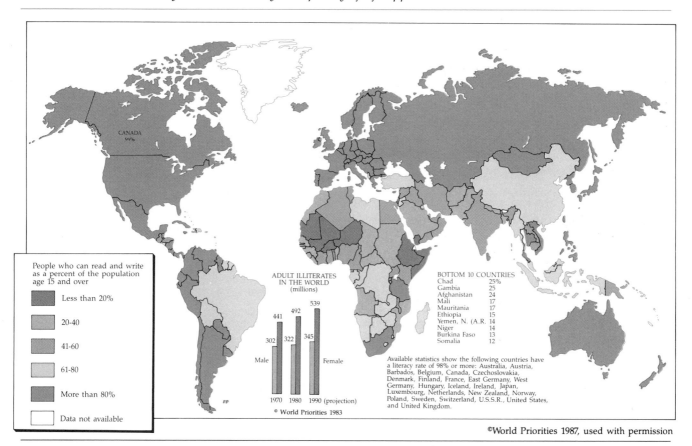

©World Priorities 1987, used with permission

In a country with a low level of literacy, it is very difficult to spread information about such matters as improved farming techniques, methods of birth control, and personal hygiene. Throughout the less developed world, illiteracy is much higher among women than men—in some countries as much as five times higher. This situation is linked with the low status of women and the high birth rates in these countries.

Many Canadians take literacy for granted. But doing so is a mistake. Consider how much your quality of life might be diminished if you

were illiterate. You could not enjoy one form of recreation, reading. You would be unable to follow printed instructions, and would have great difficulty in getting an education or a job. Furthermore, you would be open to exploitation by anyone who could read and write. For example, you might sign a contract which you could not read and understand. This would make you insecure in your dealings with others. Can you think of other disadvantages caused by illiteracy?

How is literacy related to standard of living?

According to the United Nations Educational Scientific and Cultural Organization (UNESCO), only about 2 percent of Canadians cannot read or write at all. However, this figure has been questioned by recent studies, which claim that a far higher percentage of Canadians have minimal standards of literacy.

UNESCO estimates that the number of illiterate people throughout the world is growing by 7 million a year. This increase is occurring because the countries with the lowest literacy rates are usually those with the highest birth rates. The problem of illiteracy therefore expands rather than contracts. According to UNESCO, as of 1982 the world total of illiterate people stood at about 860 million. UNESCO has worked for years to reduce the level of world illiteracy, but has not been as successful as it had hoped.

QUESTIONS

1. Name three examples each of (**a**) infectious and (**b**) non-infectious diseases.

2. From Figure 3.6, explain how malaria is transmitted from person to person.

3. State three ways in which illiteracy can diminish a person's quality of life.

Nutrition

In this section, you will examine some of the differences in the quality of nutrition in different parts of the world. There are great contrasts between both the amount and the quality of the food eaten in richer and poorer countries, as you can see in the photographs.

Food is made up of three main components: carbohydrates, fats, and proteins. All three provide energy, while proteins are also essential for body growth and health. Much discussion has centred on the value of animal protein, as distinct from vegetable protein. Formerly it was thought that only the protein derived from eating meat provided the amino acids essential for growth. Now it is known that vegetable protein, such as beans eaten with rice, can provide the necessary amino

Here two families from different parts of the world are both enjoying a typical meal. Why would it be misleading to assume that one meal is more nutritious than the other?

acids. A shortage of carbohydrates and fats in the diet is just as serious as a protein shortage, however, since it has the effect of diverting protein from its normal use to providing energy for body functions.

Certain vitamin deficiencies can also have serious results. The United Nations estimates that as many as 80 000 children go blind throughout the world every year because of a lack of vitamin A in their diet. Lack of vitamin D can cause rickets, a severe malformation of the bones.

As you might expect, people in different parts of the world obtain their carbohydrates, fats, proteins, and other nutrients from different sources. Table 3.2 shows the types of food which make up the average diet on each continent. It is obvious from this graph that western countries consume more of all these nutrients than what is available in the less developed world. Western diets are particularly high in protein from animal sources.

TABLE 3.2   *Diet by Continents. In what part of the world do people most rely on cereals as food?*

		Cereals	Starchy roots	Sugar	Pulses, nuts, fruit and vegetables	Meat, fish, eggs and milk	Oils and fats	Total supply	Total daily needs
North America Europe and Oceania	Kilojoules	4465	764	1772	920	3398	1987	13 306	10 880
	Grams of protein	29.9	4.4	—	7.6	49.3	0.3	91.5	39.8
Africa		4939	1852	479	958	664	609	9501	9870
		33.3	5.2	—	10.4	12.1	—	61.0	41.5
Asia		5796	571	479	777	643	378	8644	9660
		31.7	1.7	0.2	10.6	9.7	—	53.9	37.8
Latin America		4200	1205	1789	1142	1663	832	10 831	9996
		24.8	3.2	0.1	12.6	24.5	—	65.2	37.7

Source: UNFAO

Food Requirements

It is difficult to set precise standards for good nutrition. Food requirements vary according to climate, lifestyle, and other factors. A common way of expressing food needs is in terms of energy requirements, which are measured with a unit called the *kilojoule.* An absolute minimum for survival seems to be about 6250 kJ (kilojoules) of food energy daily on the average, but for a working lifestyle about 9375 kJ would be a more realistic minimum. Men generally require more than the average, and

TABLE 3.3 *World Food Supply. The figures in this table show* per capita *food supply as a percentage of requirements. What indicators are there in the table that the world is producing sufficient food for the needs of its people?*

	1969/71	1980
Developing countries (market economies)	95.5	98.6
Africa	93.5	94.0
Asia	92.8	94.1
Latin America	105.8	109.4
Near East	97.2	112.1
Others	100.0	105.3
Asian centrally planned economies	90.7	106.6
Total Developing Countries	93.9	101.2
Least Developed Countries	88.3	85.0
Total Developed Countries	128.4	133.4
World	104.8	110.0

Source: UNFAO

A child that experiences long periods of severe malnutrition can expect to reach adulthood with some form of both physical and mental impairment.

women less. Table 3.3 summarizes the results of a study by the Food and Agriculture Organization of the United Nations. It shows the food supply of each region of the world as a percentage of the estimated amount of food needed. The problem of the uneven distribution of food within large regions is ignored. In this table, Asia comes out almost as low as Africa overall, but Africa has a higher number of countries with critical food shortages.

Forms of Malnutrition

The lack of an adequate diet leads first to under-nutrition. The symptoms are eventual weight loss and lethargy. Prolonged under-nutrition leads to **malnutrition** which is, strictly speaking, any form of poor nutrition. Malnutrition produces clear symptoms of ill health. Kwashiorkor, one of the diseases prevalent in the less developed world, is caused by a deficiency in food energy and protein. The all-too-familiar images seen in the media of children with wasted muscles and bloated but unsatisfied stomachs show the effects of kwashiorkor. Even more serious, and often irreversible, is the condition known as marasmus, which leaves sufferers looking like bags of skin and bones.

Much more publicity needs to be given to the effects of malnutrition on mental development. A child's powers of reasoning, and motor skills such as hand/eye coordination, may be affected by severe malnutrition during the early years of growth. Yet perhaps half of the world's children suffer today from poor nutrition. A study done by the Nutrition Foundation of India in 1983 claimed, "All but 3 million of the 23 million children born in the country this year will be physically and mentally impaired by malnutrition." This form of deprivation will be

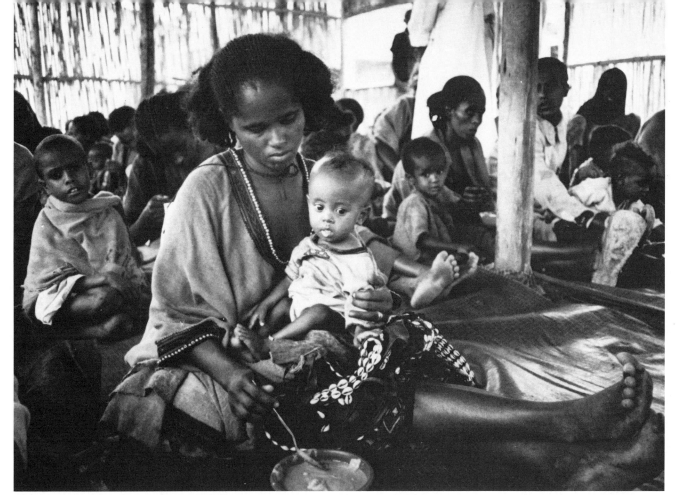

The food served in this refugee camp in northern Ethiopia during the 1985 famine was usually a high protein porridge mixture.

self-perpetuating, since the younger generation will grow up lacking the physical and mental health to solve the problems they inherit. Studies in several countries have shown some correlation between vitamin deficiencies and low scores on intelligence tests.

These forms of malnutrition are closely related to poverty. In North America, such malnutrition is common among single elderly people, low-income pregnant mothers, and young children. A study report in the February, 1987 issue of *Scientific American* indicated that 12 million children and 8 million adults in the United States experience some degree of malnutrition. These numbers show an increase over the previous decade. In Canada, malnutrition is widespread among the 3.5 million people living below the poverty line. Only a few people die directly of malnutrition in western countries. However, it is likely that many undernourished children in developed nations suffer some lack of intellectual growth.

An excessive diet is also a form of malnutrition, although you might not have thought of it as such. It has been claimed that perhaps 15 percent of the world's population put their health at risk by overeating. Particularly dangerous in this regard are animal fats. Overeating increases the risk of heart disease and circulatory problems. There is also increasing evidence linking an over-rich diet with certain forms of cancer. This form of malnutrition is common throughout the western world.

QUESTIONS

1. State the possible effects of extreme shortages of (**a**) food energy intake, (**b**) proteins, and (**c**) essential vitamins, in the diet.

2. What is (a) kwashiorkor? (b) marasmus?

3. How can malnutrition affect the mental development of children?

4. Refer to Table 3.2. What are the main differences between the average diets of people in the western world and those in Africa, Asia, and Latin America?

Chapter Summary

In this chapter, you have encountered some of the difficulties in comparing the standards of living of people in different parts of the world. Per capita income, although commonly used, is not one of the most useful measures. Quality of life indicators such as infant mortality, life expectancy, health, and literacy are more helpful in drawing contrasts among countries or societies. The amount and quality of the food people eat is also a very important aspect of their overall standard of living. By any of these measures, a wide gap in living standards exists between the developed and less developed worlds. However, the most acute problems of famine and poverty exist in a group of countries referred to as the least developed countries (LLDC's).

IN REVIEW

1. What comparisons can you make between the location of the First and Third Worlds, and the map of world birth rates (Figure 2.3)?

2. Distinguish between LDC's (less developed countries) and LLDC's (least developed countries).

3. What is meant by the term "standard of living"?

4. Why is it misleading to compare Canada's $12 000 *per capita* with Indonesia's $600 *per capita* as a measure of the contrast in standards of living?

5. Give three examples to show how your standard of living is related to your health.

6. (a) Which parts of the world have the greatest food shortages? Which have the greatest surplus?
   (b) Why can North Americans be considered malnourished?

7. Give three specific examples of ways in which illiteracy restricts economic and social development in the Third World.

APPLYING YOUR KNOWLEDGE

1. Explain why a "poor" person in Canada might be considered "rich" in countries such as Sudan or Afghanistan.

2. Giving specific examples, describe the problems involved in comparing standards of living in different parts of the world.

3. Most of the standard of living data in this chapter are averages for whole countries. What are the limitations of using national averages in identifying the problem of poverty in countries?

4. The definition of literacy varies from one source to another. Suggest criteria to define a functional standard of literacy for Canadians.

FURTHER INVESTIGATION

1. Choose one of the LLDC's shown in Figure 3.2 and do research to find out about the standard of living experienced there.

2. Investigate the relationship between (a) literacy, (b) nutrition, (c) general health, and (d) poverty in Canada. Which groups of Canadians are most likely to have a lower quality of life?

CHAPTER 4

World Food Supply

Decide, mother,
who goes without.
Is it Rama, the strongest,
or Baca, the weakest
who may not need it much longer,
or perhaps Sita?
Who may be expendable?

Decide, mother:
kill a part
of yourself
As you resolve the dilemma.

Decide, mother,
decide
and hate.

—*APPADURA*

This poem was written during the severe famine which struck India during the 1960's. The kind of choice involved in saving one member of a family by sacrificing another is something which most of us in North America know nothing about. Death by starvation is indeed a tragedy, but it is also unnecessary. As you will see, enough food exists in the world to solve this problem.

In this chapter, you will first consider the world food supply in general, then take a closer look at the continent of Africa, parts of which suffered a serious famine in the early 1980's. This famine raised many issues. Was it caused by prolonged drought, or by human factors such as overpopulation and mismanagement of the land? How can the food supply be expanded where it is needed, to avoid repetitions of this kind of problem? Some other questions you will look at in this chapter include the following:

- *How serious is the problem of malnutrition in the world?*
- *Why does famine occur, and can the problem of famine be solved?*
- *How has science helped to increase food production?*

How Serious Is the Food Supply Problem?

Sir John Boyd Orr, the first director of the Food and Agricultural Organization of the United Nations, wrote in 1950 that "A lifetime of malnutrition and hunger is the lot of at least two-thirds of mankind." This dismal view was based on a pre-World War II Food Survey which was finally published in 1946. It now appears that the picture is slightly less pessimistic. Global food production has been more than keeping up with population growth in most years (Figure 4.1(a)). However, at the same time there has been an increase in the number of very poor countries (LLDC's), where famine conditions are present, or threatened. Most of these countries are in tropical Africa, as you saw in Figure 3.2.

One current problem is that the major food exporting countries are very few in number. They are the United States, Canada, Australia,

Photographs such as this one, which shows starving Ugandan children, remind us of the need to understand the causes of famine.

France, and Argentina. The number of importing countries, on the other hand, has risen to over 100. Imports are essential because the urban populations of most of these countries cannot be fed by the surrounding rural land. The people in importing countries quite literally live "from ship to mouth". Consider the consequences of a drought in all the exporting countries, or of a decision to withhold food for political reasons.

FIGURE 4.1a   *Food Production* per capita *in the Developed and Less Developed World*

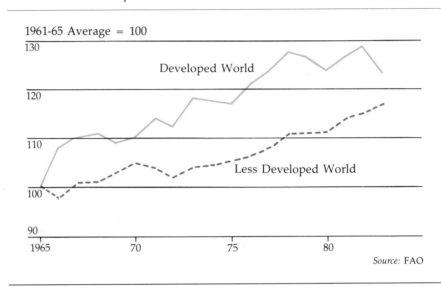

Source: FAO

FIGURE 4.1b   *Food Production* per capita *for Selected Regions in the Less Developed World*

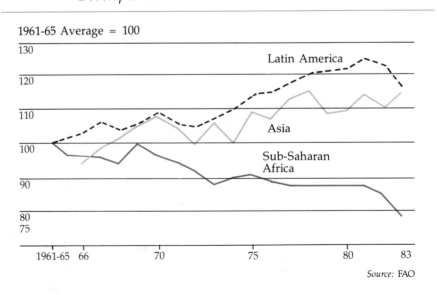

Source: FAO

Trends in Food Output *per Capita*

You can see from Figure 4.1(a) that the developed world has achieved a remarkable increase in *per capita* food production. The trends in the less developed world are not so favourable. A partial reason is that the more rapid increase in population growth in these countries uses up most of the increase in food supply. Yet the graph does show a slow increase in food production per person even in the Third World, except between 1970 and 1972.

When these trends are examined by continent (Figure 4.1(b)), the picture for the Third World becomes clearer. All continents except Africa have been steadily increasing their *per capita* food production since the 1960's. In several individual African countries, the decline in *per capita* food production has been very serious. Eighteen had lower total food production in 1980 than in 1970, even before population growth was taken into account. Figure 4.2 shows the perilous position of a number of countries, most of which are in Africa.

FIGURE 4.2 *Third World Food Production. Which three nations show the largest increase in food production? The largest decrease?*

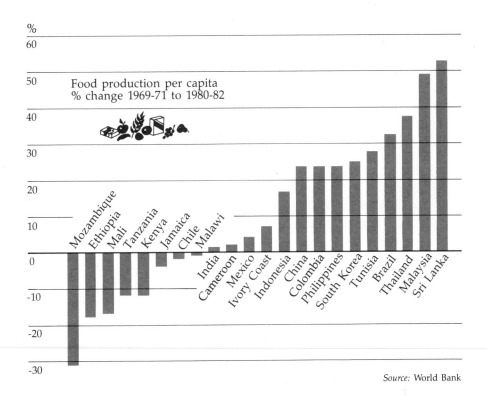

Source: World Bank

The Allocation Problem

Famine, as stated above, is a tragedy, not only because of the intense suffering endured, but also because it is unnecessary. Virtually all agricultural experts agree that the Earth is capable of supporting even the growing population totals of the late 20th century. In the mid-1980's, world food output reached a total of over 12 500 kJ daily for every person alive, which is well above hunger levels.

The problem appears to be one of allocation. Many people have more than enough food, while others have too little. This is true, as you have seen, even in the United States, which has the largest surplus of food in the world. It is equally true in those countries which you likely associate with the problem of hunger. Most of the African countries which were stricken with famine during the early 1980's actually produced enough grain to feed their populations. In Mexico, where 80 percent of the children in rural areas are undernourished, beef cattle consume more grain than the human population.

Why, then, is malnutrition so widespread? The simple answer is that, throughout the world, the people who are most in need of food usually cannot afford to buy it. A factor which contributes to this situation is that landowners in less developed nations often find it more profitable to grow crops or to produce animals for markets in western nations than to grow the food which is needed locally. Moreover, they are often encouraged to produce these **cash crops** by their own governments. In less developed nations, the money which the governments gain from the export of cash crops is needed to pay for imports of manufactured goods.

The Hunger Cycle

As you have seen, hunger and poverty are closely related. It is common today to speak of a "hunger cycle", shown in Figure 4.3. This cycle has also been described as the "vicious cycle of poverty". Poor and malnourished people may have neither the energy nor the education to improve their own circumstances. Unless this self-perpetuating cycle is broken, it is clear that the well-being of the people trapped in it will steadily decrease.

FIGURE 4.3   *The Hunger Cycle. If you were the leader of a Third World country, at what point would you propose to try to break this cycle? Why?*

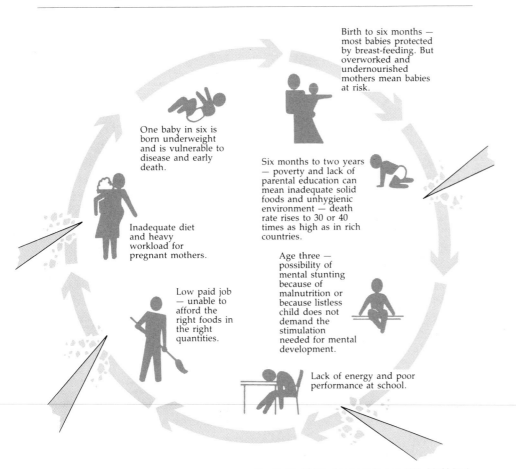

Birth to six months — most babies protected by breast-feeding. But overworked and undernourished mothers mean babies at risk.

One baby in six is born underweight and is vulnerable to disease and early death.

Six months to two years — poverty and lack of parental education can mean inadequate solid foods and unhygienic environment — death rate rises to 30 or 40 times as high as in rich countries.

Inadequate diet and heavy workload for pregnant mothers.

Age three — possibility of mental stunting because of malnutrition or because listless child does not demand the stimulation needed for mental development.

Low paid job — unable to afford the right foods in the right quantities.

Lack of energy and poor performance at school.

Source: World Development Report 1985, *World Bank*

Is the Problem Physical or Human?

You have probably been wondering about this very question as you read the past few pages. Are outbreaks of famine caused mainly by natural disasters such as droughts or floods, or by human beings themselves? For example, has the persistent famine in Africa been caused by the 18 years of lower-than-average rainfall in the Sahel area south of the Sahara Desert? Or are its main causes population growth, political factors, and mismanagement of the land? To find answers, it is necessary to take a closer look at the continent which has suffered most from famine for the past two decades.

QUESTIONS

1. Refer to Figure 4.1(a) and (b).
   (a) What is the trend of world *per capita* food supply?
   (b) In which continents is the trend most favourable? Least favourable?

2. Why do many Third World farmers grow some cash crops for export as well as traditional food crops for local consumption?

3. (a) According to the diagram of the hunger cycle (Figure 4.3), what is the cause of inadequate diet and unhygienic environment for some young children?
   (b) Suggest how the hunger cycle might be broken.

How might a preference for imported cereals contribute to lower grain production in Africa?

Africa—Continent of Famine

Hunger and malnutrition exist in all parts of the world, but Africa is the one continent whose *per capita* food output has declined since 1970. By 1984, as many as 35 million Africans were threatened by famine. This is a number greater than all the casualties in World War II. Yet the World Food Council claimed in 1974, "In ten years no child will go to bed hungry." The extent of the crisis in Africa was unexpected. The continent actually has a lower population density and more potentially arable land per person than Asia.

Africa's problems are related to its exceptional rate of population growth. The birth rate, 45 per thousand in the early 1980's, is much higher than that of any other continent. Population growth has averaged 3 percent a year, with no immediate sign of a decline. According to Edouard Saouma, director general of the Food and Agriculture Organization, "Many African countries, if they do not take positive action to encourage a drop in fertility rates, are speeding headlong towards disaster."

Africa also has a very high rate of **urbanization**. City dwellers have increasingly turned to imported cereals such as wheat, instead of the traditional millet and sorghum. One reason for this trend is a desire to consume "western" foods. Another is that, for political reasons, some African governments have deliberately kept down the price of the

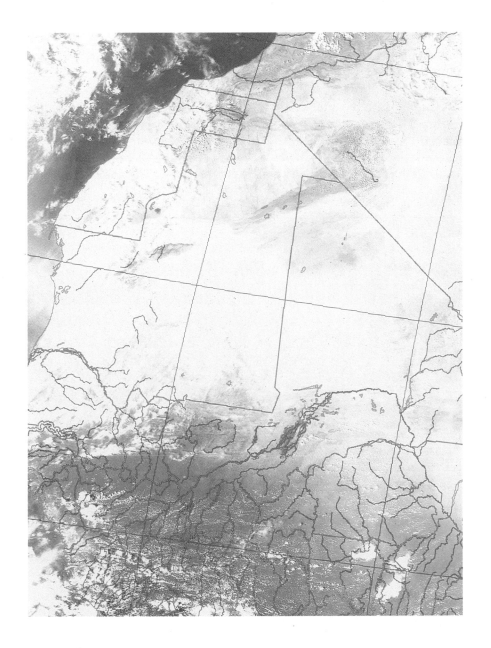

The vegetation of the grasslands of northwest Africa stands out in visible contrast to the bordering desert.

imported cereals consumed in the cities. Local farmers can therefore earn more by producing cash crops for export rather than food crops for local consumption. The result of all these factors is that many African countries have been importing food at an increasing rate while local agriculture stagnates.

Desertification: The Expanding Deserts

The African continent's main problem areas lie in two broad belts. In both locations, the desert has been expanding into the drier part of the **savanna**. The problem zone in the north of the continent is south of the

Sahara desert. Here, the Sahara has been pushing southward into what is known as the Sahel zone. The problem area in the south of the continent is north of the Kalahari. The Kalahari has been reaching northward into a wide area stretching from Angola to Mozambique. Figure 4.4 shows these belts and the countries which lie entirely or partially in them.

FIGURE 4.4 *Famine-struck Nations of Africa (early 1980's). Identify the nations affected by the advance of the Sahara.*

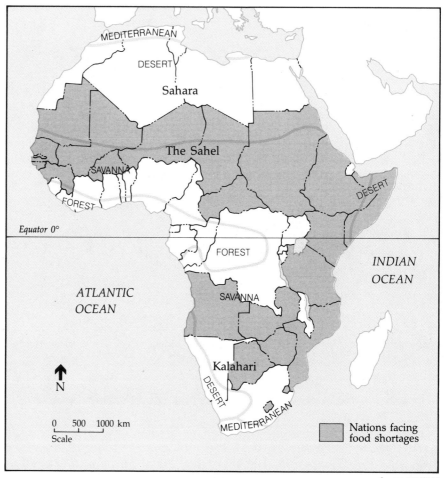

Source: UNFAO

Several of the affected countries have no access to the ocean. Indeed, Africa has half of the world's land-locked nations. Examples include Mali, Niger, and Chad. Without direct access to the ocean, their transportation problems are considerable. In addition the boundaries of most African countries have very little to do with natural features or tribal lands. They are the legacy of the scramble for colonial territory in the late 19th century.

FIGURE 4.5   *Rainfall Trends in the Sahel Zone*

Sahel rain

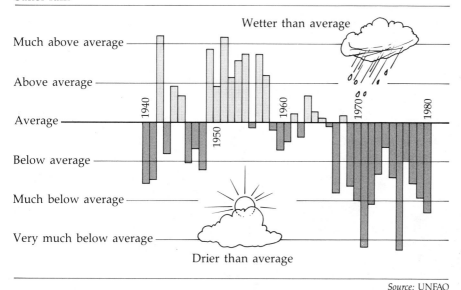

Source: UNFAO

The deserts have been steadily expanding since 1970, as the margins of the savanna have dried out and been replaced by sands. Satellite photographs show the southward march of the Sahara into the Sahel. The "green line" of well-watered vegetation has retreated south at the rate of several kilometres a year.

What can account for the rapid advance of the deserts at the expense of the savanna? The situation is a prime example of the issue raised earlier: Is nature to blame, or are people?

Figure 4.5 indicates a drier-than-average period since 1968. Rivers have dried up, and even large Lake Chad has shrunk to about one-third of its former size. Yet experts say that the drought alone would not have caused the advance of the desert. Human action has affected the vegetation and has intensified the drought.

Africa's rapid population growth has put pressure on the land in various ways. The first source of trouble is deforestation. Trees have been cut down at an alarming rate, and the wood used for fuel. Very little replanting has been done, with the result that there is now a massive shortage of wood. In addition, the absence of trees has exposed the soil to wind and sun, and reduced its capacity to retain moisture. Secondly, overgrazing has further depleted the soil and exposed it to wind erosion. When rain comes, it runs off quickly, rather than soaking into the soil. Drought can therefore be followed by flooding which carries the soil away. A third form of pressure on the

Why is desertification a serious problem for the people of the Sahel?

land, overcropping, is perhaps the most serious cause of soil erosion. Many Africans earn their living by cultivating crops. Cultivation exposes the soil more fully to the elements and causes further erosion.

Changing lifestyles have also had their effect on the soil. Many African countries now have border patrols, with the result that fewer people are nomadic. Migratory herding has been replaced by more permanent settlement near water holes. Migratory herds tended to move on before an area was overgrazed, but now the land around the waterholes is suffering badly from overgrazing. It is ironic that these watering points become the spreading centres in the process of **desertification**.

It is unfortunate that the warnings which were sounded after the first phase of the long drought (1968–1973) were largely ignored. Even though a Conference on Desertification was held by the United Nations in 1977, deforestation continued to exceed tree planting many times over. In many African nations, government funds were often devoted to status projects instead of land conservation. Skyscrapers were built in the cities, national airlines were established, and lavish embassies were built. Many countries also spent heavily on arms.

International aid was frequently diverted to urban projects, while the rural poor, who have little political power, were ignored. Tragically, very little money was earmarked for research into the farming problems of the continent. It is not surprising, therefore, that the second phase of severe drought in the Sahel (during the early 1980's) brought an even greater famine than the first.

It has been claimed that desertification is irreversible. First, land which has no vegetation reflects more of the Sun's heat than forest or grassland does. As a result, hot, dry air tends to remain near the ground. Thus, through overuse of the land, people may directly affect the climate of the dry belts. Second, the trend of the prevailing winds in the Sahel is southward, from desert to forest. The reseeding of dried-out areas in wetter years is prevented by this natural condition. However, in the late 1980's, reforestation of some parts of the Sahel seemed successful in preventing further desertification.

Why are migratory herds of cattle a better farming method in the Sahel than permanent farm settlements?

A Visit to Timbuktu

In the inland republic of Mali, near a bend of the Niger River and just south of the Sahara Desert, lies a small city. This is Timbuktu, once a thriving centre of caravan routes carrying salt, dates, and gold (Figure 4.6). Today Timbuktu is threatened with extinction as the Sahara spreads southward. The Niger's waters are irregular, wood for fuel is scarce, and grazing land yields almost no fodder.

Here is an excerpt from the eyewitness account of Marcia Pérez de Cuéllar, wife of the Secretary General of the United Nations, upon her visit to Timbuktu on February 22nd, 1984:

"My first impression was of sand....It was everywhere, hiding our feet ankle-high as we walked, and in the colour of the sky—all around us this gray-brown sand.

FIGURE 4.6 *Location of Timbuktu*

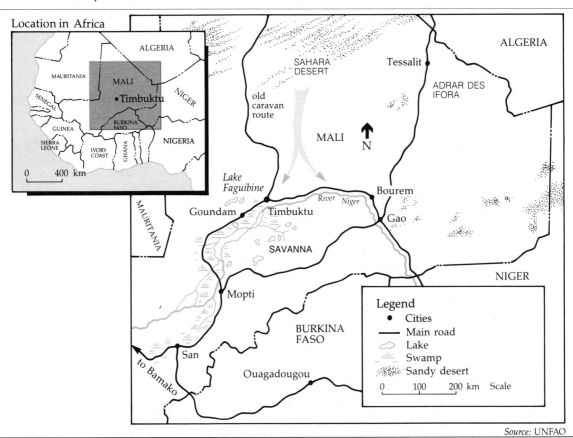

Source: UNFAO

The spread of the Sahara to the area surrounding Timbuktu is threatening the future of this historic centre.

When we turn on the water tap we never think that a place like Timbuktu exists where there is no tap to turn on, no well to fetch water from. There is simply no means of getting water. Walking through the earthen streets, we witnessed the most terrible misery, and I could feel the tears growing inside me. The children had enormous stomachs and sunken eyes, with flies crawling on their faces. . . .

. . . .I have seen misery before and know it well. I have seen it at first hand many times in my country, and in other places in the world—but misery as I saw there, never. And Timbuktu lies at the heart of a world of dark sand, heavy and thick, with no chance of escape.

There are not many who believe in miracles, but I am one. I also believe that only a miracle can save those fellow human beings of ours who live in such conditions. They themselves are resigned to their fate, but we who are so privileged cannot resign ourselves to allowing even a single Timbuktu to exist in this world."

QUESTIONS

1. Name two problems being created by the high rate of urbanization in Africa.

2. Why do some African countries import wheat?

3. (a) Where is the Sahel?
   (b) List three problems experienced in the Sahel, and explain what caused them.
   (c) What can be done to overcome them?

4. Describe the disadvantages faced by land-locked countries such as Mali and Chad.

5. Why is Timbuktu threatened with extinction?

Famine Relief

In the early 1980's, the continent of Africa experienced a famine of massive proportions. Yet the full force of the disaster was not brought home to the world at large until October 3rd, 1984, when BBC correspondent Michael Buerk gave an eight-minute televised report on Ethiopia. Within a few days, the report had been seen in an estimated 490 million households throughout the world. Though the world's attention was captured mainly by media images of the starving in Ethiopia and the Sudan, over a dozen nations were equally affected.

The international response was immediate and generous. Millions of dollars in aid were given by governments and private aid organizations. The fundraising event which received most publicity was the Live Aid Concert, held simultaneously in London and Philadelphia in July, 1985. This concert, given by over 60 rock singers and groups, raised $71.5 million (U.S) for famine relief. About 40 percent of this sum went to short-term relief, including the purchase of trucks and the chartering of ships to carry food. The remainder went to longer-term development schemes. Numerous other efforts, such as the recording made by the Canadian group Northern Lights, "Tears Are Not Enough", added to the volume of aid. One especially interesting fact emerged from the aid statistics. The Inuit community at Frobisher Bay, N.W.T., itself used to hardship, donated more aid per person than any other community in the world.

There are commonly many difficulties in making the most effective use of funds raised by international aid organizations. Some of these problems are political; others are related to the actual transporting of food and other aid to those who need them.

Name two problems faced by famine relief workers such as Jean Babcock and Sister Helene Lemay of Canada, and suggest a solution for each.

Midge Ure, a member of the British group Band-Aid, helps to load famine relief supplies destined for Ethiopia. These supplies were paid for out of the more than 5 million dollars the group raised for famine relief.

Political Problems

Helping any country can be made very difficult by internal political problems. Ethiopia, for example, has experienced a long-running civil war. The conflict is between the Marxist government of Colonel Mengistu Haile Miriam and the rebel provinces of Tigre and Eritrea in the north (Figure 4.7). The Ethiopian government considers access to the Red Sea via Eritrea a vital interest. As a result of the war, much of the government's limited money has been diverted to military spending.

FIGURE 4.7   *Famine Areas of Ethiopia and Sudan. Why would it be more difficult for relief workers to provide aid to the people of Al Fashir?*

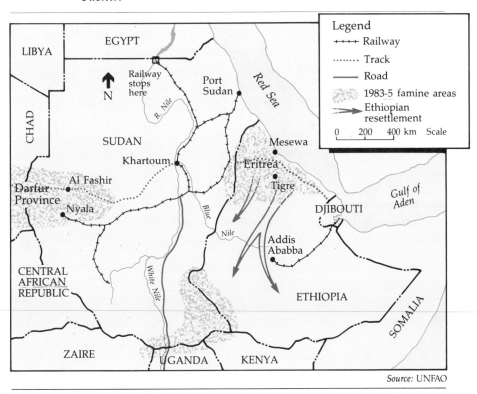

Source: UNFAO

The Ethiopian government's strategy for coping with the famine was to resettle starving people from the northern provinces to the better-watered south. (Here, coincidentally, they were less likely to take up arms on the side of the rebels.) This scheme, which moved perhaps half a million people in 1984–1985 alone, was highly controversial. Red Cross field workers claimed that up to 10 percent died as a result of unsanitary conditions and infectious disease in the resettlement camps. On the other hand, the Ethiopian government has described the resettlement as an almost complete success. To avoid the risk of expulsion, the western aid agencies working with the United Nations were obliged to cooperate with the Ethiopian government. They found themselves unable to channel aid as they wished, yet they could not criticize the policies of the government.

As a result, little aid reached the northern provinces, which were the hardest hit. There were some emergency relief camps, so often pictured on Canadian television screens. It was aid from non-governmental organizations which first reached the famine-stricken north. Canadian government aid did not reach these provinces until public awareness in Canada caused a change in policy.

Transport Problems

To the west of Ethiopia lies the huge nation of Sudan (Figure 4.7). If anything, drought and desertification have been even more serious here. In 1984–1985, food aid was rushed to Port Sudan from where it could be easily transported by road to the capital, Khartoum. The famine regions lay far to the west of Khartoum, however, and aid organizations quickly learned that the "roads" shown on maps were no better than desert tracks. One railway line heading west did exist, but it was in such a poor state of repair that only one train each three days could make the journey, carrying a small fraction of the food urgently needed.

The cost and availability of transport are major problems in any food aid project. In 1984–1985, food could be shipped from Montreal to Port Sudan for $90 per tonne, but the UN paid $260 per tonne to move the same food to Nyala in western Sudan. Delivery by air would have cost $20 000 per flight. The airplanes would have had to carry enough fuel for the return journey, reducing their food payload to a mere eight tonnes. Transport by truck was therefore adopted as the least unsatisfactory alternative. Live Aid money helped to finance it.

Is Food Self-sufficiency Possible in Africa?

The continent of Africa had been close to self-sufficiency in food production in 1970. By 1985 about one-quarter of its entire population depended upon imported food, much of it in the form of aid. Yet there are signs that African countries have begun to recognize the gravity of

their situation. According to Stephen Lewis, Canada's former ambassador to the United Nations, there is a new spirit of willingness among African nations to take responsibility for agricultural reform. Long-term programs such as the World Bank Special Fund for Sub-Saharan Development are now in place. These programs are aimed at removing the causes of famine rather than supplying short-term aid, however necessary this may be on humanitarian grounds.

Longer-term economic development plans for African countries include more state investment in agriculture, the creation of food reserves, and improved transport and marketing facilities. Scientific and agricultural programs call for a massive effort to improve soil conservation, together with more irrigation projects, flood control, and drainage measures. Livestock herds are to be improved, fish production encouraged, and forestry better integrated with farming. All these advances need to be accompanied by improvements in health and education.

Delivering food aid to areas of Western Sudan poses many problems.

The Harare Declaration

At the UN Food and Agricultural Organization conference held in Harare, Zimbabwe in July, 1984, African ministers of agriculture made the following declaration:

"WE, THE AFRICAN MINISTERS, RESPONSIBLE FOR AGRICULTURE AND RURAL DEVELOPMENT, AND FOR FOOD PRODUCTION AND DISTRIBUTION....

....solemnly resolve to overcome the crisis of food and agriculture in Africa and achieve our priority objective of raising the level of food security, and to this end declare as follows:

We fully accept that the burden of developing our agriculture and rural areas and raising the nutritional standards of all our peoples rests substantially on the efforts of our own Governments and peoples.

We pledge ourselves to continue to give the highest priority to agricultural and rural development among our national priorities, plans, budgets and programmes....we shall adopt more effective policies for food and agricultural development....we shall carry out these policies....on the basis of country specific strategies:

1. Allocation of adequate resources to support agricultural production at all levels with a special emphasis on smallholders.

2. Establishment of improved incentive systems through higher producer prices, more efficient marketing systems....and greater involvement of farmers in decision making.

3. Provision of credit facilities and timely payment of farmers' entitlements.

4. Improvement....of irrigation schemes and rural roads.

5. Intensification of training and research....in appropriate technologies, crops, livestock, fisheries and forestry.

6. Expansion of pest control and measures to reduce post-harvest losses.

7. Eradication of animal diseases and pests.

We appreciate the attention and support being given to help in solving the African food crisis by multinational and bilateral organizations, in particular the FAO.

We call on all international organizations and donor agencies to increase their financial and material assistance to accelerate agricultural development in the region.

Harvesting wheat in Kenya.

We solemnly put forward this...declaration...in the conviction that we possess the will and capacity, and have the full support of the international community, to feed all our peoples and to lay the foundation for greater economic prosperity and self-reliance in Africa."

It is much easier to list the problems of Africa than to solve them. The Harare Declaration may not easily be translated into action. It will require a great deal of political will and outside help to be achieved. The process is likely to be slow, but for the 35 million threatened by famine there is not much time.

QUESTIONS

1. Why do you think the response to the appeal to help alleviate Africa's famine was so great?

2. Politics often make the delivery of aid difficult. How did the Ethiopia aid program demonstrate this?

3. Why is the distribution of food aid within a country such as Sudan a major problem?

4. List five ways in which aid money can be spent on long-term development projects in Africa.

Solutions to the Problem of World Food Supply

There are four main factors involved in the problem of world food supply:

- population numbers

- population growth rate

- the amount and quality of arable land

- yields of food per hectare.

The first two were examined in Chapter 2. You have seen that the less developed countries contain the majority of the world's people, and have the highest population growth rates. You will now look in turn at the other two elements of the situation: the amount and quality of the world's farm land, and the techniques that can be used to increase the yield of food from a given area.

Is More Farm Land Necessary?

You read earlier that the world's food-producing land can be classified as arable (ploughed to grow crops) or grazing (used to feed animals). Since crop-growing usually produces a larger amount of food, the better land tends to be used for this purpose. Grazing is usually relegated to poorer, marginal land, in which the rainfall is too low or the soil too poor to permit crop production.

Table 4.1 shows how the amount of the world's arable land has changed in the three decades 1950–1980. The figures at left refer to the total of arable land. About one-third of this land is usually left fallow

Traditionally, how would the land needs of a cattle rancher compare with those of a crop farmer?

North American grain growers have increased the size of their individual holdings as farm technology has improved.

(temporarily unused) every year. Note that the area devoted to crops also includes **industrial crops** such as cotton or tobacco, and **fodder crops** grown to feed animals. The area devoted to growing food for people is probably under a thousand million hectares, as the figures on the right of the table reveal.

You can readily see from Table 4.1 that the developed world has

TABLE 4.1 *Availability of Arable Land (1950 to 1980)*

	All arable land				Area under Major Food Crops			
	1950*	1980*	% change	Hectares *per capita*	1950*	1980*	% change	Hectares *per capita*
Africa	228	181	-20	0.27	58	99	+71	0.19
Asia	348	452	+30	0.16	338	393	+16	0.14
Latin America	86	171	+99	0.41	42	87	+99	0.22
Total Developing	662	804	+21	0.21	438	579	+32	0.16
Europe	148	140	-5	0.29	92	86	-7	0.18
North America	220	236	+7	0.89	124	127	+2	0.49
Oceania	17	46	+171	1.92	7	17	+143	0.71
USSR	175	232	+32	0.84	109	142	+30	0.52
Total Developed	560	654	+17	0.62	332	372	+12	0.35
Total World	1222	1458	+19	0.30	770	951	+23	0.20

* 1950 and 1980 data in million hectares
Note: Africa's figures include fallow in 1950, but not in 1980.

Source: UNFAO

more than twice as much land for food crops *per capita* as the less developed world. The world average of one-fifth of a hectare per person is perhaps more easily imagined as a square of land 45 m by 45 m. This is "your share" of the world's food crop land. Figure 4.8 shows the amount of arable land *per capita* in several countries, including Canada.

FIGURE 4.8   *Land Distribution* (per capita)

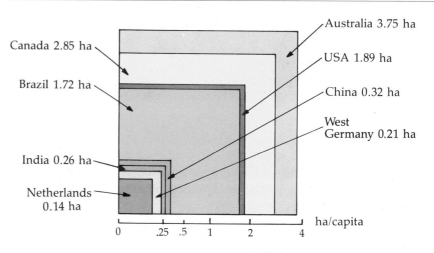

Source: World Development Report 1985, *World Bank*

Various estimates have been made as to how much potential arable land there is in the world. Some experts claim that any small increases in arable land will be offset by losses to urban and other non-agricultural uses of land, leaving no net increase. Others suggest that the total could be doubled—to over 3 thousand million hectares.

The wide gap between these estimates is easily explained. To achieve a figure of 3 thousand million hectares, vast sections of tropical rainforest would have to be cleared for agriculture. Also, large areas of grazing land would have to be changed over to crop land. Can you think of some difficulties with turning either of these areas over to growing food crops?

From Chapter 1, you are already familiar with the environmental problems of clearing the tropical forests. It now seems unlikely that the rainforests will be the scene of major agricultural developments, except perhaps in silty areas close to rivers.

The second main possibility for extending arable land, reclaiming grazing land, would involve mainly the tropical grasslands. Achieving this would require substantial amounts of irrigation, using **groundwater** or surface supplies. It is possible that falling groundwater levels might result, which would be counterproductive in the long run.

Irrigation schemes using surface water are expensive. A final barrier to reclaiming grazing land is that the farmers must be willing to change their way of life from herding to crop farming. In fact, they are often reluctant to do so. Can you suggest some reasons for their reluctance?

Higher Yields from Existing Farmland

Until the 1950's, most increases in world food production came from the expansion of the farmed area. But now most of the world's good land is already in production. The steady increases in food production since the 1960's have come from more intensive use of the land. Yields per hectare have been raised by the use of fertilizers, mechanization, improved irrigation, and scientific plant and animal breeding. Note that most of these innovations demand increased use of energy, particularly in the form of fossil fuels such as oil.

Yields per hectare are also likely to increase when farmers expect to receive a higher price for their crops. Take the example of China. For two decades, China has been committed to producing its food crops in collective communes in which large groups of farmers work an area of land. Wheat output grew very slowly until 1978, when the government allowed farmers to produce food grains on private plots. Simultaneously, it increased the prices which farmers would receive for their crops. In the seven years after 1978, China doubled its grain production and now surpasses the U.S.S.R. as the world's largest wheat producer. One journalist proclaimed that the vicious cycle of poverty had been replaced by a "virtuous cycle of plenty"!

Irrigation

Irrigation is the supplying of supplementary water to crops where precipitation is lacking or unreliable. Almost one-fifth of the world's crop land was irrigated in the mid-1980's. Irrigation schemes may be simple measures which allow high-level river flow to flood onto fields—in which case the irrigation water may be as unreliable as precipitation. Much more costly, but more reliable, are schemes based on storage dams which can provide regular water supplies. Water is delivered by canals or pipes, and applied to fields by either surface channels or sprinklers. Good drainage is essential on irrigated land, to avoid the problem of salts being left on the surface by the evaporation of water.

The Green Revolution

In the 1960's, much agricultural research was dedicated to breeding **high-yielding varieties** of crops. These were intended to meet the food needs of Third World countries. Scientific crop breeding has been going on since the turn of the century. However, in the 1960's experimental results indicated that a doubling, or even tripling, of crop yields was possible. The projects, which received extensive publicity, were heralded as a **Green Revolution**. The term was coined by journalists, not by the researchers themselves.

The high-yielding varieties (HYV's) were to be supported by increased use of fertilizers, insecticides, and water control, as well as by improved transportation, storage, and marketing facilities. Figure 4.9 shows how the new varieties can help farmers to break out of the cycle of poverty.

FIGURE 4.9 *Diagram Showing the Benefits of the Green Revolution*

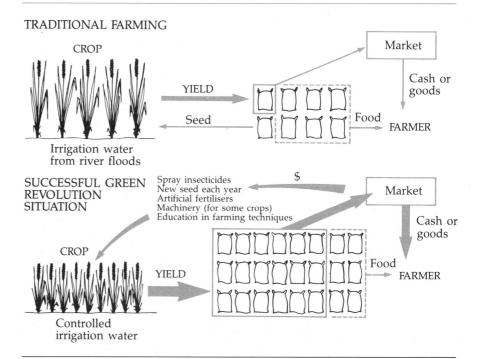

Wheat and rice are the world's most important grain crops. Therefore, research was concentrated on them. The results obtained from the planting of the new varieties of each differed considerably, however, as you will see.

Northwest India (the Punjab) and Pakistan became the focal points of attempts to improve wheat production. Most of the varieties planted

Harvesting high-yield wheat in Zambia.

Experimental rice being grown at the International Research Station in the Philippines.

were bred in Mexico at the International Wheat Institute. High-yielding wheat varieties usually have short stems to reduce the problem of *lodging* (flattening by wind and rain). These dwarf wheats were bred to be adapted to the relatively low latitude of the Punjab, where the shortness of the summer days would prevent Canadian varieties from completing their life cycles.

High-yielding wheats take more nutrients out of the soils than traditional varieties, and therefore require more fertilizer. Much of the additional water they need has come from cheaply drilled tube wells. Thus, as mentioned earlier, the introduction of the new varieties has its price—the increased use of technology, which requires both money and energy.

Both India and Pakistan experienced quick successes. India expanded its wheat output from 10 to 26 million tonnes in the 1964 to 1972 period, and in the early 1980's achieved 35 million tonnes. Wheat production doubled in Pakistan between 1963 and 1975. Both countries have been able to dispense with wheat imports, except in bad years.

Critics of the Green Revolution claim that the increase in grain production has been achieved at the expense of social justice. Rich farmers have gained most, since they are the ones best able to pay for the necessary fertilizer, machinery, and tube wells. In some places the gap between rich and poor has widened as a result. People who must buy food therefore end up paying more for it—and can least afford to do so. Nevertheless, wheat production continues to expand, not only in India and Pakistan, but also in many other countries.

Rice, the other major food grain crop in the world, accounts for half the total diet of 1.6 thousand million people. It has been more difficult to raise the output of rice than of wheat, despite a succession of new varieties from the International Rice Research Institute (IRRI) in the Philippines. Water control is the main barrier to the successful cultivation of the new varieties. Rice spends much of its life cycle growing in water, during the **monsoon** or wet season. The dwarf varieties produced by the IRRI require very precise water control, which is lacking in much of flood-prone eastern India. Pests and diseases have also proved more of a problem in the humid rice-growing areas than in the

How can the building of a tube well improve local crop yields?

How can traditional conservation methods such as terracing be combined with the new technology of the Green Revolution to produce higher rice yields?

drier wheat lands. Finally, the colour, texture, and taste of the new rices were not well received by people used to traditional varieties.

Rice production increased in India by only about one-fifth during the period in which wheat output tripled. Most of this increase can be attributed to irrigated rice growing in the Punjab, where existing irrigation facilities make water control easier, and the intense sunshine helps to increase the yields.

The Problem of Gene Shortage

The Green Revolution raised hopes that world hunger would soon end. The results have been rather mixed so far, as the above examples indicate, but plant breeding remains at the centre of the struggle to increase crop yields.

Agricultural experts have sounded an urgent warning, however. One great risk is attached to the large-scale adoption of the new HYV's. If people cultivate only these varieties, there is a great danger of losing the stock of plant genes from which further new varieties can be bred. When farmers come to rely on just a few strains of any plant, a new disease can wipe out a large portion of a nation's harvest. This has already happened—in 1970, parts of the U.S. lost almost their entire **hybrid** corn crop. Some areas of the Third World are especially rich in the genes of food plants. In fact, virtually all of the world's food crops originated in these regions. During the famine in Ethiopia, which is a major centre of genetic diversity, some important varieties became extinct because all the seeds were eaten and none was stored for future use.

One solution is to maintain genetic banks where seeds from a great diversity of plants can be frozen and stored. Such storage banks already exist. Most of them are run by companies in western countries, which have invested millions of dollars in genetic research. Developing nations, which are the source of most of the plant genes, are seeking a greater degree of control of these genetic banks.

QUESTIONS

1. What are the four main factors in the problem of world food supply?

2. Define "arable land", "marginal land", and "yield per hectare".

3. Refer to Table 4.1, which shows data on arable and food crop land.
   (a) Which continents have shown the biggest percentage changes in arable land? What reasons can you suggest for this?
   (b) Why do you think the amount of farm land in Europe decreased during 1950–1980?
   (c) Which continents are best off for crop land *per capita*? Which are worst off?

4. (a) State four ways in which farming can be intensified to produce higher crop yields.
   (b) Why have these techniques been more successfully applied to growing wheat than to growing rice?

New Food Sources

The situation in Africa suggests that much remains to be done to increase food production. Among the ways of doing this are improving farming techniques and creating a better economic environment for farmers. But there are various possible means of producing food other than by conventional agriculture. The world's food needs may also be met by the introduction of new types of food, including synthetic foods.

Food from the Waters

Fishing has long been a major source of food for many of the world's people. However, modern fishing is not very energy efficient, since one tonne of oil is used as fuel in catching one tonne of gutted fish. Overfishing is another problem. The world's *per capita* catch of fish has been falling since 1970 as a result. Many of the best areas have been overfished, endangering future stocks. The Grand Banks off Canada's Atlantic Coast, for example, are fished by vessels from Canada, the U.S.S.R., Europe, and the United States. Canada's 320 km limit does not extend far enough to offer full protection for these fishing grounds. In addition, international treaties to limit catches are often broken, and are difficult to enforce.

Alongside traditional fishing, there is now **aquaculture** , the fishing equivalent of agriculture. Fish hatcheries increase the supply of fish in rivers, lakes, and the ocean, while fish farms both produce and grow fish to the point of harvest. Aquaculture is practised in many western countries, including Canada, but is perhaps best developed in eastern Asia. Fish farms appear to have considerable potential in the tropics, especially if species like carp, which can tolerate dirty water, are produced.

Why are traditional fishing methods such as the two pictured here not able to meet the current demand for fish?

*State one advantage and one
disadvantage resulting from
aquaculture.*

Fish are an excellent source of protein. Nevertheless, fish farming often produces less protein in a given area than growing beans does, or the same amount but at a higher cost. Another problem is that aquaculture may be responsible for water pollution. Numerous fish farms have been established along the coast of British Columbia north of Vancouver. The volumes of waste produced by the concentration of fish have become a cause for concern. Another danger is the threat of disease, which could not only devastate the farmed fish, but also spread to natural stocks.

Other ways of using the world's water resources as a source of food depend on the enormous rate of photosynthesis which takes place in water. Aquatic weeds such as the water hyacinth could be used as a source of protein or as animal fodder. The oceans also produce vast amounts of micro-organisms. Attempts have been made to grow certain of these, such as blue-green algae, on plastic screens hung from rafts. In the Bahamas, such experiments yielded five times as much organic material per unit area as could be achieved by prairie farming. You may not find the prospect of eating algae particularly appetizing!

Indeed, it would cause problems for your digestive system. However, algae would make a protein-rich animal fodder.

While it may be too early to speak of a "Blue Revolution", then, the world's water resources do offer some promise for improving the overall food supply.

New Food Crops

At the present time, people consume only a very limited percentage of the world's edible food plants. About 20 000 such plants exist, of which only 100 are eaten. A mere 22 of these feed the bulk of the world's population. Nutritionists claim that several of the main food plants could be replaced, or at least supplemented, by other plants which are at least as nourishing. One of these, tarweed, has the potential to rival the soybean, the world's leading protein-rich vegetable. Another, amaranth, offers both protein-rich leaves and a very nutritious grain. Both come from the Andes Mountains of South America, an area of very rich plant diversity. The bean of the lupin, a flower which grows in gardens and fields, has been found to be rich in protein. Lupin flour has been developed for pasta, bread, and cakes.

Most people enjoy foods which are familiar, and resist change. Yet, given the rapidly growing world population, it is likely that new food crops will supplement traditional sources of food, for at least some of the world's people.

Synthetic Foods

Popular mythology has suggested that our daily food intake could be replaced by a diet of pills. This will never be possible, since our bodies require a certain minimum amount of both dry matter and liquids to function properly. But synthetic foods, foods made by chemical rather than biological processes, are a definite possibility. Vitamins, for example, are already being made more cheaply from chemicals than they could be from natural sources.

The main element in food is carbon. Therefore, today's research into synthetic foods centres on the economical conversion of compounds of carbon, such as petroleum and methane, into edible protein. The idea of such a conversion is not new—it was done in Germany during World War II. As you know, however, these carbon-based fuels are themselves in limited supply. Future research is more likely to examine ocean sediments, shales, tar sands, and possibly even atmospheric carbon dioxide as sources of carbon for synthesizing food.

The main obstacle to the development of synthetic foods is that the developed countries, which can afford the necessary research, have no real need of the products. They already possess large surpluses of food. Accordingly, the pace of development has been slow.

The Reduction of Waste

Continued research into new food sources is valuable. Still, it should be kept in mind that the world's existing food sources could be used far more efficently if the amount of waste were reduced. At present, the world's food trade goes largely to support the lifestyle of the western countries. Meat forms a large proportion of the diet of developed nations. Vast amounts of high-protein fish meal are fed to animals kept for food. The United States and West Germany buy large amounts of this meal from protein-deficient Peru. Protein from oil seed crops such as soybeans is also exported in great quantities from protein-poor Third World countries to the west in the form of poultry feed. Above all, since animals are inefficient converters of energy, the meat industries of western countries use several times more land than would be necessary if their populations consumed a mainly vegetable diet (Figure 4.10).

How does the Third World support the developed world's demand for beef?

FIGURE 4.10   *Plants and Animals as Converters of Energy*

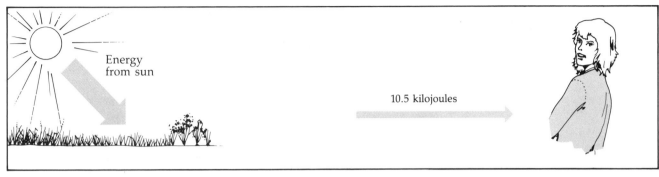

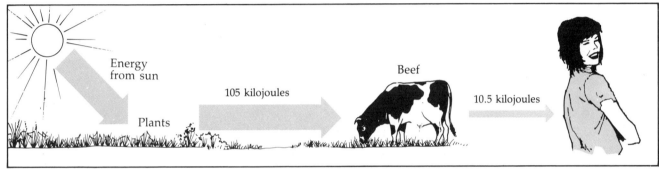

One of the marks of a high standard of living is that a nation can afford to use land exclusively for fodder crops. This is a luxury which most of the world does not enjoy.

Huge volumes of nutrients are also disposed of in the form of sewage. This is another luxury which is taken for granted in western countries. The Chinese, on the other hand, have long recycled human waste instead of disposing of it. Their crop yields are greatly increased by this practice. The processing of sewage waste into fertilizers could be an option in developed nations as well, especially if chemical fertilizers, which are based on oil, become very expensive.

QUESTIONS

1. What are three possible new sources of food?

2. Why are fish a valuable part of the diet?

3. Canada is a leading exporter of fish. What problems does it face in maintaining that position?

4. Why has there been so little progress in the introduction of new sources of food in North American diets?

Chapter Summary

In this chapter, you have seen just how complex the problems of food production and distribution are. While many people blame drought for the period of famine in Africa, the real causes are human in origin. Population growth, mismanagement of the land, and political problems combined to turn drought into famine.

Droughts and other natural disasters will recur. However, improvements in farming techniques and the application of scientific plant breeding and plant genetics to farming can keep food production ahead of population growth. There is also the possibility of developing new sources of food. However, a more positive political environment is necessary to prevent further outbreaks of famine.

IN REVIEW

1. The world's food supply is expanding faster than the growth of population. Suggest three reasons why famine still occurs despite this progress.

2. Define the following terms: food self-sufficiency, the hunger cycle, desertification.

3. Describe the causes, other than drought, which hasten desertification.

4. (a) What is the Green Revolution?
   (b) Describe two problems created by the Green Revolution.

5. Explain why the world can support more people on a diet of vegetable foods than on a diet of animal foods.

6. Discuss the problems which must be overcome to provide new food sources as a solution to the world's food problems.

APPLYING YOUR KNOWLEDGE

1. Suggest three long-term development projects in Africa on which money could effectively be spent.

2. In this chapter, a number of reasons were given to explain why desertification was allowed to continue, despite knowledge of the problem. Can you think of a Canadian environmental problem on which action is needed? What reasons are there for lack of action in this area?

3. The text states that in Mexico, 80 percent of the children in rural areas are undernourished. How do you think such data are obtained?

4. At what point in the hunger cycle is intervention likely to be least expensive and most effective?

5. This chapter opens with a poem about hunger.
   (a) What responsibility do you think Canada has to alleviate world hunger?
   (b) How can individuals best contribute to this effort?

FURTHER INVESTIGATION

1. (a) Use a food energy intake chart to try to estimate your total energy intake for a 24 h period. From what sources do you obtain your proteins?
   (b) Compare your food energy intake and diet to those frequently found in Third World countries. What differences are there?

2. Do research to discover what resources Africa has which might lead to long-term economic revival.

3. (a) Find out how much Canadians contribute to international aid at the federal level.
   (b) What restrictions are placed on these funds or goods?

4. Find out what world aid projects raise money in your area, and if possible, try to discover what uses the funds are put to. Do you agree with the priorities selected? Why or why not?

CHAPTER 5

Resources

Have I Left the Eagle to Soar in Freedom?
The time will soon be here when
my grandchild will long for the cry of
a loon, the flash of a salmon, the
whisper of spruce needles, or the
screech of an eagle. But he will not
make friends with any of these
creatures and when his heart aches
with longing he will curse me.
    Have I done all to keep the air
fresh? Have I cared enough about the
water? Have I left the eagle to soar in
freedom?
    Have I done everything I could
to earn my grandchild's fondness?

                    —CHIEF DAN GEORGE

Chief Dan George

Chief Dan George was leader of
a native Indian band resident
on the shores of the Burrard
Inlet near the Second Narrows
bridge in Vancouver. He became
famous as an actor and won an
Academy Award for a film
performance. Towards the end
of his life he published several
books of poetry, mainly on the
theme of living in harmony with
nature. Chief Dan George died
in 1981.

You have already seen examples in this book of ways in which the environment is being disrupted by human actions; for instance, acid rain and the destruction of the tropical forests were discussed in Chapter 1. In fact, the growth of the world's population puts pressure on resources of all kinds. Obviously the Earth is no bigger today than it ever was, nor are its physical resources greater. Yet for every person living in the year 1800, when the Industrial Revolution was just beginning, the Earth now has to support ten. Furthermore, the population of today consumes more of the world's resources per person than did the much smaller population of 1800.

Food is only one of the resources which the world's population is demanding in increasing quantities. Resources include all the materials needed to sustain a way of life: minerals, fuels, fibres, timber, building materials, and numerous others. All of these are needed in ever-larger amounts throughout the world. In this chapter, you will explore the subject of world resources in light of the following questions:

- *How do the levels of culture and technology of a society affect its use of resources?*

- *What are the consequences of an unequal distribution of the world's resources?*

- *Who makes the decisions as to how the world's resources are used?*

- *How should resources be managed and conserved?*

- *Will there be resources available for future generations?*

The Link Between Resources and Culture

The first thing to realize in discussing resources is that the way you use resources depends upon the nature of your culture, including its level of technology. An illustration will help clarify this statement.

Imagine that you, like Robinson Crusoe, have been shipwrecked on some remote island. Since you may be there for some time, you have to make yourself a shelter as quickly as possible. What are your resources?

The world depends on resources for the goods people need and want.

Not all cultures make the same use of the Earth's resources. What resources were used by these Berbers to prepare their meal? What resources are needed to prepare your evening meal?

Obviously they include all the materials available on your island. But how useful is a tree, unless you managed to salvage a tool kit containing a saw to cut it down? And if you happened to salvage a chain saw, it will not help you unless you also managed to retrieve some gasoline. But even if you have a complete tool kit and a fuel supply, the shelter will not be built unless you use the most important resource of all—your brain.

This has been true throughout the ages. The materials of the physical world are useful only when people have both the technology and the skill to use them. Over the centuries, human beings have assembled a "tool kit" of technology which now enables us to use a remarkable list of the Earth's materials. The kit becomes more powerful as each generation inherits the skills of those before it, and adds some of its own. This accumulated range of skills has been the greatest resource of humankind. It clearly separates us from the animals, which do not have this ability to acquire and pass on technology.

All this suggests that the materials which people find useful may change over time. Some examples of resources that were formerly more important than they are today are shown in the table below.

TABLE 5.1 *Some Changes in Resource Use*

Resource	Age	Use	Modern Equivalent
Flint	Stone age	Starting fires	Matches
Furs	Pre-medieval	Clothing	Natural and synthetic fibres
Leather	Pre-Industrial Revolution	Containers, hinges	Metals, plastics
Tallow (fat)	Pre-1900	Lamps	Electric lights
Salt	Pre-1900	Preserving food	Refrigeration, irradiation
Horses	Pre-World War I	Travel	Cars, buses

Try to construct a list of the skills and technology which must be developed before a power station can be built. The list will include the smelting of metal ores and the invention of electricity. What else can you add?

Electricity is produced at this nuclear power plant at Chapelcross, Scotland.

Resource Use and Material Wealth

You have read that the way resources are used depends upon culture as a whole. Technology is one element of culture. Another is the entire system of values shared by the majority of people within a society. For example, how do you regard the world around you? Do you see the world as waiting to be exploited for people's material gain? This has been a fairly typical North American attitude for over two centuries. Early lumber companies, for example, extracted the maximum profit from the land, and when all the trees were cut down, moved on to do the same elsewhere. Coal mining companies often devastated the landscape by **strip mining** without restoring the land. As you will see later in this chapter, human beings continue to pollute the environment in many ways in the pursuit of an affluent lifestyle.

Not everyone in North America shares the view that nature should be controlled for material profit. Your view of the natural world may be more like the one expressed in the poem by Chief Dan George at the start of this chapter. Moreover, it should be kept in mind that the desire to use resources for material profit lies behind the astonishing progress

Strip Mining

Strip mining (or open-pit mining) is the extraction of minerals from the surface rather than by means of shafts and tunnels. Surface materials are first removed, then the desired mineral is extracted by large excavators. Strip mining is generally cheaper and safer than underground mining. It does, however, create large unsightly holes in the ground, which may be filled later on with waste, but at considerable expense to the company.

made on this continent during the past century. Economic and techno-logical progress bring many benefits. Think of modern advances in transportation, household appliances, and medicine, to name just a few areas. Yet many of the world's peoples do not have the luxury of such facilities.

Each culture has its own particular glasses through which it views the world. Bedouin Arabs and African Bushmen, for example, are more accustomed to sharing their material possessions than Canadians are. A tree might be so many cubic metres of timber to a North American lumberman, but it might be an object of worship in another society.

Research and development have led to both new and more efficient use of the world's resources.

QUESTIONS

1. Name three resources other than food for which there is increased demand.

2. In what ways does the use of resources depend on technology and culture?

3. Chief Dan George listed the things in nature which he valued but feared his grandchild might not be able to enjoy. What parts of nature do you value and wish to protect for future generations?

Types of Resources

The great variety of natural resources available to human beings may be divided into two main types: renewable and non-renewable. **Renewable resources** are those which will continue to supply materials indefinitely as long as the system that produces them is not disrupted. Renewable resources are biological or organic, that is, they come from living things. **Non-renewable resources,** on the other hand, are those which cannot be replaced once they are used up. Most of them are inorganic, that is, non-living. Such materials have been created by nature over millions of years. Metal ores are a good example. One group of non-renewable resources, however, is organic in origin: the **fossil fuels.** Coal, oil, and natural gas were formed over millions of years from various living organisms. Because they take such a long time to form, the fossil fuels, too, are considered non-renewable.

Renewable Resources

Each biological resource is produced by a natural system (Figure 5.1). A system, as you know from Chapter 1, is an interrelated set of elements. A change in any element usually affects the whole system.

The *forest resources* will last indefinitely only if replanting takes place at an adequate rate. Otherwise, the soil is exposed to the weather, and is liable to erode. Forests are being over-exploited in many parts of the world; the rainforests are particularly at hazard, as you read earlier. Clearcutting has serious consequences for future timber supplies. It

FIGURE 5.1 *The Physical Environment as a System*

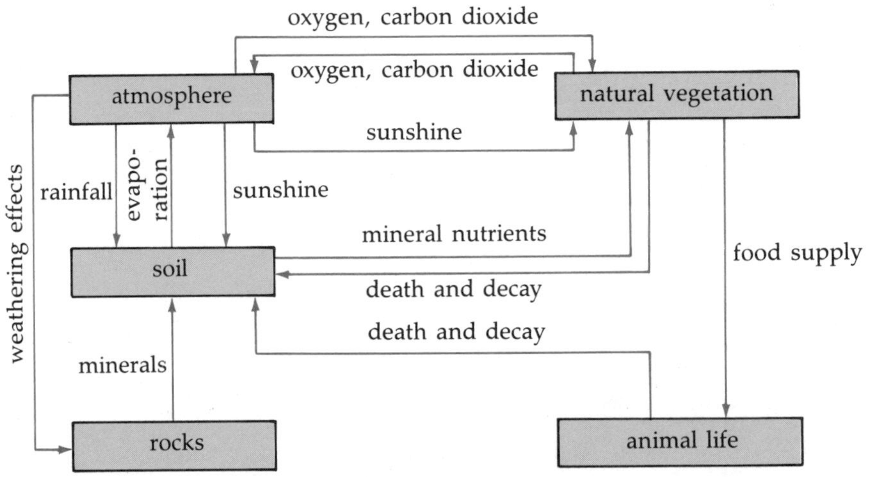

also changes river flow patterns, because rainwater drains more quickly into rivers where there are no tree roots to absorb it. Deforestation may also bring about a reduction in the world's oxygen supply, as discussed in Chapter 1.

The *fisheries* will contribute to food resources as long as stocks are not reduced by over-fishing, or as long as some of the catch is replaced by fish farming. The world's *per capita* fish catch appears to have peaked in about 1970. Since then it has fallen by 15 percent. The volume of fish caught has actually increased since 1970, but the world population has increased at a greater rate.

Farming must be done in such a way that the soil is preserved for future production. Soil erosion, a major problem in many parts of the world, has serious consequences for future food supplies. So does the loss of soil fertility, which can result from misuse of the soil. Advanced farming technology, which is meant to improve the world's food supply, may also present a risk to the farming resource. Over-dependence on certain very productive plant varieties may diminish the gene pool from which plants evolve.

From all this, you may conclude that the greatest care must be taken in using any renewable resource, to ensure that the system which produces the resource is not disrupted.

The management of forest resources is obviously important to such communities as Campbell River, British Columbia. How might it be important to communities not directly tied to forestry?

Non-renewable Resources

Under this heading, you will examine only one type of resource: metal ores. (Fossil fuels will be discussed in greater detail later in this chapter). Most metallic mineral resources are found in the form of *ore* (metal mixed with rock). An ore must contain a high enough concentration of some metal to make mining worthwhile. Such high concentrations are actually freaks of nature and are relatively rare. For example, copper accounts for about 0.006 percent of the Earth's crust, but it takes a concentration 85 times greater to reach even a low-grade 0.5 percent copper ore. Mining companies are motivated to explore for reserves only until they have an adequate supply to meet foreseeable demand. Exploration has therefore never been pushed to the limit and the Earth has by no means been fully explored. Table 5.2 shows the average concentration of some well-known minerals in the Earth's crust.

TABLE 5.2 *Concentration of Minerals in the Earth's Crust. How might these figures influence the value placed on a specific mineral?*

Element	Percent
Aluminum	8.1
Copper	0.006
Gold	0.000 000 2
Iron	5.0
Lead	0.000 1
Magnesium	2.1
Nickel	0.008
Potassium	2.6
Silver	0.000 008
Zinc	0.008

QUESTIONS

1. List three fossil fuels. Why are they considered to be non-renewable resources?

2. (a) What is a natural system?
   (b) How can unplanned tree cutting disrupt a natural system?

3. Referring to Figure 5.1, describe how soils and vegetation are related. How do they both depend on climate?

4. Using Table 5.2, rank copper, iron, magnesium, and silver from highest to lowest concentration in the Earth's crust.

5. Classify the following resources as renewable or non-renewable: fish, oil, trees, iron ore, natural gas.

The Distribution of Resources

The world's natural resources are very unevenly distributed. This is as true of minerals and fossil fuels as it is of fertile soils and timber. Recall from Chapter 2 that only about one-fifth of the world's land area appears to be capable of sustaining a high population density, whether on the basis of farming or of industry.

The world's most productive agricultural lands are located mainly in warm temperate areas such as the midwestern United States, or in valleys fed by silt from major rivers such as the Nile. Many less developed tropical nations have virtually no highly productive land. They also tend to experience climatic extremes which lead to erratic food production.

Mineral resources are even less evenly distributed. This is a matter of geology, as noted above; only in small parts of the Earth's crust are minerals concentrated enough to justify mining. The Canadian Shield and the South African plateau are among the richest locations of ore deposits. It follows that the supply of many minerals is dominated by a

The Canadian Shield is rich in mineral resources. How does the terrain affect transportation and development?

FIGURE 5.2 *The concentration of some key mineral resources*

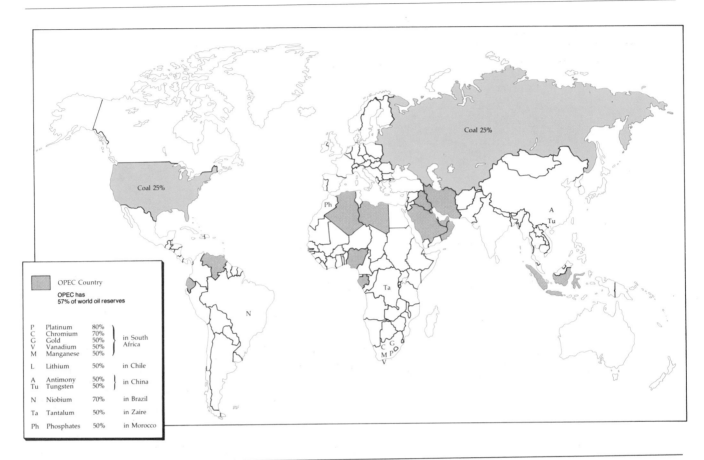

few countries, as shown in Figure 5.2. The map also shows the uneven distribution of fossil fuels. About half of the world's coal is located in the U.S.S.R. and the United States. Even more conspicuous is the concentration of almost 60 percent of the world's petroleum in the Persian Gulf area. However, reserves of oil sands and oil shale are heavily concentrated in Canada and the U.S., respectively. The uneven distribution of the world's resources suggests a need for close interdependence among all nations. It is the major impetus for international trade.

Security of Supply

When a large share of the world's supply of any resource is located in a single country, the question arises of how secure that supply will be. A country owning a strategic rare metal may not wish to export it to a nation which competes with it politically or economically. Other threats to supply can arise out of internal political problems. Take the following example. South Africa's racial policies have led other countries to attempt to boycott its exports. South Africa could retaliate by withholding from export an important material such as chromium, which is used for plating metals.

The interrelationship of resources and politics is well illustrated by the **Organization of Petroleum Exporting Countries** (OPEC). See Figure 5.2. In the early 1970's, OPEC supplied over half of the non-communist world's oil. That figure has now dropped below 40 percent. In late 1973, OPEC put a temporary embargo (ban) on petroleum exports to those western countries which were not supporting the Arab side in the Arab-Israeli War. The embargo precipitated a panic in the western world, which depends heavily on Middle Eastern oil. The fear of a shortage enabled OPEC to quadruple the price of oil within three months. Since that time, the power of OPEC has been greatly reduced, partly because the world recession of 1981–1982 lowered the demand for oil and therefore its price. Another reason is that nations which

The most noticeable effect of OPEC's 1973 petroleum embargo for some Americans was the long line-ups for gasoline.

depend on petroleum imports have taken steps since the 1973 crisis both to conserve on the use of oil and to invest in alternate sources of supply. OPEC's political power is therefore clearly linked to the price of and demand for oil.

QUESTIONS

1. Where are the world's most productive soils found?

2. From Figure 5.2, name three OPEC nations located on the Persian Gulf, and three located elsewhere.

3. Which country has the largest world reserves of (a) gold, (b) platinum, (c) tungsten, (d) phosphates, and (e) coal?

4. Explain how political factors can influence the supply of natural resources.

Trends In Resource Use

Changes in Technology and Resource Use

The demand for a resource may be altered by changes in technology. This can happen as a result of either technical improvements in production, or the development of more economical substitutes. Take the example of copper.

In the second millenium B.C., early copper mines in the Middle East extracted ores containing from 3 percent to 15 percent copper. Anything less was not considered worth mining. Yet many copper mines today, including those in Highland Valley near Kamloops, B.C., exploit ores which contain only 0.5 percent copper. This change in demand results from improved mining technology. Large-scale equipment operating in open-pit mines makes possible the mining of low-grade copper ores, as shown on page 116.

The demand for copper is affected in another way by the new technology of fibre optics. These fine filaments or fibres of glass which transmit light waves can carry hundreds of times more information than copper wires can. Fibre optic cables are also less liable to corrosion. For these reasons and more, fibre optics are taking the place of copper in telecommunications. The drop in the demand for copper causes a drop in its price. This may make some mines uneconomical to operate—despite the improved mining technology.

On the other hand, an increased demand for a metal will cause a rise in its price and possibly lead to the reopening of mines previously considered uneconomic. For example, the sharp increase in the demand for gold in the late 1970's caused the price to rise to over $800 (U.S.) an ounce in January, 1980. Many gold mines were reopened, but some closed down again when gold prices fell in the mid-1980's.

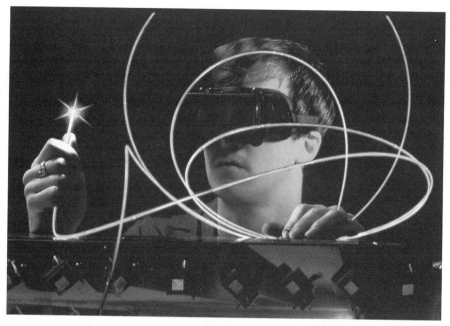

Technological innovations can determine the value placed on a resource. For example, the increased use of fibre optics has decreased the demand for copper wire. How would this situation affect the price of copper ore?

Resource Supply in the Future

Geologists have made estimates of **probable reserves** of mineral resources, on the basis of their knowledge of the Earth's crust. This measure assumes that new discoveries of reserves will be made well into the future. On this basis, most world resources would last for many years, if not centuries, at present rates of use. The reserves which have already been established by drilling are known as **proved reserves.** Each year, the measure of proved reserves changes, since the discovery of new reserves adds to the total. On the other hand, some reserves are used up and have to be subtracted from the total.

The key question is this: Are new reserves being discovered at a faster rate than existing reserves are being used up? In general, the answer is "Yes". For many minerals, such as phosphates, potash, and platinum, world known reserves were 10 times as large in 1981 as in 1951, in spite of the rapid use of these minerals during that period. But for gold, silver, mercury, and tin, world reserves increased by less than a factor of 2. In addition, the costs of exploring for resources are rising year by year. Geologists believe that the age of easy discoveries is past.

The Lifespan of Resources

A common way of estimating the quantity of any resource is to calculate its lifespan, assuming that present reserves continue to be used at present rates. In the case of oil and gas, this calculation is called the **R/P Ratio.** To obtain the ratio, proved reserves are divided by annual production. The idea can be applied to any mineral. Note, however, that the ratio does not allow for new discoveries. Figure 5.3 shows the projected lifespans of selected minerals, based on 1980 estimates of reserves and rates of production. The graph gives a general picture of how scarce or abundant each mineral is at present.

FIGURE 5.3 *Lifespan of Resources. These figures are based on 1980 known reserves and rates of annual use. Suggest one way the lifespan of any of these resources could be increased.*

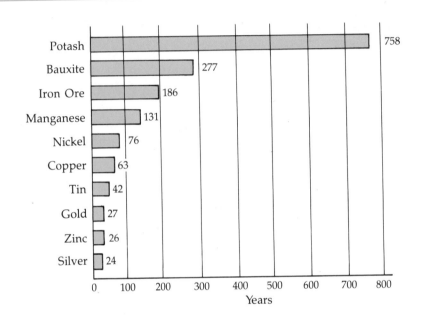

QUESTIONS

1. How have changes in mining technology made possible the mining of lower-grade ores?

2. Give an example of a case in which changing technology has reduced the demand for a resource.

3. What is the difference between "probable reserves" and "proved reserves"?

4. Name two scarce and two abundant mineral resources, as measured by their possible lifespan.

5. In what sense can it be said that world resources of metals are larger in the 1980's than in the 1950's?

6. Explain what is meant by the statement that Canada's R/P Ratio for oil is 10.

Energy—A Study in Changing Patterns of Resource Use

No other group of resources has received so much attention in recent years as energy resources, oil and natural gas in particular. The demand for oil and gas, in relation to other sources of energy, has fluctuated greatly since 1970. The world price of oil has moved sharply up and down in response to changing demand.

The Energy Crisis

Western countries had become accustomed to cheap oil during the 1950's and 1960's, following major new discoveries in the Middle East. However, this trend was abruptly reversed in 1973 after the Arab-Israeli War, which led to an oil embargo and the quadrupling of prices (Figure 5.4). Western countries felt threatened by both the scarcity and the high price of oil. Two results followed.

First, coal became once again an economical alternative to oil, especially for the generation of electricity, which is the main market for coal. The long decline in the use of coal ended, because consuming industries preferred using secure coal supplies to relying on expensive oil from the politically troubled Middle East. The second result was that nuclear power came to be seen as the hope for future electricity needs. Not only did it require much smaller amounts of fuel, but technological progress held out hopes of further reductions in cost.

Then in 1979, the Iranian Revolution disrupted oil exports from that country and led to a second large rise in the price of oil (refer to Figure 5.4). Western countries were forced to adopt further measures to cope with an erratic and expensive supply. Conservation in the use of oil was brought about by the better insulation of homes and the use of more fuel-efficient cars. The search for new sources of oil was accelerated—regardless of the high costs involved—since it was assumed that oil prices would continue to rise indefinitely. Research into renewable sources of energy, such

FIGURE 5.4 *World Oil Prices from 1970 to 1987*

$ U.S. per barrel

40

30

20

10

1970   1975   1980   1985
Arab-Israeli   Iranian   Saudi
war 1973   revolution   Arabians increase production

Since Alberta is an oil-producing region, its economy is affected by the world price of oil.

as solar, wind, and tidal power, was also stepped up. Finally, the use of coal continued to increase.

The Oil Glut

In the years following 1981, the pendulum swung the other way: oil prices fell significantly (Figure 5.4). This trend was not foreseen, though perhaps it could have been. The rise in oil prices until 1980 was so steep that it produced a recession in 1981–1982. The recession was severe enough in itself to reduce the demand for oil. Coupled with the new oil conservation measures and the switch to alternate fuels, it brought world oil consumption to a new low. At the same time, new sources in Mexico and the North Sea were increasing world supplies. OPEC was forced to reduce its price in early 1983 from $34 (U.S.) per barrel to $29. An even more dramatic decrease in 1986 to $10–$12 per barrel was the result of increased oil production in Saudi Arabia.

Unfortunately, the plummeting prices were not predicted by bankers, industrialists, or governments, all of whom were looking for continued price increases. Their lack of foresight was costly in many ways. First, banks in western countries had lent massive sums of money to less developed countries such as Mexico on the security of future oil output at rising prices. When the price fell, these countries found it very difficult to repay their debts. On a more local scale, some oil companies, such as Canada's Dome Petroleum, went heavily into debt to finance ambitious oil projects or takeovers. Dome would probably have gone bankrupt, if it had not been rescued by major banks which would have lost too much money in the bankruptcy. In addition, several major energy projects, some of them backed by the government of Canada, fell through because of the low oil prices. The low prices, in turn, reduced the tax revenues of the Canadian government.

On the other hand, consumers benefited from the decreased prices, as well as from the lower overall rates of inflation which followed. Larger cars began to sell once again, and some of the oil conservation measures of the 1970's were quietly dropped. The latter effect raises a question: Although it benefits consumers, is a fall in the price of oil likely to help in the conservation of a valuable resource for future generations?

Figure 5.5 shows the location of the world's oil reserves. The dominance of the Middle East has not changed much over the last decade, though some reserves in other areas have been added. But the list of leading producing countries has changed markedly, as you can see from Figure 5.6. OPEC countries have cut their output as a means of trying to keep the price up. Non-OPEC countries with newly discovered reserves, such as Mexico and Britain, have increased their output quite sharply.

FIGURE 5.5 *World Proved Oil Reserves (1982). What percentage are in the Middle East?*

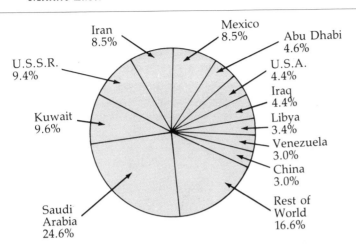

Source: Duncan L. Gibson, *Energy Graphics,* Prentice-Hall Series in Energy, Englewood Cliffs, 1983

FIGURE 5.6 *Top Eight Oil Producers (1984). In the period 1978-1983, why did Iran's and Saudi Arabia's oil production drop but Mexico's and the United Kingdom's rise?*

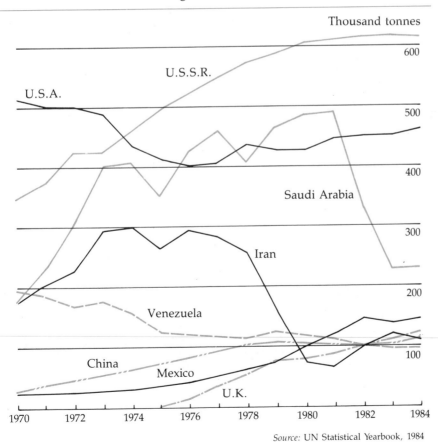

Source: UN Statistical Yearbook, 1984

Canada's Frontier Oil

The changing demand for oil, and the resulting price fluctuations, have seriously affected Canada. The conventional production of oil in Alberta is now limited by a lack of reserves. Canadian companies have therefore been exploring for new "frontier" oil, both off the coasts of Newfoundland and Nova Scotia and in the Beaufort Sea. Oil or gas has been discovered in each of these areas, but because of very high development costs, production appears unlikely before the mid-1990's.

FIGURE 5.7   *New Techniques in Heavy Oil Production (Huff and Puff Techniques)*

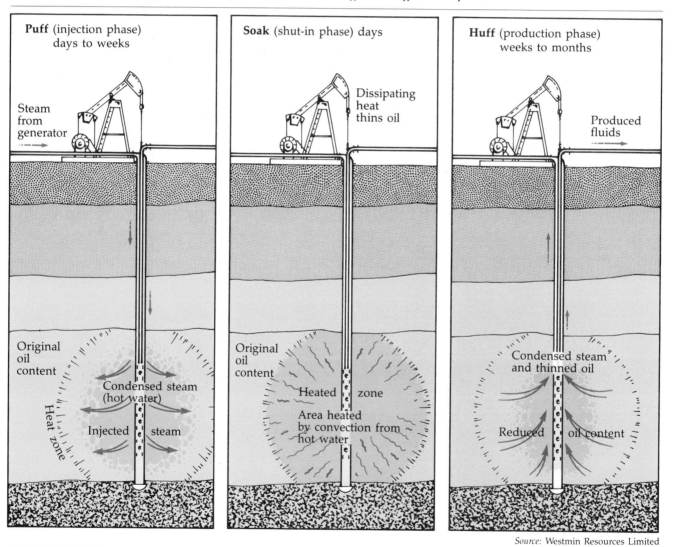

Source: Westmin Resources Limited

The demand for oil has made it economically sound to invest in off-shore drilling.

Alberta is, however, the site of Canada's other fossil fuel frontier. The conventional deposits, which are reached by drilling wells, are now limited. The other source of supply is the heavy oil fields and oil sands of Alberta. These reserves contain many times more oil than all of Canada's conventional oil fields. Two oil sands projects already exist, Suncor (started in 1968) and Syncrude (1978). But the extraction of the heavy tar-like oil is a costly business. It appears that further development of these resources will require either new technology or a significant rise in the price of oil. Currently, less efficient open-pit methods are being used. New technology in heavy oil production includes fire-flooding or steam injection to liquefy the oil (Figure 5.7). Canada will certainly require oil from these frontier sources before the start of the next century.

New patterns of supply are likely to emerge in the energy industries throughout the world as technology develops and demand rises once again.

QUESTIONS

1. **(a)** What was the energy crisis of 1973–1980?
   (b) What were the effects of the energy crisis on coal and nuclear power?

2. State three results of the very high world oil prices reached after the Iranian Revolution.

3. What factors caused the drop in oil prices from 1981–1986?

4. State two advantages and two disadvantages of the fall in world oil prices for Canadians and the Canadian economy.

5. How has the development of the Alberta oil sands been affected by the changing price of oil?

6. List three factors which could move the price of oil either up or down.

FIGURE 5.8 *Division of Townships/ Ranges. What percentage of the land in this township was set aside as individual homesteads?*

☐ School land

☐ Hudson's Bay Co.

☐ Railway grants

☐ Free homesteads (four per section)

31	32	33	34	35	36
30	29	28	27	26	25
19	20	21	22	23	24
18	17	16	15	14	13
7	8	9	10	11	12
6	5	4	3	2	1

0   3 km
Scale

Access to Land as a Resource

Most of the world's resources are controlled by a tiny fraction of its 5 thousand million inhabitants. One of the most valuable resources is land. In less developed countries, 80 percent of the land is owned by 3 percent of the landowners. Much of the land in Latin America, for example, is controlled by the owners of large estates; very few other people own any significant amounts.

In contrast, the *Homestead Acts* of the 19th century in the United States and Canada were designed to create a pattern of privately owned family farms. Figure 5.8 shows that about half of the land in the Canadian prairies was allocated to homesteaders, who could buy a quarter section of land (65 ha) for $10. The *Acts* gave many more people the advantage of possessing their own land. In recent years, however, the situation in North America has begun to resemble that in much of the rest of the world. An increasing percentage of the land in North America is now owned by corporations rather than families.

More than two-thirds of the world's people earn their living by cultivating the land. Yet only a small minority of farmers enjoy the privilege of owning the land they work on. The rest fall into several categories, depending on their relationship to the landowner. Many are **tenant farmers** who rent small plots of land. Some are **sharecroppers** who have to give as much as half of their crop to the landlord. Yet others are **landless labourers** who may work for long hours on other people's land for very small reward.

Brazilian farmers with large land holdings can take advantage of the local environment to raise herds of cattle; however, rural people such as those pictured on page 133, who own no land often face a life of poverty.

A Third World family that owns or has a secure tenancy for a piece of land will almost certainly grow its own food on it as a first priority. The same land, owned by a landlord or a company, is more likely to be devoted to growing cash crops for sale. It has been claimed, therefore, that the world's food production would rise if more of the world's farmers actually owned the land they work on. For this reason, land reform is high on the agenda of many agencies, such as the World Bank, which operate in less developed countries.

Land Reform

Land reform can take several forms. Large estates can be broken up and the land redistributed to farmers with no land of their own. Tenancies can be improved by making land available on long-term leases at manageable rents. Fragmented plots of land can be consolidated into fields of reasonable size, to save farmers a great deal of time and effort.

Attempts have been made in many countries to distribute land more equitably. The process is not easy. Owning land gives people social and political power, and people do not give up power readily. Some development agencies say that the political power of large landowners is one of the main obstacles to agricultural progress. One such agency, OXFAM, was for years a mainly technical agency which concentrated on methods of producing more food. OXFAM now emphasizes the

The World Bank

The World Bank is actually two distinct organizations: the International Bank for Reconstruction and Development (IBRD) and the International Development Association (IDA). The objectives of the World Bank are to provide advice and technical and financial assistance to less developed countries. The World Bank supports many projects in areas such as agriculture, rural development, land reform, education, health, transportation, and water supply. It is itself supported in part by contributions from wealthier nations and in part by funds raised through borrowing in international money markets.

FIGURE 5.9   *Land Reform Scheme Within a Large Estate. Before land reform this area was marsh and range land. What changes had to be made to ensure the success of dividing this land into individual farms?*

6   Plot number
□   Farm house
▨   Trees and windbreaks
—   Irrigation canal
⇢   Irrigation channel
═   Farm road
════   Farm track

Source: Russel King, *Land Reform: the Italian Experience,* (London, Butterworth, 1973).

political and social aspects of food production. Its argument is that the poverty of so many farmers throughout the world is caused by the system of land ownership and tenancy, and by the control of farm credit and marketing. Without improvements in these areas, the Green Revolution will benefit only the better-off farmers and large landowners.

Figure 5.9 shows a land reform scheme in Sardinia, Italy. Large estates were broken up, and compensation was paid to the owners. Small holdings were created from the estates and distributed among farmers who had no land of their own. In addition, irrigation facilities were constructed, and transport and marketing facilities improved. Land reform schemes such as this have also been applied in Mexico, Tunisia, and China. They must be comprehensive to be successful, and they are very expensive for governments to undertake. It is often for political reasons that governments carry out land reform, since these changes are popular with large numbers of people.

QUESTIONS

1. Why do you think the availability of land attracted immigrants to Canada in the 19th century?

2. (a) Why would an organization such as the World Bank support land reform?
   (b) What are the difficulties in carrying out land reform programs?

3. Why is ownership of land by farmers likely to improve food production?

4. Suggest possible disadvantages of a land reform scheme which involved dividing large holdings into relatively small plots.

Suggest reasons to account for the difference in size of the individual landholdings in these two photographs. The first photo shows Asian rice fields; the second, a North American wheat farm.

FIGURE 5.10 *World Resource Consumption. What do these figures tell you about opportunities in the developing world?*

The developing world has . . .

75% of the world's people

but only

17% of the world's GNP

5% of world science and technology

15% of world energy consumption

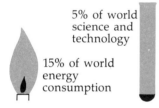

30% of the world's food grains

11% of world education spending

6% of the world health expenditure

18% of world export earnings

8% of world industry

Resources and Development

Inequality of Resource Use

You have already seen that the developed world consumes a larger share of the world's food than its population would suggest. Figure 5.10 gives some idea of just how little of the world's spending on goods and services takes place in less developed nations, which contain at least 75 percent of the world's population.

Some less developed nations are well endowed with natural resources, as Figure 5.2 showed. However, the possession of natural resources does not guarantee a high standard of living for a nation. Some countries which abound in resources are far from being among the most highly developed. Examples of less developed but resource-rich nations, such as Zaïre and Brazil, might be contrasted with Japan, which lacks most minerals and is short of fossil fuels. However, Japan has a high level of education and has been the scene of enormous volumes of capital investment. It is these factors, essential for industrialization, which are lacking in less developed countries.

Resources and International Trade

In theory, international trade ought to benefit all countries which engage in it. Trade enables countries to specialize in those forms of production to which they are best suited. Nevertheless, international trade has usually operated to the benefit of western countries, which have been able to buy their raw materials cheaply from Third World suppliers. The benefits felt by these suppliers are relatively low. This is because the cost of the resources used in making an article such as a

Japan has become a world leader in manufacturing technologically advanced goods, such as these Minolta cameras.

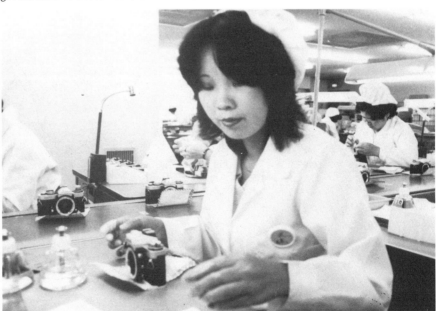

computer or bicycle is very much less than the final cost of manufacture. Most manufactured articles require several stages of processing before final consumption. Then there are the costs of marketing the finished product. Thus, only a few dollars of the price of a typical $200 article would go to the cost of the original raw materials. If these materials came from a Third World country, they might well have been bought by a company which paid only a royalty to the government, and probably low wages to its workers there.

Third World countries often sell their resources at such low cost because they are in competition with each other. Except during the oil crisis period (1973–1980), world prices in recent years have been low for both minerals and agricultural commodities. For instance, how much of the price you pay for a banana actually goes to the Third World producer? A look at Figure 5.11 might surprise you. Thus, the benefits from the use of these resources have been felt more in western industrialized nations than in the less developed countries of the world. The problem is worse for those nations that depend on a single product for much of their exports. For example, copper accounts for over 90 percent of Zambia's exports. If the price of this commodity falls, the whole nation is adversely affected.

Other aspects of trade also have adverse effects on the Third World. Foremost among these are trade barriers—import tariffs and quotas. **Tariffs** are taxes on imported goods. **Quotas** are restrictions on the amount of goods which may be imported. Both may be described as *protectionist* measures. Tariffs may be imposed by developed countries in a way that discourages manufacturing industries from setting up in less developed countries. For example, in the early 1980's raw cocoa could enter the European Economic Community (EEC) almost free of

Here, Brazilian cotton is being loaded into trucks.

The European Economic Community (EEC)

The European Economic Community was formed in 1957 when six nations (France, West Germany, Italy, the Netherlands, Belgium, and Luxemburg) signed a treaty to reduce trade barriers and increase political co-operation. Six more countries have since joined the EEC: the United Kingdom, Denmark, Ireland, Greece, Spain, and Portugal.

FIGURE 5.11   *The Price of a Banana. Can you think of any way that the grower could increase his share of the money from the banana's final selling price of 20 cents?*

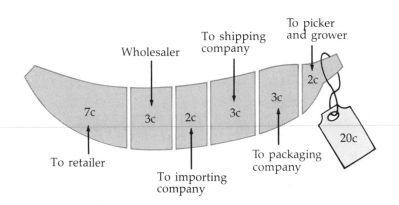

These Bolivian miners can mine ores more cheaply than their Canadian counterparts. Why is this true?

duty. Manufactured chocolate, on the other hand, was taxed at 19 percent. This encouraged the manufacturers to keep their plants in the EEC rather than set them up in places like Ghana where the cocoa is grown.

Manufacturing countries are increasingly trying to protect their industries from similar products made in the Third World, where labour is much cheaper. Canada, for instance, has imposed both tariffs and quotas on clothing in an effort to protect the jobs of workers in these industries, which are located mainly in Quebec.

Can the Third World Catch Up?

If the rest of the world were to catch up to the standard of living of the developed world, how much additional pressure would be brought to bear on the world supply of resources? Assume for a moment that the United States were to continue to use the same amount of resources as it does now, and that the world population were to stabilize at

10 thousand million. If this many people were to use resources at the current U.S. level, the following would be true:

Copper	would last	2 years
Gold	would last	22 years
Lead	would last	9 years
Tin	would last	18 years
Zinc	would last	57 years
Iron ore	would last	309 years
Nickel	would last	245 years

Note that these estimates are based on the total amounts of each resource which geologists calculate to be present in the Earth's crust, *not* on the much smaller amounts already discovered. If the lower figures were used, the lifespans would be much shorter than those shown here.

Furthermore, if all the world used resources at the U.S. level, world water consumption would increase by 13 times, requiring more water than is available from all accessible rivers on Earth. World timber production would rise by 7 times; fertilizer use by 13 times; and all energy use by 14 times. At these rates of consumption, the world's supply of oil would last only 4 or 5 years, and even coal would disappear after a little over a century. The rate of atmospheric and water pollution would also increase sharply as a result of the greatly accelerated world economic activity.

Obviously there would be an unimaginable resource crisis if the majority of the world's people began to live like North Americans or

What North American attitudes towards resource use are illustrated by this photo?

Europeans. But, in the present situation, Third World countries face the added frustration of seeing their non-renewable resources exported at small profit just to maintain western living standards. The United States, with under 5 percent of the world's population, will have consumed 30 percent of the world's oil by the time the supply runs dry. As you have seen, Third World soils also help to maintain western lifestyles. One might argue that they would be better used to grow food for the world's hungry people.

Views on How to Improve Conditions in the Third World

In 1974, representatives of 77 less developed countries presented a set of reforms to the UN General Assembly. They called these reforms the New International Economic Order. The reforms included a plan for stabilizing commodity prices, measures to promote industry in the Third World, and easier access for Third World manufactured goods to western markets. High on the agenda were debt relief and technical and economic aid. Unfortunately for the less developed countries, very few of these objectives had been achieved by the mid-1980's.

Many people have concluded that there is no hope that poorer countries can raise their living standards to the current level of the rich. Therefore, the only way to improve conditions in developing nations is for the rich to change their priorities away from economic growth. In this view, western consumers should not be encouraged constantly to buy more, and thereby use up more of the Earth's resources. The pressure on less developed countries to grow cash crops and sell their minerals at low prices to industrialized countries would be reduced as a result. The developing nations might then be able to put their own needs first.

Much would have to change before this view would be accepted by a growth-oriented society such as that in North America. Any government which proposed that Canadians should make substantial cuts in their living standards in order to help Third World countries would likely stand little chance of being re-elected. However, public opinion on this issue might change in the future.

The opposing point of view is that the western world does not have to become poorer to make the Third World richer. In this view, strong economic growth in developed nations would increase the demand, and therefore the price, for Third World resources. Obtaining a better price for their exports would help the Third World countries to pay for the imports which they need. From this perspective, resources are not seen as a limiting factor. If any resource should prove to be in short supply, alternate resources or new technology would likely be developed to solve the problem. The possibility of replacing some uses of copper by fibre optics, mentioned earlier, is a prime example.

QUESTIONS

1. List four resources of which North Americans use more than do people in Third World countries.

2. What is the difference between a quota and a tariff?

3. Why does Canada impose quotas on clothing imports?

4. Why is it a disadvantage for a country to rely on one or two export commodities?

5. State one reason why manufacturing companies in developed countries have been able to acquire raw materials cheaply.

6. Describe the resource supply problems which would occur if the rest of the world were to attain present North American living standards.

Problems of Resource Use

Natural resources are scarce enough that people must use them as efficiently as possible. Yet the record in this respect is not a good one. In the western world particularly there have been many examples of greedy and thoughtless use of resources. The attitudes which caused these abuses still affect resource use today.

Until recently, the main test in deciding whether or not to use a resource was a simple matter of economics. If short-term profit was

Pictured here is one example of environmental pollution caused by resource use; pollution from a zinc smelter being dumped into a local water system.

likely to be increased, the resource would be used. The greater part of the gains from using the resource went to the owners of the resource, usually large landowners and industrialists. The effects on society in general or on the environment were not usually considered. The landscape in western countries shows many traces of this type of approach to using resources, in the form of derelict (unused) land, heaps of mine waste, polluted water, and unplanned land use.

Pollution—Misplaced Resources

Pollution has been defined as "misplaced resources". What exactly does this mean? Many resources are, in a sense, not consumed by industry; rather, they are used in some process, then discharged in a different form and in the wrong place. For example, various heavy metals such as cadmium, mercury, nickel, and lead are present (and indeed necessary) in the natural environment. They are also required for thousands of products useful to people. But if any or all of them are discharged irresponsibly into the environment, they can cause cancer or disorders of the nervous system. You read in Chapter 1 that when heavy metals enter the food chain, they can become highly concentrated. As a result, the organisms in which they are concentrated, such as fish, may be quite unsafe to eat (Figure 5.12). Numerous toxic chemicals, such as polychlorinated biphenyls (PCB's), cause exactly the same problem. These chemicals are very dangerous to transport and are difficult to dispose of.

In many ways, however, the developed nations have made great progress in dealing with the problems of resource use. Most resource projects now require detailed planning and permission before going

FIGURE 5.12 *Mercury Build-up in Wildlife (parts of mercury per million)*

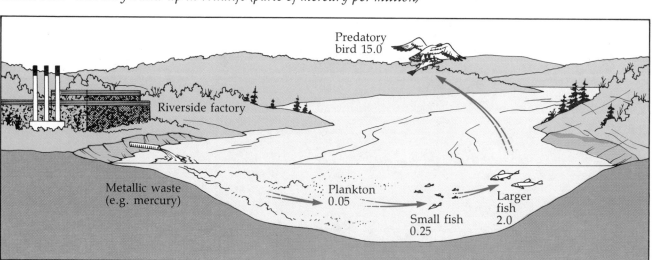

Why are fragile environments, such as those in Alaska or Canada's far north, especially vulnerable to damage caused by the oil and gas industry?

ahead. Public inquiries and pressure from people with something at stake can exert real influence on decision-makers. For instance, drilling for oil and gas off the coast of British Columbia has been banned for many years because of concern for the environment.

The process of inquiry can create costly delays; yet the benefits can be real and long-lasting. While American courts were deliberating about the vast Alaska Pipeline project in the 1970's, the submissions were so extensive that they would have made a pile of paper 17 km high! But when the courts eventually approved the pipeline, they insisted on the inclusion of many environmental safeguards.

Many environmental problems which plague the world today are the result of the opposing attitude—a lack of planning. Consider the following Close-up on the pollution of the Niagara River and Lake Ontario.

CLOSE-UP

The Problems of the Niagara River and Lake Ontario

Lake Ontario provides drinking water for about eight million Canadians and one million Americans. Large quantities of pollutants are added to the lake from industries and sewage plants along its shores, particularly in the Greater Toronto area. The Niagara River carries three-quarters of all the water that enters Lake Ontario. It, too, is a source of pollution, bringing in chemicals which have been discharged into it, mainly from the American side.

Figure 5.13 shows the locations of several large chemical waste dumps near the banks of the Niagara River. At Hooker Chemical Company's dump on the Love Canal, and at Hyde Park dump, some of the most toxic substances known, including mirex and dioxin, are now known to have been seeping for years through the fractured underlying rocks into the river. In 1978, after a higher than normal number of birth defects was observed in the area,

Dioxins

Most toxic chemicals are measured in units of parts per million (ppm); dioxins are so highly toxic that they are measured in units of parts per billion (ppb)—that is, parts per thousand million. There are many types of dioxin. One of them, 2, 3, 7, 8-TCD dioxin, is perhaps the most deadly poison produced by the chemical industry. At least one tonne of this material lies in the chemical dump at Hyde Park. According to the U.S. Environmental Protection Agency (EPA), at least 159 t of "priority organic pollutants" are discharged into the Niagara River every year, as well as 246 t of heavy metals, many of which are also highly toxic.

Most residents of Love Canal abandoned their homes, but one family chose to move their house to a new location—leaving the foundation behind.

two hundred homes were temporarily evacuated. Public anxiety remains high. Attempts to contain the chemicals have not proved satisfactory; they continue even now to leak from the bedrock into the water.

The companies have resisted the expense of moving the dumps elsewhere. In the event that the dumps were moved to a more suitable site, do you think people would willingly agree to have them located near their homes? It is a sobering thought that there are many less publicized examples of toxic waste dumps throughout North America. Such dumps have been called LULU's (locally unwanted land uses)!

Both Canada and the United States have come to recognize the seriousness of the problem. In February, 1987, the two governments signed an agreement to cut the flow of toxic chemicals into the Niagara River by at least half.

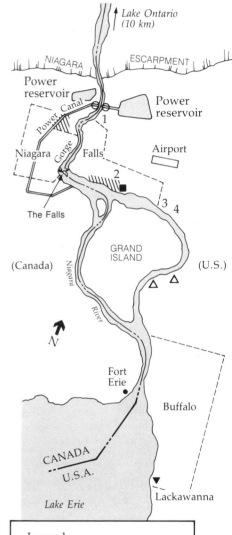

FIGURE 5.13 *Niagara Falls Area. Why does the location of the Niagara River make anti-pollution steps more difficult?*

Legend

O Hydro electric power station
■ Water treatment plant
△ Petro chemical works
▼ Steel complex
\\\\\\ Industrial area
Chemical dumps
1 Hyde Park dump
2 Hooker Chemicals dump
3 Love Canal
4 102nd Street dump
(Hooker and Olin)

0   5   10 km
Scale

QUESTIONS

1. How do toxic chemicals get into Lake Ontario?

2. The proposed solution to the chemical pollution of the Niagara River is the complete removal of the dumps to a safe location. What problems does this solution pose?

3. Cadmium, mercury, nickel, and lead are essential industrial elements. Why are they frequently described as environmental hazards?

4. Do you think that environmental concern (in the area of resource use) is increasing? Give an example to support your answer.

5. Suggest two things that you can do to help ensure a safe environment for yourself and others.

Nuclear Waste

The first nuclear power station, completed during the 1950's, was hailed as a breakthrough. Civilization seemed to be on the verge of a period of cheap, safe electrical power. Some enthusiasts even claimed that electricity bills would be a thing of the past.

The past 30 years have brought a more sober view. Nuclear power stations are expensive to build and are often plagued by technical problems. Depending on how the figures are calculated, nuclear stations produce slightly more power than coal at the same cost—or just

Three Mile Island

At the Three Mile Island nuclear generating plant near Harrisburg, Pennsylvania, a technical failure occurred in March, 1979 which came close to causing a melt-down in one of the reactor cores. Clouds of radioactive gases were released into the atmosphere. Opinions are divided as to how much harm was done by the Three Mile Island incident—certainly much less than by the serious accident at Chernobyl in the U.S.S.R. in 1986. Nevertheless, it is claimed that cancer deaths in the surrounding area have increased six-fold since the accident.

break even. Perhaps the main problem is the disposal of nuclear waste. The wastes from the uranium which produces the energy must be removed at regular intervals from reactors. These materials are highly radioactive. They also contain plutonium, a particularly deadly substance, which takes millions of years to decay into harmless substances. Plutonium is also a raw material in the nuclear weapons industry.

Some nuclear waste was originally dumped at sea. Much of it is now stored underground in containers which are intended to be leak-proof. However, at just one underground location, near Hanford, Washington, there have been 20 leaks since 1958. Two solutions have been proposed: either shooting nuclear waste out into space, or burying it deep underground. One of the sites proposed for the second solution is the Canadian Shield, whose bedrock is very geologically stable. Can you think of any problems in connection with either of the proposed solutions? As in the case of chemical waste, most people strongly object to having nuclear waste buried near their homes.

It is, however, unfair to dwell upon the problems of disposing of nuclear waste without mentioning the hazards involved in generating electricity from other sources. For example, it is possible that as many as 20 000 Americans die prematurely every year as a direct or indirect result of the coal industry. Some deaths occur in the mining and transporting of coal. Far more occur because of health problems resulting from air pollution caused by the burning of coal. Burning coal also

Some people are starting to question the value of nuclear power when the supply of energy is measured against possible environmental pollution. (Pickering Nuclear Power Plant, Ontario.)

Solar panels were developed in response to the need for a pollution-free energy source.

releases amounts of radioactive material into the atmosphere which are several times higher than routine emissions from nuclear power stations. Finally, coal-fired power stations are a major cause of the environmental problem of acid rain.

Even "clean" sources of power such as solar energy create some environmental problems. The source of solar power—sunlight—may be pollution-free, but it is a very dilute form of energy. Generating solar power on a large enough scale to solve energy supply problems would require vast numbers of solar collectors made of materials such as steel, aluminum, glass, and copper. The manufacture of each of these materials would, in itself, create pollution.

Given that gas and oil are scarce resources, nuclear power is still seen by many as an important stopgap until the time when more energy can be obtained from renewable resources. These will likely include a combination of solar, wind, and tidal power. A longer-term possibility is harnessing **nuclear fusion** rather than **nuclear fission,** which is the technology now being used. The great advantages of nuclear fusion are that it uses hydrogen, which is in unlimited supply in the form of water, and that it produces few radioactive byproducts.

QUESTIONS

1. (a) What has emerged as the major problem with nuclear power?
   (b) What is its major advantage?

2. Plutonium decays slowly; that is, it loses its dangerous radioactivity slowly. Why does this increase the nuclear waste disposal problem?

3. Accidents at nuclear power stations such as the one at Chernobyl, U.S.S.R., in 1986 can create worldwide danger. Why is this so?

4. Identify one advantage and one disadvantage of generating electricity by means of each of the following:
   (a) hydroelectricity
   (b) burning oil
   (c) burning coal
   (d) solar power

Resource Management and Conservation

You are aware that renewable resources will be available only as long as the natural system of which they are part is maintained. It is now time to see to what extent people are succeeding in conserving resources.

"Resource conservation" is not an easy concept to define. At one extreme it might mean that people should consume no resources at all for fear of using them up too quickly. But if the use of resources is sharply reduced, the world's large and growing population will not be able to sustain itself.

A much better definition of "resource conservation" would be "using resources in such a way as to ensure continued supply in the future". Thus, farmers should not risk future soil fertility by trying to maximize one particular year's crop yield. Fishermen should not deplete fish stocks to the extent that natural replacement cannot take place quickly enough.

Land Conservation

It is often possible to use a certain resource in different ways. Land, for example, has many possible uses, but generally it may be put to only one use at a time. How is the use of a particular piece of land decided? Two factors must usually be considered to answer this question.

One factor is price. Land is often sold or rented to the highest bidder. Those who expect to obtain the highest profit or the greatest usefulness from a piece of land are likely to be willing to pay more for it than other possible users. Therefore, if price alone is taken into consideration, land will be bought by the users who are likely to profit most from it.

What problems result from urban encroachment on good agricultural land?

The ability to pay the necessary price for land has influenced land use on a grand scale throughout this century. Cities have been spreading out into the surrounding countryside. Farmers close to cities have found far more profit in selling out to real estate developers than in continuing to work the land. A factory on ten hectares will employ more people and generate far more income than the same area of farmed land (Figure 5.14). But you may well ask whether it is in

FIGURE 5.14   *Farm and Factory Output Comparison (10 ha of land)*

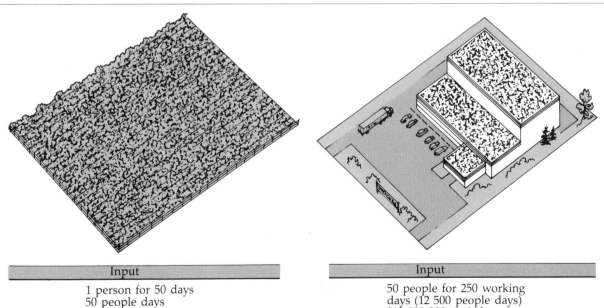

Input
1 person for 50 days 50 people days $90 000 capital

Output
45 825 litres of wheat or 2000 kg of beef value $4000

Input
50 people for 250 working days (12 500 people days) $12 000 000 capital

Output
manufactured goods (e.g. typewriters) value $3 000 000

Canada's long-term best interests to allow profit to be the main motive in determining how land will be used. The result of doing so will be the rapid loss of much of the best Canadian farm land. This has already occurred in the Niagara fruit belt in Ontario. In British Columbia, on the other hand, much rural land around urban centres is protected under the Agricultural Land Reserve legislation.

The second main factor influencing land use is government regulation. Governments have usually taken the power to control land use when they see that it is in the public interest to do so. The need to preserve the best farm land is an example of such a situation. Another is the need to prevent undesirable users of land from locating in the middle of residential areas. This often happened before restrictions applied. The **zoning** of land for industry, commercial development, and residential use is intended to keep apart land uses which do not easily mix, such as petrochemical works and housing, or airports and hospitals. Canada's cities still show many examples of such clashes in areas which were developed before land use planning came into operation.

QUESTIONS

1. What do you understand by the term "conservation"?

2. What are the possible benefits of building a factory on an area of farm land? What is the major loss?

3. What factors do the various levels of government have to consider when making decisions that affect land use?

Water Conservation

Water is a resource which Canadians tend to take for granted. There are two main factors in the conservation and management of water resources: the quantity of water and water quality. Preserving water quality through pollution control makes it possible for water to be re-used, and therefore reduces the need for expensive new water supply facilities.

Table 5.3 shows that Canada's water resources are abundant by the standards of any other country. Yet there is evidence that Canadians are about to enter a period of water scarcity. Like land, water has alternate uses, and when these conflict with each other a choice must be made. For example, the Fraser River has always been an important river for salmon. To build hydroelectric dams on it would seriously damage the fishing resource. This happened on the Columbia River in both Canada and the United States. The installation of fish ladders would allow

TABLE 5.3 *Canada's Share of World Fresh Water Supply*

	$km^3/year$	$000\ m^3$ per capita
Canada	3 122	121.93
Brazil	5 190	38.28
U.S.S.R.	4 714	16.93
Indonesia	2 530	15.34
U.S.A.	2 478	10.43
China	2 680	2.52
India	1 850	2.43
WORLD (Approx)	41 000	

some fish to bypass the dams, but the movement of fish upstream to spawn would still be restricted. Obtaining the power means sacrificing the fish. Preserving the fish means foregoing the power. Some resource uses are, like this one, mutually exclusive. We may have one or the other, but not both.

Which interest groups might be the most concerned about the impact of dams on the environment? (Shasta Dam, California.)

Water in California

Much can be learned from the experience of California, where water supplies have been scarce for some time. Water is relatively abundant in northern California, as you can see in Figure 5.15. But it is very scarce in the more arid southern half of the state, where the demand for water is greatest because of the farms and cities. Two major schemes, the Central Valley Project and the State Water Project, bring water from north to south (Figure 5.16).

FIGURE 5.15 *Rainfall and Stream Flows in California. Why is the location of Los Angeles unfortunate when you consider California's water resources?*

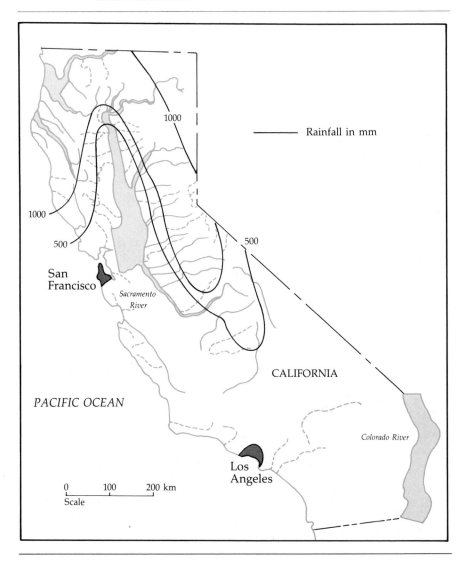

These schemes were built on the principle that, if there was a demand for water, it was the duty of governments to build the necessary facilities to supply it. In the 1970's, this principle began to be questioned. No more water was available within the state. Even water from the huge Colorado River was likely to be reduced as other states such as Arizona began to claim their share.

For a time, California examined the possibility of bringing water from Canada via a grand scheme called NAWAPA (North America Water and Power Alliance). It would have dwarfed all other schemes already in existence and cost thousands of millions of

FIGURE 5.16   *California Water Schemes*

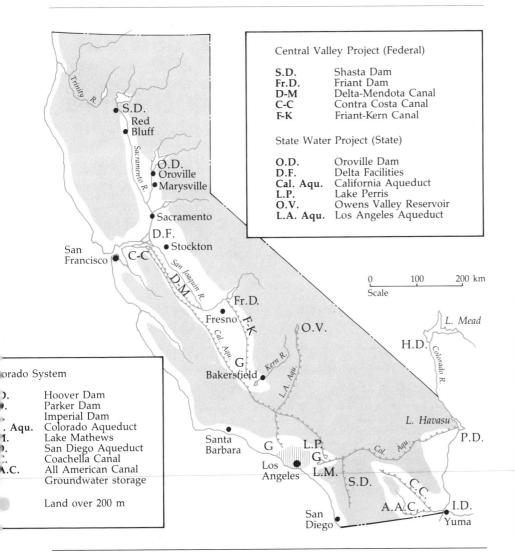

Central Valley Project (Federal)

S.D.	Shasta Dam
Fr.D.	Friant Dam
D-M	Delta-Mendota Canal
C-C	Contra Costa Canal
F-K	Friant-Kern Canal

State Water Project (State)

O.D.	Oroville Dam
D.F.	Delta Facilities
Cal. Aqu.	California Aqueduct
L.P.	Lake Perris
O.V.	Owens Valley Reservoir
L.A. Aqu.	Los Angeles Aqueduct

...orado System

).	Hoover Dam
).	Parker Dam
1.	Imperial Dam
. Aqu.	Colorado Aqueduct
1.	Lake Mathews
).	San Diego Aqueduct
.	Coachella Canal
A.C.	All American Canal
	Groundwater storage

Land over 200 m

Dos Amigos pumping station (California Aqueduct).

Beware the Water Bandit! (An extract from a school workbook in San Francisco.)

dollars. Other proposals included the nuclear desalination of seawater. This scheme went rapidly out of favour after the near-disaster in 1979 at the Three Mile Island nuclear plant in Pennsylvania. Another was the interesting, but impractical, idea of towing icebergs from Antarctica to California via the cold currents to the west of South America.

Today the emphasis has changed. It is now known that it costs much less to persuade people to save a million litres of water than to build reservoirs to supply an additional million litres. Conservation measures are therefore emphasized both on the farms (by far California's largest water users) and in the cities. New methods of irrigation and the lining of canals to prevent seepage are among

What does this photograph suggest about some Californians' attitude towards water conservation?

many measures used to conserve water on farms. In their homes, people are encouraged to use space fillers in toilet tanks to reduce the flush, as well as more economical shower heads. To further encourage conservation, water prices have been raised.

The issue remains as to whether Canada should sell water to the United States, assuming that transporting it becomes feasible. Perhaps your first reaction might be that Californians should manage their own water resources in such a way that they do not need to import more. On the other hand, if Canada already sells non-renewable resources, such as metal ores, to the United States, why should we not be prepared to sell water? It is, after all, a renewable resource which nature will continue to supply long after metal ores are worked out.

QUESTIONS

1. List the main sources of water which have been used by southern California. List three schemes which have *not* been adopted because of high costs or other risks.

2. State three methods of water conservation which are increasingly being used by Californians.

3. What are the arguments for and against making California farmers pay more for their irrigation water?

Chapter Summary

In this chapter you have learned that both renewable and non-renewable resources must be carefully managed. Renewable resources such as fish and timber are the products of natural systems which can easily be upset by human interference or overuse. Non-renewable resources such as minerals and fossil fuels have a limited lifespan which careful use can prolong. The resource crisis is likely to get worse as the less developed world progresses technologically and increases its demand for energy and materials. At present, resource use is leading to serious environmental problems such as water pollution and the disposal of toxic wastes. The solutions to these problems are both complex and costly.

An important issue is "Whose responsibility it is to ensure that the resource needs of future generations are met?" It is sometimes said that if you can afford to buy something, you can do with it whatever you wish. Consumers in the western world can afford to buy large volumes of world resources without much thought of the future. This, however, is a short-term view which could lead to a resource crisis. People should be considering the needs of not just the next generation, but the next several generations. Short-term profit may make some people rich, but it will leave the world as a whole poorer.

IN REVIEW

1. Explain how technological change can affect the use of natural resources.

2. (a) What are Canada's main renewable resources?
   (b) For each of them, suggest two measures which will help maintain levels of production for future generations.

3. Some countries have abundant natural resources, but nevertheless are less developed nations. Give reasons why this is so.

4. Describe how each of the following non-renewable resources can be conserved:
   (a) fossil fuels   (b) minerals

5. Discuss the inequality of resource use between rich and poor countries.

6. What are the advantages and disadvantages of allowing price to be the sole factor in deciding how a resource should be used?

APPLYING YOUR KNOWLEDGE

1. What might visitors to Canada from a less developed country find different in the use of resources and energy in comparison to their own nation?

2. (a) List the advantages and disadvantages of keeping the Fraser as a salmon river.
   (b) Identify groups who would support or oppose changing the use made of the river. Give reasons to support your choices.

3. (a) What examples of a wasteful use of resources can you think of from your own daily life?
   (b) What would have to change to make you use these resources more carefully?

4. (a) What is land zoning?
   (b) Find examples in your area where land zoning might have improved present land use.

5. Predict how each of the following situations might affect the world price of oil:
   (a) a major oil find off the coast of Alaska
   (b) peace in the Middle East
   (c) a major natural disaster in a leading oil producing country.

FURTHER INVESTIGATION

1. List Canada's five most important mineral resources. How many of these are found in significant quantity in British Columbia?

2. Look at the photograph on page 131 of oil drilling in the Beaufort Sea. In what ways might the development of Canada's offshore oil affect the lives of people who live in these regions?

3. The pollution of the Niagara River is only one of many environmental problems caused by improper resource use. Do the necessary research to find details of another environmental problem of interest to you, and suggest some solutions.

4. Do research, then debate the issue of whether Canada should build further hydroelectric power stations to export power to the United States.

CHAPTER 6

Industrialization and Technology

Resources and technology are the bases of industrialization. Technology enables people to use resources in new and more efficient ways. Two centuries ago, the Industrial Revolution brought in a set of new technologies, including the use of mechanical power and the ability to smelt iron ore with coal. Another revolution is underway today which is changing patterns of production and the nature of employment. It is perhaps better called a Technological Revolution, since the number of people actually employed in manufacturing industries has been steadily decreasing in most industrial countries. This second revolution is altering at an astonishing pace the way we work, shop, travel, and communicate with each other.

The Industrial Revolution created a great deal of human suffering as the price to be paid for progress. Millions of people, including children, worked for long hours in appalling conditions in the new mines, mills, and factories. You may well ask whether there is a price to be paid for the advances brought by the Technological Revolution of today. Keep this question in mind as you read through this chapter. Other questions which are examined throughout this chapter include these:

- *What factors encourage industries to locate where they do?*

- *How is high technology changing industrial processes and the workplace?*

- *What patterns and trends of industrialization exist throughout the world?*

- *How do current trends in information and global communications affect economic and political power throughout the world?*

The Organization of Industry

The word "industry" is normally used in connection with the manufacture or production of goods. Table 6.1 shows the various categories of production of both goods and services in Canada, together with the numbers of people employed in each category. The **primary** group depends upon the direct use of natural products. Examples are mining ores and farming the land. The **secondary** group consists of all types of manufacturing industry, as well as construction, which, like manufacturing, has a tangible end-product. The **tertiary** group involves the performance of services rather than the production of goods. This group includes transportation, utilities, the selling and servicing of goods, all professions, public administration, and the whole range of personal services. Activities related to research and development of technology are sometimes separately listed in a fourth or **quaternary** group.

TABLE 6.1 *Categories of Production in Canada (1981 Census). Which category employs the most people?*

			000's	%
Primary	1	Agriculture	486	4.1
		Forestry	104	0.9
		Fishing and Trapping	37	0.3
		Mining (including oil)	216	1.8
Secondary	2	Manufacturing	2278	19.2
		Construction	767	6.4
Tertiary	3	Transport and public utilities	960	8.1
		Trade (wholesale and retail)	2005	16.9
		Finance, insurance and real estate	638	5.4
		Community, business and personal service	3478	29.3
		Public administration and defence	910	7.6
		CANADA	11 879	100.0

Precision is a vital component in today's high-technology industries.

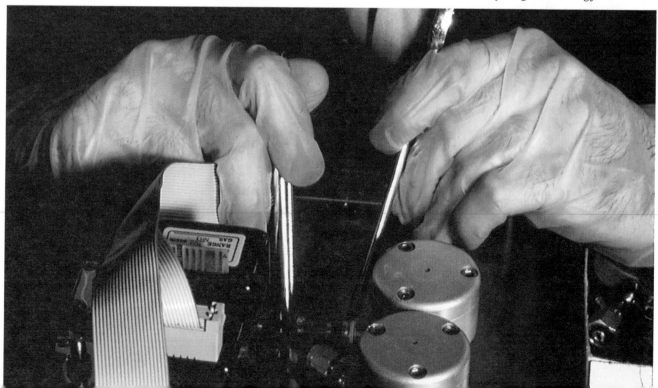

In this century, employment in most western countries has moved strongly in the direction of services and away from the production of goods. This trend is evident in Figure 6.1. Most students who are now in high school and university will find employment in the service sector, though this was not true for their grandparents. Manufacturing is still essential, however, for generating money that can be spent on services.

FIGURE 6.1 *Increase of Tertiary Activities. In which activity sector have all the countries actually dropped? Which country has the greatest proportion of services?*

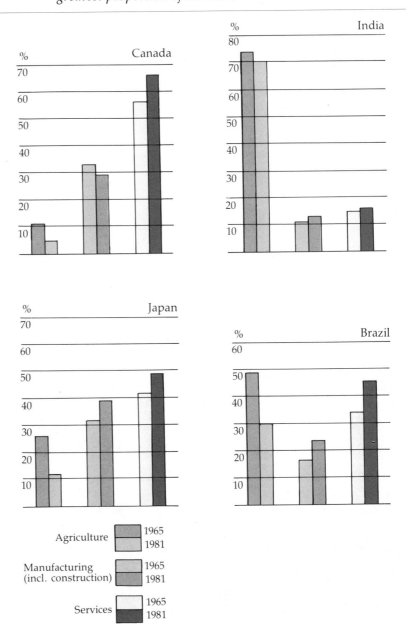

FIGURE 6.2   *Cost Structure Diagram*

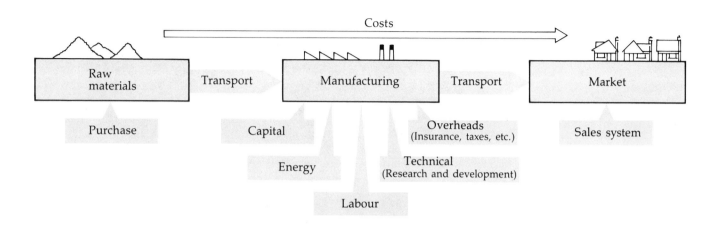

The general aim of manufacturing industries is to produce goods at a profit. To do this, the sales value of the output has to exceed all the costs of production. These costs are numerous, as you can see in Figure 6.2. First of all, raw materials must be purchased. These may be literally "raw" in the sense that they have been directly produced by nature, as in the case of apples for the apple juice industry. Alternatively, they may have been partly or completely processed by someone other than the industry using them. An example is semiconductors used in the computer industry.

The process of manufacturing is in itself costly, including as it does labour and energy costs, interest payments on borrowed capital, and overhead costs such as insurance and land tax. Then there are the costs of setting up and operating a sales system. All these costs have to be met before an article can be sold profitably.

The Effects of the Industrial Revolution on Production

Throughout the world there is an enormous variety of types of industry. Some operate on a domestic scale, using local materials to supply local needs. Others draw on worldwide resources and distribute their products internationally (see Figure 6.3). Small-scale industries were at one time very common in all countries, but the Industrial Revolution set in motion a trend toward larger-scale production, in western countries at least.

One aspect of production which was affected by the Industrial Revolution was the division of labour. Most workers in a factory do a single task, using equipment to help them do it efficiently. This practice

Consumer Goods and Capital Goods

Industries which manufacture goods for sale to consumers are known as consumer goods industries. Those which sell their products for further processing, or make machinery to be installed in factories, are called capital goods industries. As an example, the making of car components is classified as a capital goods industry, but the actual assembly of the car is a consumer goods industry.

Decide whether each of the following is the product of a consumer goods industry or a capital goods industry: car transmissions, kettles, steel beams, aluminum cans, cameras.

How did the Industrial Revolution affect the cost of manufactured goods?

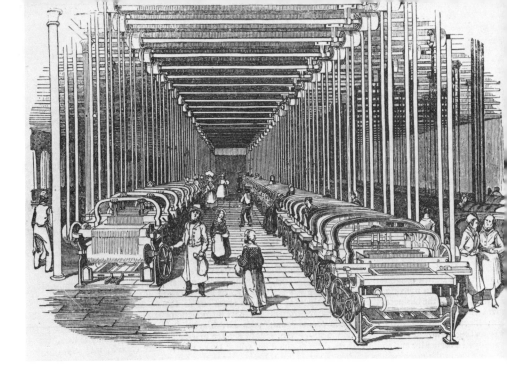

yields a far higher output than if each worker is involved in every stage of production.

The costs of producing a single item usually fall as the number of items produced rises. The costs involved in setting up a factory are so high that the only way to recover these initial costs is to spread them over a large output. Another trend brought by the Industrial Revolution, therefore, is mass production, which is said to lead to "economies of scale". The costs of all the goods you buy would be much higher but for the fact that they are produced in large quantity.

FIGURE 6.3   *Domestic and International Production. Which type of industry requires large amounts of money to start up?*

DOMESTIC

For sale in local market

Local clay

Fuel from local supplier

Family

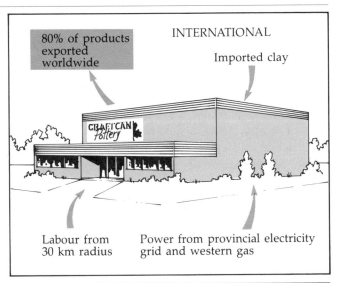

80% of products exported worldwide

INTERNATIONAL

Imported clay

CRAFTCAN Pottery

Labour from 30 km radius

Power from provincial electricity grid and western gas

A final trend is the necessity for large markets. The large-scale industries associated with the Industrial Revolution require international markets to achieve the high sales volume necessary to keep costs down and remain competitive. Unfortunately, this type of production may put small-scale local producers out of business, and people out of work.

The various types of industry can be divided into many categories. Table 6.2 classifies the main groups of industries by product, according to the system used in Canada.

Just as the Industrial Revolution replaced handcrafted goods with machine-made goods, so modern technology is changing the type of goods available to today's consumer.

TABLE 6.2 *Industry Classification*

INDUSTRY GROUP

Food and beverage industries
Tobacco products industries
Rubber and plastics products industries
Leather industries
Textile industries
Knitting mills
Clothing industries
Wood industries
Furniture and fixture industries
Paper and allied industries
Printing, publishing, and allied industries
Primary metal industries
Metal fabricating industries (except machinery and transportation equipment industries)
Machinery industries (except electrical machinery)
Transportation equipment industries
Electrical products industries
Non-metallic mineral products industries
Petroleum and coal products industries
Chemical and chemical products industries
Miscellaneous manufacturing industries

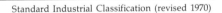

Standard Industrial Classification (revised 1970)

QUESTIONS

1. Why can it be said that a Technological Revolution has occurred during the past 20 or 30 years?

2. Give an example of primary industry.

3. Why is transportation considered a tertiary industry?

4. Why do most modern companies need to produce goods on a large scale?

5. Why are increasing numbers of people finding employment in the tertiary sector?

The Location of Industry

Industries can also be classified by their location. The decision about where to locate an industrial enterprise is an important one, since the costs of production, including transport, will be different for every site chosen. Industrial locations fall into several different categories, shown in Figure 6.4.

Materials-oriented Production

An industry that comes under this category is located near the source of the main raw material it uses. This choice is made for two major reasons. First, the raw material may lose weight or bulk during manufacture. It is therefore economical to locate the factory near the raw material, and transport only the less bulky product. For example, low-grade ores are always upgraded (concentrated) in a processing plant near the mine. Second, the raw material may be fragile or perishable. Tomatoes must be canned near where they are harvested, and fish preserved at the fishing ports or on the fishing boats themselves.

FIGURE 6.4   *Various Location Diagrams. How does the nature of the raw materials used by an industry influence its location?*

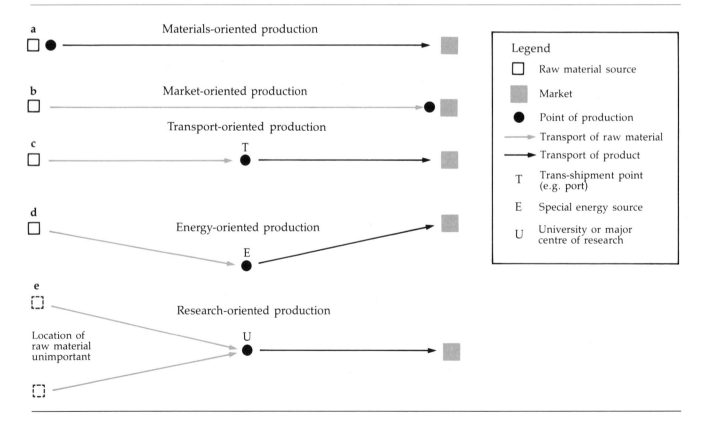

Market-oriented Production

An industry in this category is located where a market exists for the product(s). There are three good reasons for selecting a site on this basis. First, the raw material may gain weight or bulk in manufacture. This is true of industries as widely different as farm machinery assembly, piano making, and soft-drink bottling. Second, the end product may be fragile or perishable, as in the production of furniture or baked goods. Finally, some industries need to be in constant touch with their markets. For example, much of the fashion industry is located near Paris, New York, or London.

Transport-oriented Production

Many industries are located neither at a resource point nor at the market, but at some intermediate location. Such points are frequently lake or ocean ports, where materials can be transferred from ship to train, or the reverse. They may be called **trans-shipment points** or **break-of-bulk points.** Examples of Canadian locations based on favourable transport facilities include Hamilton, Ontario and Vancouver, B.C. Most port cities come into this category to some degree.

Energy-oriented Production

Sometimes a specific factor becomes all-important in the location of an industry. Take the case of aluminum smelting in Kitimat, B.C. Aluminum smelting requires sixteen times as much energy as steel making for every tonne of metal produced. The availability of cheap electricity, especially hydroelectricity, is likely to outweigh other location factors in

Kitimat, B.C. aluminum plant, and the hydro-electric plant that supports it in nearby Kemano.

such a situation. In fact, Alcan Aluminum built its own hydro power station near Kitimat. The town exists almost entirely on the basis of the employment provided by the smelter.

Research-oriented Production

Modern high-technology industries, especially those based on electronics, use small quantities of raw materials. Light in weight and small in bulk, desk-top computers and digital watches are typical high-tech products that can be widely distributed at relatively low cost. But high-technology industries rely heavily on **research and development** (R & D). They are therefore likely to be found close to major universities and centres of research. A major example is the cluster of high-tech producers located near the University of Texas (Austin). The so-called "Silicon Valley" near San Jose, California is the best-known North American centre of electronics industries which rely heavily on R & D. A smaller group of similar industries located in the suburbs of Ottawa has been called the "Silicon Valley of the North".

Other important factors that can affect the location of industry include the availability of skilled and unskilled labour, the water supply, and waste disposal facilities. However, governments at the local or national level can also influence the location of industry by the decisions they take over land zoning and by incentive schemes that include grants, tax concessions, and ready-built factories.

QUESTIONS

1. Give two reasons why an industry might be located near the source of its raw materials.

2. Why is the market usually the most important factor in the location of ready-mix concrete companies?

3. The presence of a labour force is usually a minor factor in locating industries. Why do you suppose this is so?

4. Suggest what the major location factors are likely to be for each of the following industries: oil refining, Coca-Cola bottling, flower growing, jam making, sawmilling.

The Advance of Technology

Since the Industrial Revolution there has been a continual advance in the technology of production. The result has been a larger output of goods in relation to the amounts of capital and labour supplied. Technological progress therefore makes a higher standard of living possible. It also creates new patterns of industry, as well as new

Today's industries, like this smelter in Belgium, must keep up with technological advances if they are to remain competitive.

situations for people at work. The pace of these changes has sped up over the past two decades, in what was called the Technological Revolution earlier in the chapter. Technological changes have affected long-established industries and stimulated the creation of many new industries.

In the iron and steel industry, for example, the technology of smelting ores has improved greatly since the Industrial Revolution. In the 19th century three tonnes of coal were needed to smelt one tonne of iron ore. As a result, steelmills were almost always located on coalfields. Today, less than one tonne of coal is required for the same product. The optimum site for an iron and steel plant is therefore on an iron ore deposit, or at a deep water port where ore can be imported cheaply in bulk carriers. Technological change in the steel industry has thus created growth in these locations. At the same time, other areas, especially those inland and away from cheap water transport, have fallen into decline. The location diagram for the steel industry is shown in Figure 6.5.

FIGURE 6.5   *Location Diagram for the Steel Industry. What advantage might a steel industry on a water body enjoy over an inland location?*

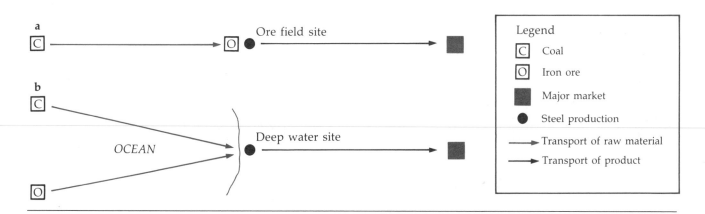

Technology has also led to the emergence of completely new industries. The term **high technology** is perhaps most often used to refer to the microelectronics industry, but it includes others such as **biotechnology** and **materials technology.** Biotechnology involves scientific efforts to improve plant and animal species. It also refers to new ideas such as the use of microbes to recover metals in the mining process. Materials technology often involves the use of new materials to accomplish traditional functions. A familiar example is the transmission of signals by light waves through fibre optics instead of by electrical impulses along copper wire. The most important area of change in modern industrial society continues to be the field of microelectronics.

The Microelectronics Revolution

Today's Technological Revolution is mainly the result of the use of electronics to replace moving parts in machinery, and the use of electrical impulses to perform complex mathematical calculations. In fact, you might well equate the Technological Revolution with the Microelectronics Revolution. Since the first commercial use of computers in the early 1950's, extraordinary progress has been made in microelectronics. The first computers, with their hand-assembled wire circuits, now seem like dinosaurs; they were cumbersome and slow and had tiny memories. A sophisticated mainframe computer of the 1960's required a large air-conditioned room and cost several million dollars. Today, a portable desk-top machine with roughly the same capacity can be bought for about the same price as a good television set.

The first attempts to miniaturize computer circuitry took place in the

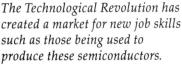

The Technological Revolution has created a market for new job skills such as those being used to produce these semiconductors.

1960's. The new technology was first developed near San Jose, California, in the area referred to earlier as Silicon Valley. Since that time, the silicon chips or semiconductors containing the microcircuitry have become ever smaller, yet able to contain ever-increasing numbers of circuits. **Integrated circuits (IC's)**, which include both processor and memory chips, are so important today that they have been called "the crude oil of the 1980's and 1990's". In recent years IC's have become vastly more powerful in the information they can handle, and constantly smaller in size.

The semiconductor industry is now enormous, with an estimated world output of $27.3 thousand million (U.S.) in 1984. The steady decline in the price of semiconductors has further stimulated demand and has led to the application of electronics to virtually every industry imaginable. The United States and Japan currently dominate semiconductor production, as Table 6.3 shows.

TABLE 6.3 *World Semi-Conductor Production (1982). Why are electronics and precision instrument manufacturing known as "knowledge intensive" industries?*

U.S.A.	Japan	W. Europe	Others
50%	30%	17%	3%

Source: OECD Observer

Microelectronics and the Environment

The microelectronics industry makes much lower demands on energy resources than, for example, steel making. However, the industry is not entirely free of polluting byproducts. Some of the chemicals used in semiconductor production are now thought to be unsafe, on the basis of reports of unusually high rates of birth defects in Silicon Valley and elsewhere. Another potential danger is related to the video display terminals associated with computers. Frequent use is alleged to cause health problems from prolonged exposure to very low levels of radiation. It must be noted, however, that people willingly tolerate this risk every time they switch on the television. A more likely danger from video terminals is strain on both eyes and nerves!

The Impact of Computers on Industry

It would be hard to overestimate the potential effects of computers on industrial production. In some cases the impact is direct and obvious. Both the telecommunications and the aerospace industries make such great use of electronic equipment as to be virtual extensions of the electronics industry. In fact, many of the early advances in computing arose from the demands of the aerospace and defence industries. But there are many ways in which new computer-based technology can improve the efficiency of all kinds of manufacturing industry.

The use of **computer-assisted design (CAD)** systems has largely replaced pen and paper in engineering design. CAD is to drafting and designing what the word processor is to the handling of verbal information. For instance, blueprints and architectural drawings can be made quickly and accurately by the use of CAD systems. In fact, CAD systems are used to design other computers! Computers can also replace the endless paperwork in business planning and stock control.

Microprocessor chips, which are shown being tested here, have brought the computer industry into every aspect of our daily lives.

FIGURE 6.6 *Computers and Increased Efficiency. Based on this chart, how can the high cost of computer equipment be justified by a company?*

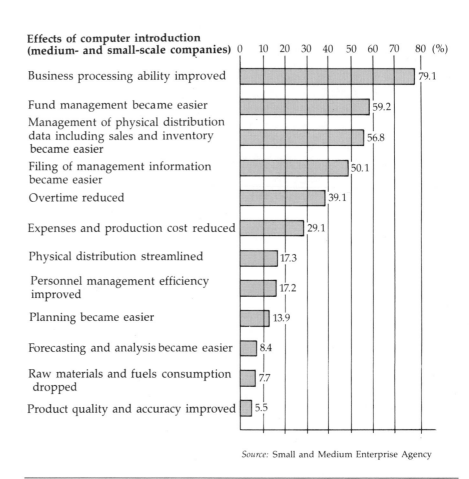

Effects of computer introduction (medium- and small-scale companies)

Effect	Percentage
Business processing ability improved	79.1
Fund management became easier	59.2
Management of physical distribution data including sales and inventory became easier	56.8
Filing of management information became easier	50.1
Overtime reduced	39.1
Expenses and production cost reduced	29.1
Physical distribution streamlined	17.3
Personnel management efficiency improved	17.2
Planning became easier	13.9
Forecasting and analysis became easier	8.4
Raw materials and fuels consumption dropped	7.7
Product quality and accuracy improved	5.5

Source: Small and Medium Enterprise Agency

JIT (Just in Time) inventory control, for example, helps to reduce the cost of maintaining expensive stocks. In general, computers can greatly assist management to become more efficient, as a survey done in Japan clearly shows (Figure 6.6).

Robotics

Machines that perform repeated operations under mechanical control are referred to as *industrial robots.* Mechanically controlled operations are said to be *automated.* The actual power used by robots may be compressed air, hydraulics, or electricity, but the operations are controlled by microcircuits.

The purposes of the introduction of robots are reducing labour costs and minimizing human error. The advantages of computer-controlled robotic systems are obvious. Computers do not tire. They do not suffer from boredom, take holidays or sick leave, or attend their grandmothers' funerals. They can maintain a constant quality of work, and relieve workers of repetitive or physically strenuous operations.

Robots are expensive both to buy and to install, however. In the early 1970's it took as long as 10 years before the initial cost of a robot was recovered by improved productivity. The current figure is about three years. This improvement is encouraging the use of robots in industry for a wide variety of operations.

Initially, welding and spray painting were the major applications for which industrial robots were used. Today, robots are increasingly being

What advantages are gained by the use of robots in car making?

used for materials handling, such as the loading, moving, and unloading of materials at factories, docks, and warehouses. They can also be adapted to do many kinds of machining (cutting, grinding, polishing, *etc.*) and the assembly and inspection of products. Their use in the manufacture of cars is well known. Finally, remote-controlled robots can do work in such hazardous environments as the interior of nuclear reactors and space stations.

The Citroën car company in France has a completely automated workshop producing automobile parts. The factory operates 24 hours per day in three eight-hour shifts. It employs 26 people, compared with an estimated 44 for a similar non-automated production unit. One person in the control tower can operate the night shift. The automated unit requires a different type of labour force, almost all technicians and skilled workers, than a non-automated unit would.

TABLE 6.4 *World Use of Industrial Robots*

	Welding	Painting and Finishing	Materials Handling	Loading and Unloading	Assembly	Other Uses	Total
Japan	8 052	1 071	6 797	2 578	6 099	7 303	31 900
United States	2 453	490	1 300	1 060	72	925	6 300
West Germany	1 916	417	587	193	122	1 065	4 300
Sweden	260	245	130	580	15	220	1 450
Italy	492	97	100	102	111	198	1 100
World	14 651	2 853	13 104	5 326	9 555	11 938	57 427

Source: Worldwide Robotics Survey, (RIA November 1983)

Table 6.4 lists the five countries of the world which are leaders in the number of installed industrial robots. Japan clearly has an enormous overall lead, especially in the use of robots for more advanced assembly operations.

QUESTIONS

1. How has increasing efficiency in the use of coal in the steel industry changed the optimum site for iron and steel plants?

2. What is materials technology?

3. (a) What material, other than copper, can be used to transmit signals?
   (b) What are the advantages of this material over copper?

4. About what proportion of the world's semiconductor production occurs (a) in the United States and (b) in Japan?

5. Name three items, apart from computers, which you use on a day-to-day basis that rely on microelectronic components.

6. Describe three ways in which computer-based technology can improve the efficiency of manufacturing industry.

7. What are the advantages of using robots in manufacturing industry? Can you think of a disadvantage?

For some workers the cost of new technology has been job loss. Should society try to balance the need for new technology with the human need for jobs?

New Technology and Employment

After reading the previous pages, you are likely wondering whether the new technology will eliminate more jobs than it creates. This is one of the burning issues of today, hotly debated by economists and politicians. But the answer may not be known for some time, according to Nobel Prize winning economist Wassily Leontief, since the Technological Revolution may last 30 to 50 years. Several factors must be considered in examining the effect of technology on employment.

First of all, industries look to high technology to cut expenses, particularly labour costs. In some fields the job loss is considerable. Telecommunications experienced job losses of about 30 percent in the late 1970's in countries such as Britain and Sweden. Other industries to face large job losses included printing and the manufacture of office equipment and television sets. However, labour displacement has been much slower in some other areas because wages are lower and there is less pressure to save on costs by introducing high technology. Examples are the textile and garment industries.

The other side of the coin is a result of the fact that automation generally reduces industry's costs of production. The lower selling prices can create new market opportunities, both at home and abroad. This can lead to further expansion of an automating industry, and the eventual employment of more people.

It must also be considered that the introduction of new technology often coincides with the introduction of new products and product design. This combination makes it difficult to tell how much of the job loss in a given industry is a result of technology. When the company Fiat introduced robots to make cars in Italy, total employment fell by about 40 percent. However, only about 5 percent of that reduction could be directly attributed to the robots. Most of the savings came from general improvements in efficiency.

Finally, at the same time as jobs are being lost through the application of technology to industry, many new jobs are being created. The most obvious example is the steady growth of employment within the microelectronics and computer industries. Jobs are also created through the sales, installation, and servicing of this new equipment. Yet another new job area involves a whole range of technology-related consumer goods industries (for example, video games) which all require labour for production and servicing.

Historically, there is little evidence that technological progress has reduced employment. On the contrary, the transformation brought about by railways and automobiles in the past led to rapid economic expansion. New areas of the country were opened up. Goods could be sold to a much wider market. Farms and factories, in turn, required many new products in the form of machinery and equipment.

It seems unlikely, therefore, that the overall effect of the Technological Revolution will be to reduce employment to any significant extent.

Some experts even claim that robots create, rather than destroy, jobs, particularly in the manufacture and sales of related equipment. Nevertheless, the introduction of new technology may cause serious problems of transition. It is not very comforting to workers who lose their jobs to know that other jobs are being created for which they are not qualified. Unemployment, for whatever reason, is undoubtedly a major cause of mental and emotional stress.

The main problem arising from new technology is that many unskilled jobs are being replaced by others that require precise forms of training. Many older workers are especially vulnerable because they have the least career time remaining in which to undertake the necessary retraining. They may also have less inclination to do so. Some younger workers, especially those with a limited education, are also at risk. Retraining is probably the major hurdle which society faces as a result of the Technological Revolution.

Another social change caused by retraining is related to the fact that it requires mobility. Many retrained people must move elsewhere in search of employment, while others with different skills arrive to take their place. Thus, there is likely to be a greater turnover of population, especially in smaller communities, than in the past. Some population experts have claimed that this trend could lead to the formation of "communities of strangers".

Technology and Less Developed Countries

Next it is necessary to ask *where* jobs are being gained and lost as a result of technology. Between 1963 and 1982, less developed countries had increased their total share of world manufacturing from 8.1 percent to 11 percent. Their lower wage rates allowed them to compete in the markets of developed countries. The spread of high technology raises questions about the future of industry in some Third World countries.

In some markets, handcrafted items can bring a higher price than manufactured goods. What goods would you consider more valuable if they were handcrafted?

Only a few less developed countries, Brazil and Korea among them, have been able to develop their own high technology industries. Some others, such as Singapore and Taiwan, have set up semiconductor assembly plants. Initially this was a relatively *labour-intensive* operation, that is, one requiring large numbers of people. However, the production of semiconductors is now a highly automated process. As a result, high technology industries are increasingly concentrating in Japan, the United States, and western Europe.

You have seen that the main reason for the competitiveness of less developed countries is their low labour costs. Yet if machines continue to replace labour in the production process, the cost advantage may well swing back to those countries which have the most sophisticated technology, particularly Japan and the United States.

QUESTIONS

1. Name four industries in which jobs have been lost as a result of advances in technology.

2. Give some examples to show how advances in technology can create jobs.

3. (a) What are the effects of high technology on (**i**) the environment and (**ii**) working conditions?
   (b) Do you think technology has in general had a positive or a negative effect in these areas?

Patterns of Industrialization

Some countries became industrialized relatively early in history; others entered the race much later; and some remain almost entirely non-industrialized. The Industrial Revolution began in the late 18th century in Britain, then spread rapidly to other European countries and the United States. It heralded the birth of the factory system of production.

In the present century, industrialization has spread even more widely. The U.S.S.R. and Japan became major industrial powers before the mid-point of the century. Industrial output has risen sharply in the centrally planned (socialist) European allies of the U.S.S.R. as well. More recently, a large group of **newly industrialized countries (NIC's)** has emerged, among them Korea, Brazil, and Singapore. Below you will examine these three contrasting patterns of industrialization.

Mature Industrial Economies

The industrialized nations of western Europe, North America, Japan, and Australia may be said to have **mature industrial economies.** Their manufacturing industries usually cover a broad range of products, especially goods produced for sale to consumers. These countries enjoy high standards of living, whether measured by *per capita* income or the physical quality of life index. In mature economies, the percentage of people who work in manufacturing has begun to decline, while the percentage in service employment has been correspondingly rising, as you saw earlier in the chapter.

The U.S.S.R.—State Planning

The U.S.S.R. and its east European allies have been striving to catch up with the west in both total output and *per capita* income. In the U.S.S.R., the government makes the major decisions about investment in industry, since it owns the means of producing and distributing goods. The steel and engineering industries, which were badly damaged in World War II, were given high priority in economic planning. The U.S.S.R. remains more committed to heavy industry today than any western country. It is the world's largest producer of coal, iron ore, and steel. However, there has been a shift from a heavy dependence on coal to a more balanced energy mix, with coal and oil or gas roughly equal in importance. Since World War II, some of the world's largest hydro power facilities have also been built in the Soviet Union.

Industry in the U.S.S.R., unlike industry in the United States, is resource-oriented rather than market-oriented. Since the largest unexploited mineral and energy resources are located east of the Ural Mountains in Siberia, the government has encouraged development in these areas of the country (see Figure 6.7).

Unfortunately, the distribution of the Soviet population does not correspond to the distribution of resources. The government has had a constant problem persuading people to live in the more remote eastern regions, with their extreme climate. Incentives, including higher wages and improved benefits, have been offered to encourage people to work in eastern industrial cities such as Novosibirsk and Karaganda.

The Soviet Union has developed numerous communities in the frontier regions, including this one in Siberia. Explain why Canada has not developed its northern frontier to the same extent.

FIGURE 6.7 *New Eastern Projects in U.S.S.R. How has the industrialisation of the U.S.S.R. been hampered by the location of raw materials? Why do you think river transportation has not been widely used?*

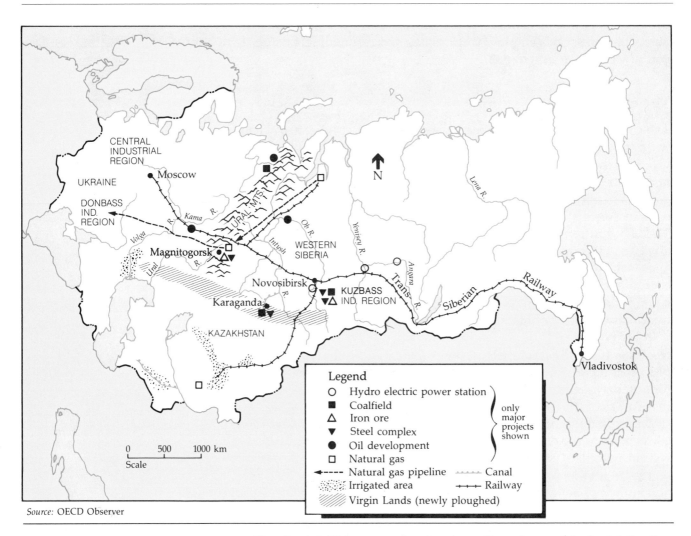

Source: OECD Observer

The Soviet Union remains in an earlier phase of industrialization than western countries. Consumer industries, which are located mainly in the Moscow area, have been held back by the government in order to devote more investment to heavy industry and chemicals. More consumer goods industries exist today than ever before, but because of the Soviet Union's lower *per capita* income, there is nothing comparable to the variety available in western countries.

Newly Industrialized Countries (NIC's)

It is clear from Figure 6.8 that some newly industrialized countries have extremely high growth rates of industrial production. Korea's volume of industrial production was eight times higher in 1980 than in 1968, and Singapore's was four times higher. The larger industrial countries obviously cannot attain such rates of expansion, since they have for

FIGURE 6.8   *Industrial Production (Selected Examples)*

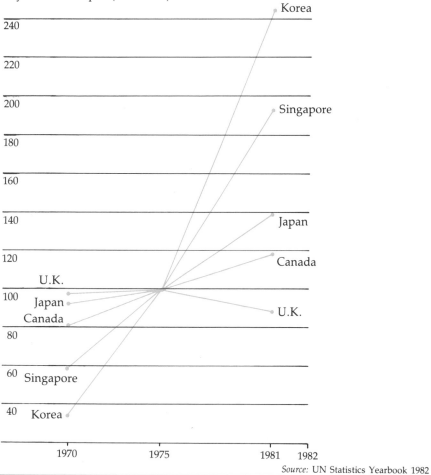

Index numbers of industrial production
in selected countries by volume output (1975 = 100)

Source: UN Statistics Yearbook 1982

This Asian street scene shows that newly industrialized countries can have a mix of new and old technologies.

many years had a high volume of production. Thus, the rapid growth of industry in the NIC's is providing western nations with intense competition.

Newly industrialized countries have very low labour costs and limited trade union organization. Many large companies based in Europe, North America, or Japan have therefore opened branch plants in NIC's to take advantage of the lower costs of production.

Countries in the early stages of industrialization have often begun with textile production because the technology is relatively inexpensive and widely available. The industry is relatively labour intensive, but low-cost labour is provided by the large populations of the NIC's. Figure 6.9 shows the top 10 nations in production of woollen goods. Woollen sweaters are now imported into Canada from several NIC's including Hong Kong, Singapore, and Mauritius, as well as from traditional suppliers such as Britain.

FIGURE 6.9   *Top Ten Producers of Woollen Yarn*

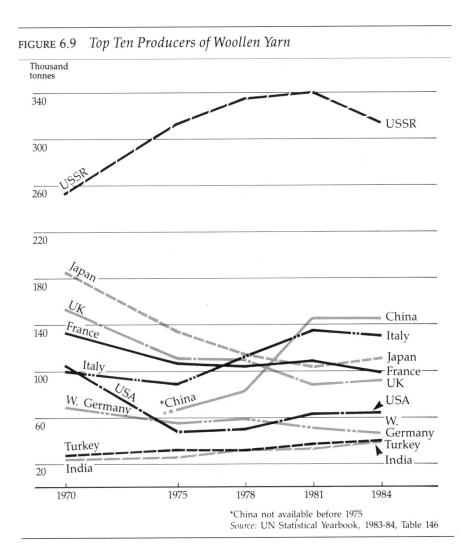

*China not available before 1975
Source: UN Statistical Yearbook, 1983-84, Table 146

The Least Developed Countries (LLDC's)

Industrialization is not an easy solution to the problems of the poorest countries of the world. These nations suffer from the cycle of poverty (Figure 6.10), which is similar to the hunger cycle examined in Chapter 4. Their inhabitants have very low incomes, and therefore can neither accumulate capital nor buy large amounts of manufactured products. Foreign investment is often deterred by the risk of low profits or by political instability. Added to these factors is the enormous problem of educating and training a labour force for an industrial way of life, which differs greatly from the routines of agriculture.

FIGURE 6.10 *Diagram of the Poverty Cycle. How can the poor break out of this cycle?*

Dire Poverty

Not enough money to buy food, medicine, seeds or materials

Inadequate shelter, malnutrition, debilitation, sickness

Inability to look for or perform work

A quick and successful means of transforming a traditional economy into an industrial economy has yet to be found.

FIGURE 6.11 *Percent of GNP in Industry. List those nations that depend on industry for the highest contribution to their GNP.*

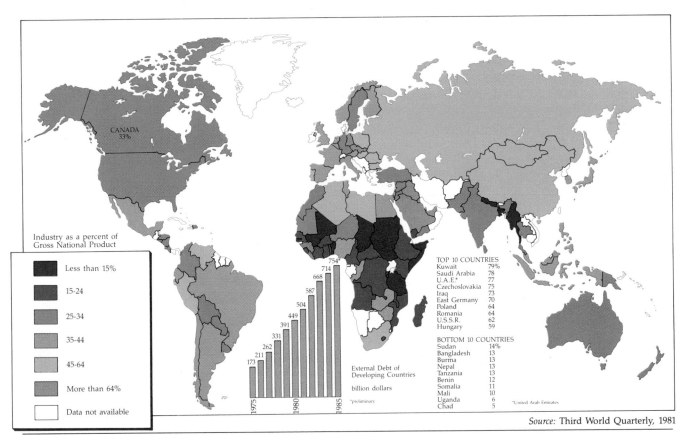

Industry as a percent of Gross National Product

	Industry as a percent of Gross National Product
	Less than 15%
	15-24
	25-34
	35-44
	45-64
	More than 64%
	Data not available

CANADA 33%

External Debt of Developing Countries

billion dollars

*preliminary

173	211	262	331	391	449	504	587	668	714	754*

1975   1980   1985

TOP 10 COUNTRIES
Kuwait	79%
Saudi Arabia	78
U.A.E.*	77
Czechoslovakia	75
Iraq	73
East Germany	70
Poland	64
Romania	64
U.S.S.R.	62
Hungary	59

BOTTOM 10 COUNTRIES
Sudan	14%
Bangladesh	13
Burma	13
Nepal	13
Tanzania	13
Benin	12
Somalia	11
Mali	10
Uganda	6
Chad	5

*United Arab Emirates

Source: Third World Quarterly, 1981

The LLDC's therefore have very little industrial output. Figure 6.11 shows that in a number of countries, industry may contribute less than 15 percent to the already very low gross national product.

Appropriate Technology

High technology may be suitable for countries having high income and education levels. In many countries, however, the capital costs of setting up modern industries are too high. Factories in such countries would have to be paid for by foreign investment, and the products would be mainly for export. Little benefit would be received by the people of these countries. Yet all countries make use of some level of technology for their domestic needs, whether in agriculture or transportation. No matter how poor a country is, there are invariably some types of technology which would enhance production and therefore improve the lives of the people.

This type of low-cost technology is often referred to as **appropriate**

These women in Sri Lanka make and assemble hand pumps using local skills and resources.

or **intermediate technology.** It can make a great contribution in less developed countries. Consider an example. Western countries use huge combine harvesters in agriculture. These machines are inappropriate in less developed countries on two counts: they are far too expensive, and they replace people with machines. Where labour is abundant and cheap, it makes no sense to import machines that require further imports of oil and spare parts to keep them going. Hand-powered devices may be more appropriate to use in very poor countries.

Low-cost devices using local materials and labour can be built to accomplish such essential tasks as raising water from wells, for instance. They may be operated by hand or pedal power, or by animals. Whereas technology is estimated to cost about $12 000 per worker in Western Europe (and more in North America), hand-operated technology in poorer Third World countries may cost as little as $4 to $10 per worker. International agencies such as the Intermediate Technology Development Group do much to foster the use of appropriate technology in less developed countries.

The foregoing is not intended to suggest that there is no place for high technology in poor countries. On the contrary, recent famine relief efforts in some African countries have been assisted by the use of computers and long-wave radio communications. As microelectronic devices become cheaper, they have a larger potential use in the Third World. Overall, technology in less developed countries, with their large populations, should put improving production ahead of saving on labour costs.

QUESTIONS

1. Name three characteristics common to industrialized countries with mature economies.

2. For what reasons have Soviet planners encouraged regional resource development?

3. Refer to Figure 6.7. Why do you think the distribution of many of the Soviet Union's resources poses a problem in terms of industrial development?

4. Refer to Figure 6.8, Index Numbers of Industrial Production.
   (a) Which country has had an industrial decline since 1975?
   (b) Which country has had the greatest relative increase in manufacturing production?
   (c) Why do mature industrial countries show lower increases in graphs of this sort?

5. What factors would encourage the establishment of branch plants in newly industrialized countries?

6. What is "appropriate technology"? How can it be judged what technology is appropriate in a given situation?

CLOSE-UP

Japan: Adaptation to Change

During the past three decades, Japan has experienced very rapid economic growth. In 1964, personal income *per capita* was only 10 percent of the level in the United States. By 1983 the gap had narrowed to 80 percent of the U.S. level. In 1987, following a dramatic rise in the value of the yen, Japan's *per capita* income exceeded that of the United States for the first time.

Japan received financial assistance from the United States to rebuild its economy after World War II. Nevertheless, the country is poor in many resources and has to look abroad for supplies of iron ore, coal, and oil. When oil prices rose so dramatically in 1973, Japan was one of the countries most seriously affected, since 77 percent of its energy needs were based on oil. By 1982 Japan reduced its dependence upon imported oil to 62 percent. The balance comes from coal, which it imports from Australia, the United States, and Canada. This trend has stimulated the expansion of coal mining in British Columbia.

Structural Changes in the Japanese Economy

Japan's industrial structure has been reshaped to a large extent since the energy crisis of 1973. The changes have been brought about by cooperation between Japanese firms and the government in the shape of the Ministry of International Trade and Industry (MITI). This partnership seems to work well in Japan.

In a recent policy change, the emphasis on industries that consume large amounts of either energy or labour in production has been reduced. Investment in high-technology industries and those with high-value products has been increased correspondingly. These shifts have been made possible by Japan's investment in research and development, which is among the highest in the world (Figure 6.12).

The rise in the value of the yen since 1985 has had a profound effect on Japanese industry. The industries which have been cut back are those considered to be less profitable or more likely to

FIGURE 6.12 *R & D Expenditures in Japan, U.S. and Canada. How does Canada's expenditure on R & D compare to that of Japan and the U.S.? Should we be spending more?*

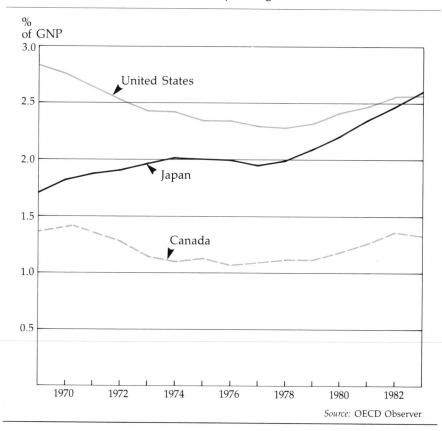

Source: OECD Observer

Japan has become a model for other nations seeking rapid modernization.

succumb to competition from the NIC's. Examples include the production of chemical fertilizers, basic (but not high-quality) steel, and synthetic fibres. Japan is now a net importer of textiles, having conceded that the lower labour costs in countries such as Korea and Taiwan would eventually prove too competitive. Japan remains the world leader in shipbuilding, but its share of world production has been reduced from 42 percent to 28 percent. Aluminum smelting has been cut back by two-thirds. Workers in the declining industries are being retrained for other forms of work.

Japan's growing industries are electronics and precision instruments, which can be called "knowledge intensive" industries. See Figure 6.13. Japan has claimed a large share of the world market for integrated circuits. Currently, Japanese researchers are concentrating on leading the way toward the production of so-called "fifth generation" or "intelligent" computers. Japan's profits from exports in electronics and high technology have been outstanding, well ahead of the value of its most publicized export, cars.

The industrial success of Japan has been attributed to a variety of factors, including the following:

- a very high level of capital investment (15 percent of GNP)

- very high nation-wide levels of education

- on-the-job training of workers straight from school

- good quality control and a minimum of poor workmanship

- the ability to foresee the most profitable sectors of production

- generally stable social relations in Japanese factories

FIGURE 6.13 *Production Trends in Japanese Industry. Suggest one reason for the rapid rise in the electronics industry in Japan.*

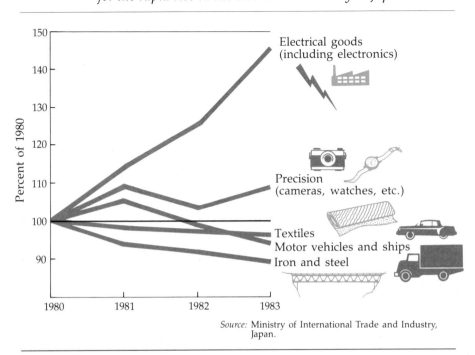

Source: Ministry of International Trade and Industry, Japan.

• relatively high spending on research and development

• a population which shares a common culture

It used to be said that Japan's success lay in copying western products. This explanation is now totally inadequate. Still, Japan remains a large importer of technology. Between 1950 and 1980 Japan purchased 30 000 production licences from companies in other countries at a total cost of $10 thousand million (U.S.). This may seem like a high price to pay, but it is only a fraction of the cost of the research and development needed to produce the technology in the first place.

QUESTIONS

1. What disadvantages did Japan face in industrializing?

2. (a) Name three industries which have recently declined within Japan.
(b) What are the reasons for the decline in these industries?

3. What do you think are the main reasons for Japan's economic success?

4. How has Japan responded to **(a)** a lack of natural resources for heavy industry and **(b)** foreign competition?

Industrial Decline

It is often said that ours is a post-industrial society. This label is applied because of the decline in the importance of manufacturing and the corresponding growth of service employment in the economies of western countries. Competition from Japan and from the NIC's has adversely affected industries in Europe and North America, including traditional heavy industries such as steel and shipbuilding. In addition, older mining areas with limited reserves cannot produce as cheaply as large new mines in developing countries. Industrial decline is a serious problem of most mature economies.

C L O S E - U P

De-Industrialization—The Case of Britain

Few countries experience an absolute decline in the volume of manufacturing output. However, in the United Kingdom, the volume of manufacturing output actually fell by 17 percent from 1975 to 1983. Britain has been the only major manufacturing nation to show a reduction.

Related to this decline in manufacturing has been a dramatic rise in unemployment in Britain's cities. In Table 6.5 you can see Britain's employment structure from 1961 to 1981. Job losses are most striking in the area of manufacturing, with a decline of 1.8 million jobs between 1971 and 1981. More than half of this loss occurred in 1979–1981 alone.

TABLE 6.5 *Employment in Britain: 1961–1981*

	1961 (000's of people)	1971 (000's of people)	1981 (000's of people)
Agriculture, forestry, fishing, mining, quarrying	1 577	828	692
Manufacturing	8 381	8 013	6 199
Services (incl. construction)	13 050	13 075	14 468
Total	23 008	21 916	21 359

Table 6.6 shows the individual industries which have been hardest hit, both in total numbers and in percentage terms, in 1971–1981.

TABLE 6.6   *Job Losses by Industry in Britain: 1971–1981*

	000's of people		% decline
1. Engineering & electrical	−298	1. Textiles	−41.6
2. Textiles	−259	2. Metal manufacture	−41.5
3. Metal manufacture	−231	3. Leather goods	−34.0
4. Vehicles	−180	4. Clothing & footwear	−31.2
5. Other metal goods	−148	5. Bricks,pottery,glass	−29.6
6. Clothing & footwear	−142	6. Shipbuilding	−25.4

To keep these depressing figures in perspective, remember that some decline in employment will take place in developed nations even if the volume of output is maintained. All industrialized nations have been steadily reducing their labour force, because technology produces an increase in productivity per worker. Two questions remain. Are new industries replacing the jobs lost in declining industries? Is the service sector of the economy expanding fast enough to absorb the people displaced from manufacturing? Earlier in this chapter, you saw that in most western countries the answer to both questions is a qualifed "Yes". In Britain, however, new industries have been slow to develop, except those which have arisen in connection with North Sea oil. (The reasons

The closing of this car plant in Linwood, Scotland is just one example of de-industrialization in Britain.

FIGURE 6.14 *U.K. Unemployment*

% of work force
unemployed

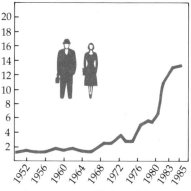

Source: Ministry of Labour, U.K.

for this are detailed below.) And the service sector, which grew steadily until 1975, has increasingly been faced with employment problems of its own. Unemployment rates in Britain have therefore risen sharply in recent years, as Figure 6.14 shows.

Several possible reasons for Britain's industrial decline have been suggested:

- over-expansion of state-owned industries (such as coal and steel), leaving little capital for other industries

- low output per worker, often the result of poor management or outdated equipment

- low levels of investment, much less than in Japan

- high labour costs, though wages are not as high as those of some of Britain's competitors

- the rise in the value of the pound, which made British exports too expensive on world markets, especially from 1979 to 1981

- the tendency for the government to support declining industries (for social reasons) rather than to invest in new growth areas

- labour/management conflicts, with many working days lost through strikes

- an educational system badly adapted to the needs of a modern economy

Not all of these reasons apply to the entire period of industrial decline in Britain, but each has contributed to a loss of export markets and increasing foreign competition in Britain's home market.

QUESTIONS

1. Refer to Table 6.5, which shows the employment structure in Britain.
   (a) Which sector showed the greatest relative decline between 1961 and 1981?
   (b) Which sector showed an increase?

2. Refer to Table 6.6. Which industries in Britain suffered the greatest decline between 1971 and 1981 (a) in total numbers and (b) in percentage terms? What reasons can you suggest?

3. Why do you think the textile and metal goods industries have fared so badly in Britain? Are there any parallels in Canada?

4. Of all the factors that contributed to Britain's decline, which do you consider the most important? Give reasons for your answer.

Government Aid to Declining Regions

Declining industries are often located in specific areas of a country. The concept of helping these areas goes back to the Depression of the 1930's when governments, faced with serious unemployment and economic hardship, began to accept some responsibility for maintaining levels of employment. Policies intended to help problem regions within countries are sometimes called **regional policies.**

This kind of program first developed in Britain. Between the two World Wars, several Acts of Parliament defined special areas of the country which would receive various forms of government assistance. One measure provided for the setting up of industrial parks, with planned sites for companies establishing factories. After World War II, further Acts extended this form of regional policy in Britain. The idea was eventually adopted in several other western countries, including France and Italy.

Regional Policy in the United States

The United States has never adopted a formal regional policy of the British type. The reason is partly that the American federal system does not provide adequate central authority to carry out such policies

Regional Policies

There are many ways in which governments can help industries in areas which are experiencing economic decline. The establishment of industrial parks in which factories are rented or sold cheaply is one method. Another is the offering of tax concessions and other financial subsidies to companies prepared to set up in problem areas. These subsidies may add up to very considerable sums and be quite effective in recruiting new companies, as in the case of the many American companies which have located in the development areas of the United Kingdom.

Regional policy can help local industries compete in world markets and can also protect local jobs.

effectively, and partly that the United States has a more persistent tradition of free enterprise.

The United States does, however, have a record of constructing major public works programs in areas where unemployment is high. The Tennessee Valley Authority (TVA), constructed after 1935, is an example. This multi-purpose project improved navigation and flood control on the Tennessee River, while generating hydroelectric power and providing for the reforestation of eroded slopes. More recently, large sums of money have been spent on improving the economy of the Appalachian Region by investment in roads, hospitals, schools, and other social programs.

In one respect the U.S. government does play a significant role in the location of industry: Look at the map of federal spending on defence (Figure 6.15). In parts of the southern and western United States,

FIGURE 6.15 *U.S. Defence Spending by State (per capita). How does this map illustrate how government spending can influence regional development?*

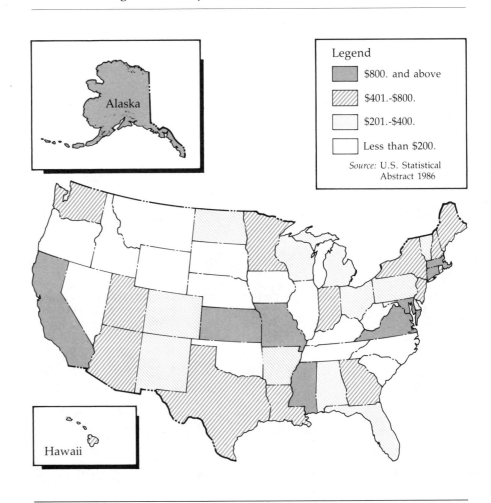

Legend

- $800. and above
- $401.-$800.
- $201.-$400.
- Less than $200.

Source: U.S. Statistical Abstract 1986

spending levels are high enough to stimulate industry in general. Furthermore, defence spending is so closely related to high technology that non-defence industries share in the benefits.

Government Involvement in Canadian Industry

The Canadian government, too, is faced with the problem of declining industrial areas. The textile industry of Quebec requires substantial import duties to help it survive fierce international competition from NIC's. The steel industry at Sydney, Nova Scotia and the related coal-mining industry at Glace Bay are now both heavily subsidized by the federal government, to maintain employment in areas where new industry is scarce.

The **Department of Regional Industrial Expansion (DRIE)**—formerly the Department of Regional Economic Expansion (DREE)—works closely with provincial departments of trade and industry. The aims of DRIE are to assist areas experiencing economic hardship and to stimulate promising industrial ventures. A notable example of a DRIE incentive is the Atlantic Assistance Program, which gives particular help to Cape Breton Island. DRIE also provided assistance in the establishment of the new Toyota and Hyundai plants in Ontario and Quebec respectively. In 1984–1985, DRIE gave a total of $21.5 million in grants to 91 projects in British Columbia, ranging from sawmill renovation to promising high-tech ventures.

Canada's Department of Regional Industrial Expansion works with a variety of industries.

Having undergone widespread industrial decine, Britain has many examples of landscapes such as the one shown here.

Industrial Decline and Industrial Landscapes

Industrial development makes a great impact on the landscape. Factories, warehouses, waste disposal dumps, and transport facilities are all highly visible signs of an industrial economy. Whereas modern industrial parks can present a neat, well-landscaped appearance, old or declining industrial areas often look run down, with disused buildings and derelict land. They often look unplanned as well, having been built before modern **zoning** restrictions.

Such areas are common in the old coal-based industrial regions of Europe, where industrial growth reached its peak early in this century. Coalfields and textile producing areas in parts of the northeastern United States are equally unsightly. Coal mining in particular greatly scarred the landscape, even where the mining was underground. Slag heaps, abandoned pit buildings, and water-filled subsidence areas were a common sight. However, much effort has been made in recent years to clean up the areas formerly scarred by coal mining, especially in Britain. The tragedy at Aberfan in South Wales in 1966 quickened the nation's conscience with regard to the problems of the coal industry. In this disaster a water-swollen slag heap slid down a hill and engulfed a school, killing 26 adults and 116 children.

QUESTIONS

1. What are the major causes of industrial decline in parts of Europe and North America?

2. Why do you think some old coal mining areas, such as Appalachia and Cape Breton, have suffered economic problems?

3. How have governments attempted to solve problems of industrial decline? Quote examples from Canada.

4. (a) What environmental hazards are created by some older heavy industries?

   (b) How can these be solved, given that such industries have limited funds to pay for improvements to the landscape?

The Information Economy

The decline in the number of people employed in manufacturing in the western countries is one of the major trends of the Technological Revolution. According to the economist D.L. Birch of the Massachusetts Institute of Technology, only 12 percent of the work force in the United States actually make anything. Most people are involved in jobs which deal with information of some type. Computer programmers, editors, accountants, lawyers, secretaries, and government employees are just a few examples. Most students now prepare for these kinds of employment. In the final section of this chapter, you will consider some of the implications of this trend towards an information-based economy.

Commodities and Information

The study of geography emphasizes location and distance. Among other things, it considers where people live and what they produce. When people exchange commodities, a process we call "trade", the ease of movement of the goods is closely related to the form of transportation available and to the physical difficulties which have to be negotiated. For instance, transport by rail through mountains is difficult and costly, as the builders of the CPR through western Canada soon found out, but bulk transport of coal from Canada to Japan by sea is relatively inexpensive.

Information is bought and sold just as commodities are. Indeed, the trade of information between countries has been valued at over $600 thousand million each year. However, as you read in Chapter 1, radio and satellite transmissions differ from the shipment of goods in that they pay no attention to international frontiers. No customs officer can stop the beaming of information into a country.

Radio and television help traditional societies to learn what is happening elsewhere in the world. The effect is to increase the desire of poor countries to share in the higher living standards of the west.

Satellites have revolutionized the communications industry.

Modes of Communication

The term "information" covers all modes of communication. Consider the following list:

- words (spoken)
- words (written)
- photographs (still)
- films (moving)
- pictures or diagrams

- music
- maps
- statistics (spoken)
- statistics (written)
- statistics (graphed)

Until little over a century ago, all these could be passed only from person to person. The invention of the telegraph and, somewhat later, the telephone, made long-distance verbal communication possible. Still later, the invention of radio liberated verbal communications from travelling along cables which could break or be interfered with, and, later still, television enabled pictures as well as words to be transmitted. Very recently, the technology of communications has leapt ahead. All

---

FIGURE 6.16   *Person-to-Person Communication. How long would it take a piece of information to reach everybody if each arrow were a 24 hour period?*

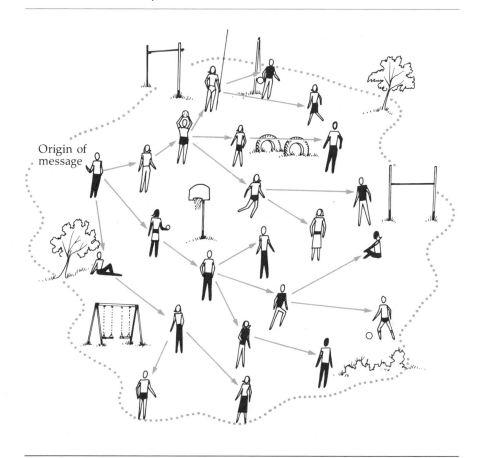

forms of communication—voice, graphic, or pictorial—can now be transmitted digitally (*i.e.,* in numerical form). Modern satellites enable information to be transmitted almost instantaneously over the entire world. Compare this with slow person-to-person spreading of information (Figure 6.16).

Information is vital to manufacturing and service companies in virtually every stage of their operations: research, design, production control, marketing, distribution, order processing, and maintenance. Not surprisingly, some large corporations maintain their information-based activities as separate subsidiary companies. McDonnell-Douglas, the aircraft and defence manufacturer, does this, while General Motors has taken over a high-technology company, Electronic Data Systems, for the same purpose. It is estimated that up to 40 percent of the costs of developing a new General Motors car will be spent on computer hardware and software.

A key point is that some forms of information can be utilized only by those who have high-technology equipment. For instance, the U.S. Landsat Program, which monitors mineral and agricultural resources, makes its data available, but very sophisticated equipment is necessary to analyze it.

The Canadarm is just one of Canada's contributions to aeronautical engineering.

Information Networks

According to futurist Robert Arnold Russel, "Information networks are the Roman roads of our time." Computer systems are now linked worldwide, so that, for example, a foreign exchange trader or stockbroker can consult several world markets simultaneously to get the best price for a stock, a currency, or a commodity. If you lose your credit card, a warning against other possible users can be transmitted to the Canadian head office, as well as to the European head office of the related company, almost before you hang up the telephone.

The network used most often is the telephone system, which is linked worldwide by direct dialling among most countries. Large companies, especially multinationals, often find the public telephone system too slow and expensive. Most have therefore installed their own **private information networks**. IBM, for example, can use its private system to change design specifications for all of its world facilities on the same day.

Another type of information network is the **limited participation network**. In such a system companies can pool the costs of expensive information. Oil companies may do this with geological information relating to their exploration activities. Most airlines belong to a network which integrates seat assignment, departure control, and meteorological information.

Public information networks are also growing rapidly. Today, several thousand data bases are available on-line to users via the normal telephone system. You can do library research for a major project through such data bases, and even get an up-to-date weather report.

Shopping at home is likely to prove popular with some people in the near future. This example of an interactive network allows consumers to select merchandise and pay for it without leaving their own homes.

The office desk of the near future will probably have an audio and video work station linking each worker to an outside world full of integrated information services. Tele-conferencing, a group of people at various locations linked by telephone, is now common. A further stage is video-conferencing, which allows face-to-face discussion among people scattered across the globe.

Consequences of the New Communications Technology

As the new communications methods spread, they will increasingly affect the way people live and businesses operate. One effect may be to thin out the concentration of businesses in downtown areas. People in certain fields, such as publishing and computer software design, will be able to work effectively from home using telephone links to a central office. Some businesses, stockbrokers' offices, for example, which until recently had to be in close contact with the financial markets, will now be able to locate in less expensive premises away from the city core. It seems likely that an increasing amount of information-based employment will be found on the periphery of cities rather than in city centres. This trend will, in turn, affect the patterns of **urbanization** in highly technological countries.

Another effect of communications technology is most disquieting. The ability to record information and obtain access to it almost instantaneously poses a threat to individual privacy. There is a great deal of information about each and every Canadian stored on computer files. These may be held by any branch or agency of government—Statistics Canada (for census purposes), Revenue Canada, motor vehicle branches, police departments. Criminal records are stored electronically, as are records of minor traffic offences. Private concerns such as banks, credit card companies, insurance firms, and even some beauty salons also keep information files. A key question is, "Who has access to this information?" Should employers or insurance agents be able to uncover every personal and financial detail of your life? It may be in society's interest to know about the record of a criminal, but would you want a potential employer to know whether you have received a parking ticket?

The information age has created a number of other problems. One of them is an up-to-date variation on an age-old theme—theft. Compiling information is an expensive task, whether the production of a video cassette or the writing of computer software is in question. The producers are entitled to be paid for their products. Yet it is all too easy to pirate electronically stored information. A related danger is the possibility of unauthorized entry into government or defence data systems. A less obvious hazard is that a major disaster, such as an earthquake in California, could put the information systems of banks and other

Production of videos is one new industry that has developed from the new communications technology.

businesses out of action for weeks. Serious financial difficulties would occur worldwide.

It is clear that the new information technology is linked to many aspects of the social and economic structure of the world. You will next examine three of the most significant.

The Emergence of a New Elite

Bankers, financiers, politicians, and senior civil servants are among the people who use global information daily. Access to highly important information—whether about money, resources, or political events—confers great power.

Thus, those who manipulate and control modern communications systems find themselves in positions of power over the majority of "ordinary" people. Power is always open to the possibility of abuse. As governments and companies become stronger and more remote, it is not surprising that many ordinary people feel alienated. A sense of alienation can affect the way people behave, and therefore affects society as a whole, as you will see in the next chapter on urbanization.

Ownership of the Media

Modern communications technology has developed as a result of massive expenditure on research and development, some of it motivated by military purposes. Not surprisingly, western countries have a near monopoly on global communications, through ownership of satellite systems and news media organizations.

In spite of Article 19 of the United Nations Universal Declaration of Human Rights, which states that "everyone has the right of freedom of opinion and expression", it would appear that most of the world's people enjoy very limited expression indeed. Just five main news agencies maintain bureaus and correspondents around the world (Table 6.7). No major Third World news agency serves the developing world. Consequently, much of what poor countries learn about themselves is determined by the market for information in North America or western Europe. To give an example of the world's lopsided news

TABLE 6.7 *World News Agencies*

Press Agency	Number of countries covered
AP (USA)	62
UP (USA)	81
APF (France)	167
Reuters (UK)	153
Tass (USSR)	110

Source: Smith A. 1980 *The Geopolitics of Information: How Western Culture Dominates the World.* Faber & Faber, 1980

How do these advertisements on a street in Delhi, India compare with those you see each day?

system, the British Reuters News Agency had 550 full-time correspondents around the world in the late 1970's, when all black African countries together did not have even one full-time correspondent in the United States.

This does not necessarily imply that there is a conspiracy to keep the less developed countries ill-informed. Nevertheless, because the western world maintains the news services it tends to interpret Third World events in the light of its own political and trade interests. Third World countries have been seeking to set up their own news services through UNESCO. This move has been resisted in the United States. Perhaps there is concern that a Third World news agency could be used by Third World leaders to maintain their authority and political control.

Keep in mind, too, that news can be presented in a highly political way, or even suppressed entirely, as in the Soviet Union. Nor is it unknown in Canada and other western nations for news to be distorted or suppressed for political reasons.

The Power of Advertising

Most companies depend upon advertising to sell their products. Advertising in Third World countries is dominated by the products of western industrial companies. Many of these products, notably cosmetics, toiletries, and non-essential foods, are not part of the cultures of many developing nations. Advertising—and selling—are made easier by the popularity of American television soap operas. Such programs are much cheaper for Third World countries to buy than local programs are to produce. Television shows from western countries

These children in Manila have their own way of using a soft drink cooler to beat the heat.

tend to popularize western culture and, consequently, the consumption of western goods.

This tendency to "westernize" has had some serious consequences. The worldwide popularity of American soft drinks has eliminated many local fruit juice industries. Perhaps the power of global advertising was made most evident by a situation that occurred in the 1970's. Because of a massive surplus of milk in western countries, several companies intensively advertised powdered milk formulas throughout the world. The advertising campaign persuaded millions of mothers in the Third World that powdered milk was the modern way and led them to switch from breastfeeding. Many serious health problems resulted, until eventually public opinion in the western world forced these companies to stop worldwide advertising.

QUESTIONS

1. In what ways does the movement of information differ from the movement of goods?

2. How can the media change the expectations of traditional societies?

3. Briefly describe two types of information networks which are used mainly by companies and governments.

4. What is tele-conferencing? What are its advantages?

Chapter Summary

This chapter has shown how new technology, especially in the field of communications, has helped to change both the location of industries and the way people work. The countries which have adapted most readily to these changes have become industrial leaders. Other nations have gone into decline.

Third World countries have the advantage of lower labour costs. However, they have less access to high technology than developed nations because of the expense of technology, the lack of research and development, and lower levels of education. Instead, it is the highly industrialized developed countries such as Japan and the United States which are changing their industrial base with the help of high technology.

Industrial change is a difficult process. It is almost always the cause of unemployment in the less successful regions of a country. Such regions may require government assistance in the form of grants, tax concessions, and subsidies.

The Technological Revolution has also changed the employment base of western countries. Manufacturing jobs have declined, while information-based industries proliferate. The ease of storing and transmitting information by electronic means has many implications for the society in which we live.

IN REVIEW

1. What evidence indicates that western nations are now moving into a post-industrial age?

2. **(a)** Explain what is meant by the term "high technology".
   (b) Give three examples of the application of high technology.

3. What two things can be done to reduce the dislocation in employment caused by technological innovation?

4. **(a)** In reviewing the reasons for Britain's industrial decline, which problems do you think can be most readily solved? Which will require longer-term solutions?
   (b) What economic advantages does Japan have which Britain does not?

5. The industrial performance of several countries has been discussed in this chapter. What positive lessons can be learned from each?

6. In what ways does the developed world's superior communications system contribute to its advantages relative to the Third World?

7. (a) Should governments try to encourage new industries to locate in less prosperous areas rather than leaving industry to locate wherever it wishes? Why or why not?

(b) In what other ways can governments encourage industrial growth?

8. List some positive and negative influences transmitted to other cultures by the advertising of developed nations.

9. How might modern communications change the travel and work habits of business people?

APPLYING YOUR KNOWLEDGE

1. What role do you feel government should have in minimizing the dislocation caused by technological innovation? Give reasons for your answer.

2. In what ways might the introduction of advanced technology, such as automation and computerization, widen the gap between developed and less developed countries?

3. (a) What factors do you think might influence high-tech industries to locate in British Columbia?

(b) What could British Columbia do to encourage such industries?

4. How can Canadians increase their ability to compete with countries such as Japan in developing high-tech industries?

5. Does Canada face problems of industrial decline similar to those of Britain? Explain your answer.

6. Discuss the advantages and disadvantages of having personal data stored on easily accessible electronic files.

7. In what respects is ownership of information a more complicated question than ownership of goods?

8. How can a news agency influence our opinion about an event?

FURTHER INVESTIGATION

1. Draw location diagrams similar to the examples shown in Figure 6.5 for two industries in your area.

2. If possible, find out what items were manufactured in your area 50 years ago. Is the list the same today? If some goods are no longer made locally, where do they come from?

3. List the ways in which your family could use modern communications systems. How would this change the way you live?

4. Some people feel that our freedom is threatened by the power of those who control the communications media. Debate this point of view.

CHAPTER 7

Urbanization

It is said that Manhattan Island, in the heart of New York City, was bought in 1626 from the native Indians for $24 worth of beads, mirrors, and other trinkets. Today, that amount of money would not be enough to rent space for a wastepaper basket in one of Manhattan's skyscraper office blocks!

This anecdote reflects the changes in society which have led to the creation of enormous cities in all countries of the western world, particularly over the past century. Both the Industrial and the Technological Revolutions have helped to produce an urbanized society. According to the most recent census of Canada, about 80 percent of Canadians live in towns and cities. This figure is equalled in several developed countries, including Australia and Britain.

As you may recall from Chapter 2, the world as a whole is becoming increasingly urbanized. In fact, the greatest movement from country to city today is taking place in the Third World. Cities such as Mexico City, São Paulo, and Calcutta have overtaken the large cities of the west in total population.

Most people have become urbanized quite willingly, since cities offer many facilities, services, and attractions. In this chapter you will explore both the growth of cities and the attraction of the urban way of life in light of questions such as these:

- How did cities originate?

- What population changes are occurring in cities in different parts of the world?

- Why are cities laid out as they are?

- What are the social and economic features of cities?

What is a City?

In the photographs you can see two very different landscapes. One is dominated by buildings and roads; the other by fields and trees. One is obviously urban; the other, rural. If you were to step into these scenes, you would notice many other differences as well—in sounds, smells, the variety of plants and animals, and the number of people. In fact, the photographs show glimpses of two entirely different environments with two very different ways of life. Although the rural environment has been influenced in some ways by human beings, cities are almost entirely the creation of people.

People often make personal judgements about a city according to what it looks like, whether its buildings are pleasing or ugly. Buildings, however, are not just there to be looked at. They exist to perform various functions, and so reflect the varied activities carried on within the city. Ultimately, then, a city is more than its buildings: it is the reflection of the people who live in it. A city can be thought of as an organic or living system, in which people provide the forces of creation and change, and buildings represent the outward expression of these forces. A city tells much about the people who live in it—their values and priorities, their degree of wealth and power.

Population Characteristics

To answer the question "What is a town or city?" you need to look at some characteristics of the population, in particular its size, density, and types of employment.

How do the life styles of rural and urban dwellers differ?

It is difficult to say how many people must live in a community before its status changes from village to town. The minimum number varies greatly from country to country. In some countries, numbers of people, alone, do not make a community into a city. Other conditions are necessary. Look at the examples in Table 7.1.

TABLE 7.1   *Conditions for Urban Status*

Country	Minimum Population Size	Other Conditions
Denmark	200	
Sweden	200	
Canada	1 000	
Ireland	1 500	
Israel	2 000	Not more than 33 percent in agriculture
U.S.A.	2 500	Settlement must be incorporated
India	5 000	Not more than 25 percent in agriculture; density over 386 people/km²
Italy	5 000	Not more than 50 percent in agriculture
Netherlands	5 000	Not more than 20 percent in agriculture
Greece	10 000	

Notice that the definition of an urban area in India includes **population density.** This is a key factor in understanding any urban community. Some cities have a very high population density: Hong Kong and the West End of Vancouver are examples that you may recall from Chapter 2. Such close proximity between people has both advantages and disadvantages. An advantage is that people have neighbours close by to satisfy social needs and provide help in times of emergency. But the housing of large numbers of people in small land areas can also create problems. People like to have their own "personal space" so that they can be by themselves or enjoy the company of family or friends. In crowded urban areas this personal space can become very cramped indeed, and privacy is limited. People in busy cities actually expend much time and effort on avoiding each other. Have you ever walked on a crowded city street, or struggled for space on a packed bus, and felt that everyone else looked either past you or through you? Such behaviour is a natural expression of the desire for privacy in a crowded world.

You also saw in Table 7.1 that another condition for urban status has to do with setting limits on the number of people employed in agriculture. For example, southern European countries such as Italy and Greece have many large agricultural villages. These settlements are not accorded urban status even though their population size has reached the minimum number for a town.

What reasons might these people give for choosing city living over rural living?

In Chapter 6, you examined the employment structure of a country (Figure 6.1). Doing the same thing for a city will give you an indication of how its inhabitants earn their living. Table 7.2 gives data for Hamilton, Ontario and Vancouver, British Columbia. In neither of these cities is farming nor any other primary occupation important, but large numbers of people find employment in manufacturing industries (Hamilton) and in services (Vancouver).

TABLE 7.2: *Employment Data, Hamilton and Vancouver*

	Hamilton	Vancouver
	%	%
Agriculture	1.7	1.2
Forestry	—	0.7
Fishing and trapping	—	0.3
Mining (including oil)	0.2	0.5
Manufacturing	32.4	14.7
Construction	5.9	6.8
Transport and public utilities	5.4	10.6
Trade (wholesale and retail)	16.8	19.3
Finance, insurance and real estate	5.0	7.2
Community, business and personal service	28.6	32.9
Public administration and defence	4.0	5.8
Total	100.0	100.0

Source: Census of Canada, 1981.

QUESTIONS

1. Make a list of the different characteristics of town and countryside that affect the way a person lives.

2. (a) At what population size does a settlement become a town in Sweden, Canada, and Greece?
   (b) What other conditions have to be met before a settlement can be called a town in the United States, Italy, and India?

3. Why is it often true that cities can be lonely places?

4. List the four main occupation groups in Hamilton and Vancouver. Suggest reasons for the differences between the two cities.

The Growth of Cities

The origins of cities go back to at least 5000 B.C. This is known from archaeological discoveries in the Middle East. While knowledge about early cities is limited, it is clear that they began to develop when farming techniques enabled people to produce more food than they required. Urban centres came into existence in places where products and services were traded for the surplus food of the countryside. Early towns remained small, however, since there was a limit to how far food could be carried by means of the transportation available at the time.

The growth of a rural settlement was accompanied by a new and more complex division of labour. Occupations such as trader, priest, and administrator appeared. These occupations had little to do directly with the growing or gathering of food. Thus, towns created an entirely new form of society in which occupations became specialized. Another feature of this new society was increased social stratification. In other words, because there were more occupations, there were also more social levels. Power and influence belonged to the upper levels of society, especially to people in professions such as religion, law, and administration.

Cities became much larger in the empires of Greece and Rome, which flourished from about 500 B.C. to A.D. 476. Rome itself was by far the largest city in the classical world, with an estimated population of 650 000 in A.D. 100. Improvements in transportation and communications had widened the area from which a city could obtain the resources it needed. Political organization also had much to do with urban growth, for it created the conditions of order and stability needed for trade.

With the decline of the Roman Empire after A.D. 476, political stability and urban life in Europe collapsed. In those parts of the world where political structures remained highly developed, however, cities continued to thrive. Hangchow in China, for instance, had an estimated population of 432 000 in A.D. 1300. In Europe, city growth became re-established with the emergence of nation states in the late Middle Ages.

Urbanization and the Industrial Revolution

Urban growth became rapid in western Europe during the Industrial Revolution of the 18th and 19th centuries. This growth was made possible by several interrelated factors:

- Increasingly efficient farming methods allowed a small labour force to produce more food. The result was a surplus of agricultural workers.

- A great deal of capital had been accumulated from successful banking and trade. The people who possessed it decided to invest in industry and transport.

Industrialization puts new pressure on land use in a community.

- The application of new mechanical technology to manufacturing led to the factory system of production, which required labour to be concentrated in towns. Many towns were located on the coalfields which provided the energy for the new industries.

- Improved transport facilities (first canals, then railways) enabled raw materials to be brought in from greater distances and finished products to be distributed to more distant markets.

Towns of the Industrial Revolution were not attractive places. There were certainly no "bright lights" to beckon migrants. But layoffs of farm workers and the possibility of jobs in town brought large numbers of poor rural labourers to live around mine, mill, or factory. Industrial towns were high-density settlements with poor housing, open sewers, and limited social facilities. Death rates were high, and urban populations were sustained only by continuous migration from the countryside.

Urbanization in the Twentieth Century

Several fundamental changes took place in cities at the start of the 20th century. Improvements in public health and sanitation cut the death rate, and urban populations increased naturally, apart from in-migration. Cities also began to grow in physical size, both outward and upward. Previously they had covered relatively small areas, since all transportation was on foot or at best by horse-drawn vehicles. After World War I, the new electric streetcars, and later, motor-driven buses, caused the formation of suburbs spreading outward from cities (Figure 7.1). Finally, the private car accelerated the geographical spread of the city to its present size.

Cities have also grown upward, mainly because of the great demand for space near the urban core. The invention of the elevator and of reinforced and pre-stressed concrete in the late 19th century made possible the construction of high-rise office blocks and apartments.

Rural-Urban Migration

Migration is the main reason for the rapid growth of urban centres in this century. There has been a movement from smaller to larger towns, but most inward migration has come from rural areas, where birth rates have exceeded death rates by a wide margin. Why have so many people migrated from rural to urban areas? The answer lies in both employment and amenities. Large towns offered more opportunities for employment, usually at a higher level of pay, than rural areas. In the 20th century cities have come to provide a greater range of facilities, such as hospitals, secondary schools, large shopping centres, and restaurants. The biggest cities are also likely to possess universities and airports, and to offer more specialized services in business, medicine, and entertainment.

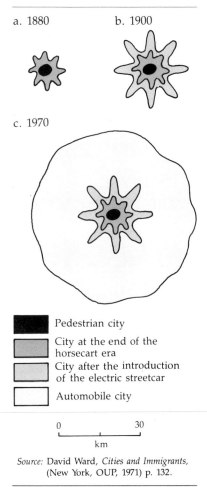

FIGURE 7.1 *City Size and Modes of Transport. How have improved transportation methods changed the size of cities?*

a. 1880   b. 1900

c. 1970

■ Pedestrian city

City at the end of the horsecart era

City after the introduction of the electric streetcar

Automobile city

0   30
km

Source: David Ward, *Cities and Immigrants,* (New York, OUP, 1971) p. 132.

FIGURE 7.2 *Stages of Rural-Urban Migration*

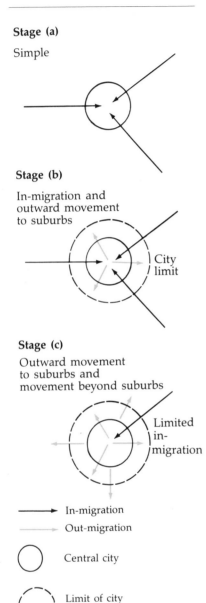

Stage (a)

Simple

Stage (b)

In-migration and outward movement to suburbs

City limit

Stage (c)

Outward movement to suburbs and movement beyond suburbs

Limited in-migration

→ In-migration

→ Out-migration

○ Central city

⌀ Limit of city (including suburbs)

Urban migration has led to the abandonment of many farms.

Rural-urban migration has had profound effects on the countryside. In the days of large rural families there was always room for some migration to the cities without depletion of the rural population. This is no longer true. First, rural birth rates have fallen. With the majority of young people leaving for the cities, the remaining rural population has an older age structure. Services in rural areas, as elsewhere, depend upon a viable population to keep in business. With the decline in population, bus services are withdrawn, stores and other amenities close, and whole rural communities face a loss of services.

In Figure 7.2 you will find a model of urban migration. Stage (a) allows for simple migration to the city, while Stage (b) shows movement outwards from the city centre to the suburbs. City centres have been taken over by commerce, while the suburbs provide the peace and quiet needed for residential life. Commuting between homes in the suburbs and places of work is a feature of modern urban life.

Decentralization

In Stage (c) of Figure 7.2 this outward movement to the suburbs has been carried further. People have begun to move out of the city as rural-urban migration has gone into reverse. This process, called **decentralization**, is common in the United States. In recent years, the central areas of American cities have been experiencing increasing problems of crime and vandalism. Employment has declined in the city centres because new industries and businesses have opened up on cheaper land near the city limits. However, even the once-safe suburbs have experienced increasing crime. For all these reasons, some city dwellers have moved beyond the suburbs to surrounding rural municipalities. Table 7.3 shows that many American cities have actually declined in population as a result. This does not mean that refugees from the city are "down on the farm". Most live in new subdivisions beyond the city limits, where they pay lower taxes but can still make use of city amenities whenever they wish. In many cases, such people will once again become city dwellers should the city limits extend farther outward, as has often happened in the past.

TABLE 7.3 *Population Change in Selected American Cities. In which parts of the United States have cities been growing? declining? Why might this be so?*

	1970 (in 000's)	1980 (in 000's)	% change
1. New York	9077	8275	–8.8
2. Los Angeles/Long Beach	7042	7478	6.2
3. Chicago	6093	6060	–0.5
4. Philadelphia	4824	4717	–2.2
5. Detroit	4554	4488	–1.5
6. Washington, D.C.	3040	3251	6.9
7. Boston	2887	2806	–2.8
8. Houston	1891	2736	44.7
9. Nassau/Suffolk	2556	2606	2.0
10. Pittsburgh	2348	2219	–5.5
11. Baltimore	2089	2200	5.3
12. Atlanta	1684	2138	27.0
13. Minneapolis/St Paul	1982	2137	7.8
14. Dallas	1556	1957	25.8
15. Anaheim/Santa Ana	1421	1933	36.0
16. Cleveland	2064	1899	–8.0
17. Newark	1937	1879	–3.0
18. San Diego	1358	1862	37.1
19. St Louis	1846	1809	–2.0
20. Oakland	1628	1762	8.2

Source: U.S. Statistical Abstract

What problems has urban expansion created for downtown areas?

Canadian cities have also experienced strong outward growth into the suburbs. Unlike many American cities, however, no major Canadian city has experienced an overall decline in population growth. There are two reasons for this. First, urban social problems are much less serious in Canadian than in American cities. Second, most Canadian cities have wide territorial limits which allow for further suburban expansion without the need for building in rural areas. It is nevertheless true that the inner areas of many Canadian cities are experiencing some decline in population.

Mexico City is now one of the world's largest cities.

Current World Trends in Urbanization

Many of the world's cities have become very large. In 1913, there were only 13 cities with populations of over one million people. Today there are over 200 such cities, of which at least 10 have over 10 million residents (look ahead to Table 7.4 on page 216). Urbanization has been particularly rapid in the Third World, where population growth has combined with high rates of rural-urban migration. In the western world, urbanization is much less rapid, and cities in some countries are actually declining in population, as you have just seen. However, this does not mean that cities are less important in the west. Western cities contain about 60 percent of the entire world's manufacturing output, and an even greater share of its service activities. Chapter 6 showed that advances in transportation and communications have reduced the need for a central city location. In many cases, businesses have followed people outward to the suburbs. All these factors contribute to the process of decentralization, which may become more common.

QUESTIONS

1. What was the first condition necessary for towns to come into existence?

2. Why did improved transportation facilities play such an important role in the historical development of cities?

3. Name three types of occupation which early towns made possible.

4. State three reasons for urban growth during the Industrial Revolution.

5. What are the main reasons for the outward spread of cities in the 20th century?

6. What is meant by "urban amenities"? List amenities found in a larger city which are not normally found in a small town.

7. Why has commuting become such a common feature of urban living in North American cities?

Urbanization in the Third World

The March, 1985 issue of the UNESCO *Courier,* a magazine published by the United Nations, made the following observations about urban growth in the Third World: "The lion's share of urban growth is taking place in developing countries whose drama of rampant urbanization dwarfs the problems of urban stagnation and inner city decay encountered in the industrialized world. With their services already overburdened by their present populations, Third World cities exercise a magnetic attraction on the people of the surrounding rural areas, luring a massive influx of migrants for whom the bitter reality is not streets paved with gold but a desperate struggle for survival in slums and shantytowns."

Two different ways of making a living in Latin American cities.

In Caracas, Venezuela squatters have settled on the slopes surrounding the city.

This description is, unfortunately, quite accurate. Cities in the less developed world are growing very rapidly, putting enormous pressure on the limited facilities and services they are able to offer. But why, if the cities have so many problems, are they so popular? What factors lead to rapid rural-urban migration in virtually all parts of the less developed world?

Migration to Third World Cities

Migration may be thought of as a "push-pull" situation. In poorer countries the main "push" factor is generally the grinding poverty of many rural areas, made worse by high birth rates and rapid population growth. In addition, rural land may be scarce and already fragmented into tiny pieces. Other possible "push" factors are natural disasters such as floods or drought. The only hope of survival may be to move in search of a better existence. The main "pull" factor is that the city appears to offer at least a chance of self-improvement. Migrants usually have enough optimism to believe that they will obtain some kind of employment. The possibility of a job is seen as better than the certainty of rural poverty. Most of the limited medical and educational facilities in many Third World countries are located in cities. Government assistance is also more likely to be available in the city than in the countryside. Some advantages and disadvantages of cities from the point of view of families with children are shown in Figure 7.3.

The result is that millions of people in less developed countries have left their rural homes and moved to the cities, frequently settling in one of the so-called **shantytowns** which are found in many cities. These go under a variety of local names: *bustee* (India), *barong-barong* (Philippines), and *favela* (Brazil). Near Johannesburg, South Africa, shantytowns have been created by black Africans who are denied homes in the city.

FIGURE 7.3 *The Child and the City*

Urban advantages

Health and education services are easier to provide in cities. And mortality and literacy statistics do show the urban areas in a favourable light.

Education

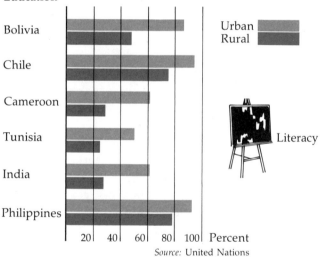

Source: United Nations

Health

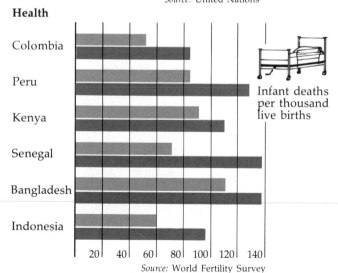

Source: World Fertility Survey

But there will be great differences between the poorer and richer parts of each city. In Lima, Peru, for example, 19% of the children overall are malnourished but this figure rises to 36% in the poorest districts.

Street children

Some 40 million children around the world spend their days on city streets — often working. The majority maintain contact with their families, but millions of children also live on the street.

Why they are there

A survey in Maputo, Mozambique, asked children why they were on the street. These are the reasons they gave.

Hunger and poverty in the home	27%
Treated badly at home	27%
Nothing else to do	27%
Sent by the family	9%
Abandoned by the family	9%
Just following other children	1%

Source: Mozambique Min. of Health

What they do

Many city children work (as well as going to school for part of the day). Research in Asuncion, Paraguay, asked children what their major jobs were:

Selling food, etc.	33%
Selling newspapers	27%
Shining shoes	24%
Cleaning and looking after cars	9%
Cleaning windscreens	6%
Others	1%

Source: Govt. of Paraguay

City children also have factory jobs — often in harsh conditions. And in rich and poor countries alike street children risk falling into prostitution.

Source: UN Fund for Population Activities

A shantytown in Bogotà, Colombia.

The photograph shows a shantytown in Bogotá, Colombia. By North American standards shantytowns may seem to be quite unfit for human habitation. Yet attempts in some countries to bring in bulldozers and remove them from the map have not proved very successful. Some governments have provided high-rise housing in cities as a substitute, only to find that many people cannot afford the rents, even though they are subsidized. The financial pressures have forced many migrants into crime and prostitution, and their community life has been broken up. The shantytowns at least provide a self-help environment where the migrants can live within their means and within their own social structures. It is therefore possible that the money devoted to destroying some shantytowns would have been better spent on providing water, electricity, and sewage facilities in the shantytowns themselves. Some Third World cities have adopted this approach.

Megacities

The rapid growth of very large cities is a striking aspect of urbanization in less developed countries. Table 7.4 shows the number of cities having over 10 million inhabitants in 1980. Their 1950 populations are given, as are estimates for A.D. 2000. A table of cities of over 5 million would likely include more than 60 cities by the year 2000. Most of these megacities are in Latin America, where Mexico City adds 750 000 per year to its population, and São Paulo, Brazil adds 500 000. Indeed, one Latin American in four lives in a city with a population of over one million. Not far behind in speed of growth come Cairo, Egypt and Bangkok, Thailand, which each add over 300 000 per year. The next pages present a detailed look at three megacities, and a Close-up on Mexico City, now the largest city in the world.

TABLE 7.4 *Cities of 10 Million People or More in 1980, with Estimates for A.D. 2000*

City	Population (in millions)		
	1950	*1980*	*2000*
Tokyo/Yokohama	6.7	19.7	26.1
New York	12.3	17.9	22.2
Mexico City	2.9	13.9	31.6
São Paulo	2.5	12.5	26.0
Shanghai	5.8	12.0	19.2
London	10.2	11.0	12.7
Los Angeles	4.0	10.7	14.8
Buenos Aires	4.5	10.4	14.0
Beijing	2.2	10.2	19.1
Rio de Janeiro	2.9	10.0	19.4

Source: UN Data

These two homes, both found in Lima, Peru, show the contrast in lifestyles possible in Third World cities.

Cairo, with a population of 8 500 000, is an ancient city whose buildings are decaying rapidly as a result of air pollution from traffic fumes and nearby factories. One-third of Cairo's inhabitants have no sewage facilities, and many live at a density of 80 000 people per square kilometre. Yet 350 000 migrants flock to the city each year.

Shanghai, with 11 800 000 people, falls into a different category. Once the port city of Imperial China, with a reputation for drug trafficking and vice, Shanghai was cleaned up by the communist government which won the civil war in China in 1949. Nevertheless, Shanghai remains a very crowded city, as 150 000 migrants enter from the countryside each year. The average house space in Shanghai is estimated at three to four square metres per person, but the inner city core often offers under two square metres. Despite the crowding, the government ensures that services such as transportation and utilities work efficiently, and that no shantytowns develop.

Calcutta, whose population is 11 000 000, was the capital of India before 1911. Though it has many fine buildings and beautiful parks, the city has gained the reputation of having perhaps the lowest standard of living of any large city in the world. About 70 percent of its inhabitants earned below $8 (U.S.) per month in 1984. Nearly half a million homeless people live—and die—on the streets of Calcutta. Yet since 1951, the city of Calcutta itself has grown more slowly than the Indian population as a whole, with more out-migration than in-migration. The main reasons for this are acute crowding and lack of amenities. The same cannot be said for the urban areas surrounding Calcutta City, which continue to grow rapidly.

FIGURE 7.4   *Growth of Mexico City. Why does the graph provide two different forecast figures?*

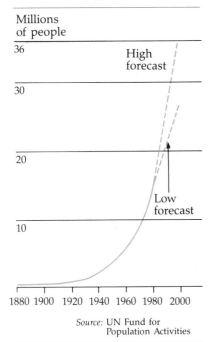

Millions of people

Source: UN Fund for Population Activities

Mexico City

Figure 7.4 shows the phenomenal population growth of Mexico City during this century. In 1986, its nearly 18 million inhabitants made up one-quarter of the entire population of Mexico. The growth of Mexico City has been generated almost equally by immigration from rural areas and by natural increase of population within the city itself. If this growth trend continues, Mexico City's population will exceed the entire population of Canada before A.D. 2000.

In many respects, Mexico City, once the capital of the Aztec Empire, is a grand city, with its sweeping boulevards and ornamental fountains. It stands on the site of an old lake bed some 2300 m above sea level. The city is encircled by scenic mountains which supply it with groundwater. Yet these same mountains trap the city air, which is continually polluted by three million cars and thousands of factories. So great is the air pollution that an estimated 30 000 children die annually of respiratory disorders and gastric diseases. Breathing Mexico City's air is alleged to be the equivalent of smoking two packs of cigarettes a day.

Like any city in the less developed world, Mexico City shows

What environmental factors contribute to Mexico City's air pollution problem?

extremes of wealth and poverty. However, Mexico City has perhaps a larger middle-class population than any other Third World city, with many good suburban residential areas. The shantytowns, by contrast, contain self-made shelters of mud brick and corrugated steel.

The city's population is swollen by over 1000 new migrants daily. Two million people have no running water in their homes, and three million are without sewers. Many suffer from ill-health and malnutrition. One-quarter of all families live in single rooms. Those who have accommodation are fortunate in at least one respect: rents have been frozen since World War II at rates as low as 25 cents per week. Unemployment rates hover around 12 percent, but if underemployment could be accurately measured the figure would be more like 40 percent.

Why Do Immigrants Come?

Immigration into Mexico City has been called "a tidal wave of irrational and irresponsible hope". Yet immigrants, including many squatters known locally as *paracaidistas* (parachutists), continue to arrive. Studies done in Mexico show that immigration is not as irrational as it first appears. First, the migrants are usually better educated than those whom they leave behind. Women also outnumber men as migrants, presumably because women have a higher status in urban areas than in rural areas. Furthermore, the studies indicate that those who leave farming for an urban life usually achieve an increase in income, even if the urban job is in the so-called "informal economy" (street peddling, shoe shining, even car minding). Some people scrape out a living by scavenging in the city's many garbage dumps. The incomes from these activities are indeed low—but not as low as would be experienced in rural poverty. Another gain is in access to health care facilities; Mexico City has numerous hospitals and over 200 health care centres.

An underlying reason for the attraction of the city is the high degree of centralization in Mexico. Half of all industry and most government offices are located in Mexico City. Until some effective regional policies for curbing this trend are implemented, the city is likely to continue to be a magnet for migrants.

One shattering event, however, might turn out to have changed all this. On the morning of September 19th, 1985, Mexico City was hit by a massive earthquake measuring 8.1 on the Richter Scale. Although the earthquake originated 400 km to the west, its effects were magnified in Mexico City because of the soft clay lake bed on which the city is built. Many buildings in Mexico City were already tilted to some extent as a result of subsidence into the lake

The Richter Scale

This scale, used for measuring the shock waves of earthquakes, was devised by Professor Charles Richter of California. It is a logarithmic scale, which means that a rise of one point on the scale implies shock waves 10 times as severe as for the previous point. An increase of a single point also implies a 31-fold increase in the total energy released by the earthquake.

An earthquake of less than magnitude 5 on the Richter scale usually causes no serious damage. The most severe earthquakes in recent history have been approximately 8 on the scale. The Alaskan earthquake of 1964 had the greatest effect on British Columbia. It produced several seismic ocean waves large enough to inflict severe damage on the town of Port Alberni.

The earthquake that hit Mexico City in 1985 demonstrated the devastation which can result when a natural disaster strikes a megacity.

bed. This insecure base shook like a bowl of jelly during the earthquake, which produced appalling devastation in parts of downtown Mexico City. About 7000 people died, and many times that number were made homeless. It remains to be seen whether this tragedy and its economic effects will choke off the supply of *paracaidistas*, or whether Mexico City will rebuild and advance towards the 30 million population mark.

To put Mexico City's experience in a broader context, it should be stated that urban growth in the less developed world, though rapid, is not always so spectacular. Studies done in India, for example, show that rural-urban movement accounts for only 15 percent of all migration. This is far fewer than the 69 percent who move from one rural location to another. Rural-urban migration has been slowing down in recent years in many parts of India. As in Mexico, it is the better-off and better educated who are most likely to migrate. The literacy rate among migrants in India is double that of the population as a whole. The exception is in the case of those who flee from natural disasters such as floods in the Ganges Delta. Many of the half million street dwellers of Calcutta come into this category.

QUESTIONS

1. Give reasons why Third World cities attract so many migrants in spite of their living conditions.

2. Describe two "push" and two "pull" factors which play a part in rural-urban migration in the Third World.

3. Why are there so many street children in some Third World cities?

4. State the arguments for and against the rehousing of shantytown dwellers in urban redevelopment schemes.

5. What are the main advantages and disadvantages of moving to Mexico City, from the point of view of a poor rural migrant?

6. Why has Mexico City shown such a rapid rate of population growth? What are its prospects of achieving a stable population in the near future?

Land Use in Cities

Western cities differ in some respects from cities in the Third World. You have already seen something of the urban chaos caused by tidal waves of migrants to cities such as Cairo and Mexico City. For the remainder of this chapter, you will concentrate on the features which are typical of many western cities.

The Economic Base of Towns and Cities

People who live in cities, from the smallest town to Mexico City, need to consume materials and products grown or made elsewhere. To pay for the resources they need, people who live in cities must earn money by making goods or performing services. In other words, cities must have an **economic base** in order to survive. The jobs of some of the people in a city help to bring in money from elsewhere. An insurance company, for example, might provide insurance coverage for farmers living across the country. On the other hand, a house painter might earn a good income solely by performing a service for other residents of the same city. If cities do not have enough jobs of the former kind, the supply of money available to pay for the latter will eventually diminish.

Earlier in the chapter, you saw that some cities in the United States have grown while others have declined. Declining cities have probably had their economic base eroded by competition from elsewhere. British industrial cities have had just this experience, as you read in Chapter 6. On the other hand, new or expanding industries (or service activities) will cause cities to grow.

The economic base of a city helps explain the different types of land use which are found there. Each type of land use is related to a different function of the city, and each has its own appearance. In the next section, you will read about some of the reasons why towns and cities are arranged as they are.

Land Use and Land Values

Price helps to sort out the demand for land in the city. Assume that each of three possible users of city land—a major bank, a medium-sized shoe shop, and a housebuilding firm—has a maximum price it is prepared to pay for the land at varying distances from the city core. These prices can be plotted on what is called a **bid-rent graph** (Figure 7.5). This graph shows why land values at the centres of cities are much higher than elsewhere. A careful look at it should show you why the bank is prepared to outbid the other two competitors for land close to the centre. Why does the shoe shop finds its affordable location a little farther out, while the housebuilder is forced to move farther still?

FIGURE 7.5 *A Bid-rent Graph. According to this graph, how are land use and land value linked?*

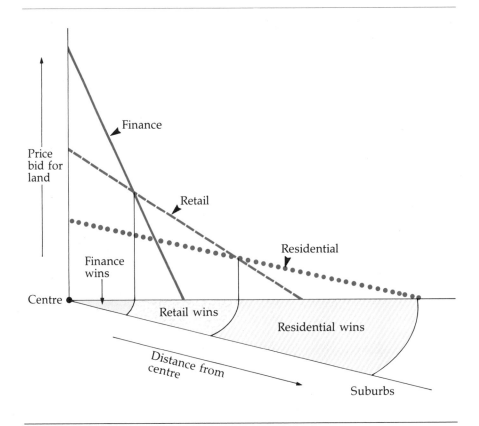

The Central Business District

In spite of movement to the suburbs, the city centre provides an ideal location for those businesses which can afford it. Since the city centre is accessible to the greatest number of people, it is where you will find large department stores, head offices of banks, and cultural centres (theatres and concert halls). The core or **central business district** is the nerve centre of any city, the focus of decision-making and communications. It is here that the intensity of land use is highest, as measured by the heights of buildings, the numbers of pedestrians, and the density of traffic (unless specifically excluded from the centre).

The central business district not only contains the principal financial offices in the city, but often has the largest amount of retail floor space (though this may be exceeded by some new suburban shopping malls). The main types of stores located downtown are large department stores and specialty shops. Neither of these is used frequently by any one customer; each therefore needs exposure to the largest possible number of people in order to stay in business. Theatres and other major places of entertainment are also often located in, or near, the central business district. Again, the key is accessibility. Parking is made easier by the departure of the daytime business population before the influx of people seeking evening entertainment.

Its central business district usually reflects the overall vitality of a city. In the case of Calgary, Alberta, increasing oil prices in the 1970's led to a surge of development in the city core. The two photographs of Calgary's central business district were taken from the same vantage point before and after the oil boom of the 1970's. The drop in oil prices in the 1980's brought an abrupt decline in demand for new office space in Calgary, with the result that many new offices remained unoccupied.

From a residential point of view many cities are like doughnuts, with many people living in the circle around the central business district but few actually living in the core. Streets of houses in the centre have been progressively taken over by businesses as the city has developed. In recent years, however, downtown living has become fashionable once more, and planners are trying to encourage increased residential land use in and around the central business district. You will return to this point later in the chapter.

You have seen that land values usually drop quite sharply away from the centre since there is less competition for land. Cities are increasingly dominated by residential land use towards the suburbs, but commercial activities (especially shopping), industry, and recreation all have important roles to play.

Left, Calgary 1968.
Right, Calgary 1984.

Commercial and Shopping Centres

Businesses tend to cluster together in cities. Shops are the most visible form of commercial enterprise in the city, but other businesses ranging from banks and health care offices to photographers and hairdressers are usually found nearby. The wide variety of shops in shopping centres allows customers to make comparisons, especially between clothing stores, where shoppers normally like to compare several items before making a purchase.

Shopping centres may be classified according to the number and type of stores and other services which they include (Figure 7.6). The central business district normally has the largest area of retail floor space in a city. It is followed by **regional centres** which draw shoppers from a wide area and require a large amount of parking space. For this reason, regional centres tend to locate in the suburbs. **District centres** survive on fewer shoppers and need less parking space. **Neighbourhood centres** contain few shops and serve only the local area. In some cities, the large shopping malls are gaining business at the expense of shops in the downtown core. However, some of the older shopping centres are, in their turn, beginning to face competition from very large "super-stores" which offer an enormous range of goods at lower prices. It is not only the number of stores, but also their size and the range of goods they offer that determines how important a shopping centre will be.

FIGURE 7.6   *Different Types of Shopping Centres in a City*

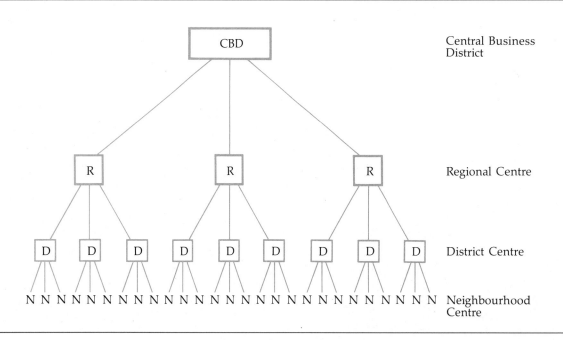

Left, Oxford Street, London.
Below, Don Mills Shopping Centre,
North York, Ontario

Residential Areas

Outward from the city centre, land use becomes increasingly residential. In general, the oldest housing is nearer the centre, with the newest on the outskirts, as might be expected. However, the pattern is not entirely regular. Some early residential districts spread outward along roads well before other areas were built up, while old low-density housing close to the central business district has often been displaced by new high-density housing.

Residential areas differ in a number of ways other than the age of housing. They differ in population density and age structure, the value of the properties, and the socio-economic characteristics of the people. Figure 7.7 shows population density in Vancouver by **census tract**—the

FIGURE 7.7 *Population Density in Vancouver (1981). Identify the areas of highest and lowest density.*

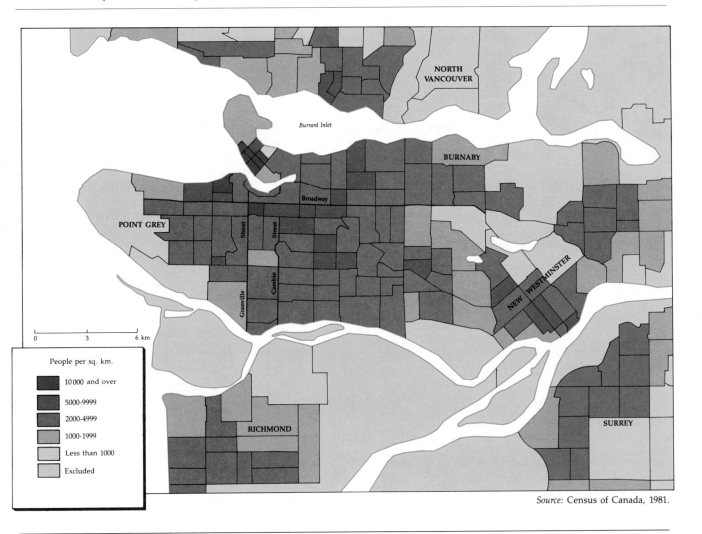

Source: Census of Canada, 1981.

unit used in the collection of census data in large cities. Figure 7.8 shows the average house value in Vancouver. The value of any individual house is influenced by its size, design, and state of repair. Its overall location also plays a major role in determining how much a house is worth. In general, the more expensive housing is found in suburban areas with many amenities such as West Vancouver. Areas of older, low-cost housing can be found closer to the centre, as in East Vancouver. However, lower-cost modern housing is also found on the outskirts of the city, where land is cheaper. Figure 7.9 gives an economic picture of Vancouver by income levels. Socio-economic indicators include levels of education and the number of cars or appliances a household owns.

FIGURE 7.8 *Average House Value in Vancouver (1981). In general, are houses cheaper in the suburbs or close to the downtown area?*

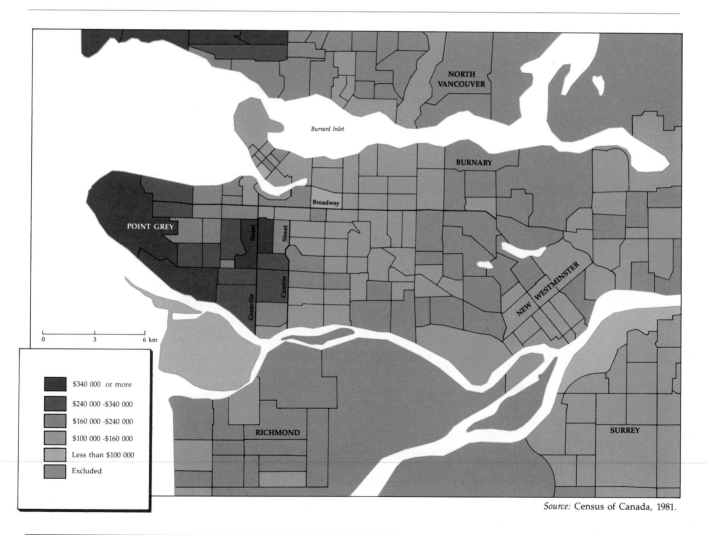

Source: Census of Canada, 1981.

Vancouver's Chinatown is one example of a unique neighbourhood within a city.

FIGURE 7.9 *Income Levels in Vancouver (1981). Where are the areas of highest and lowest income located?*

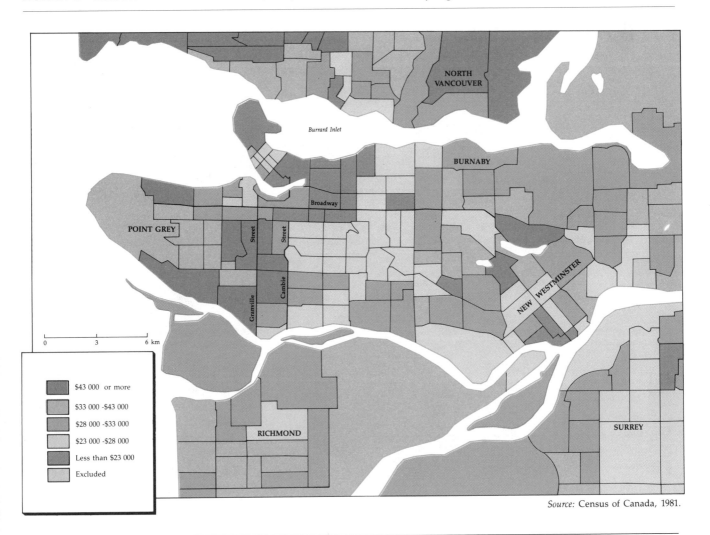

NORTH VANCOUVER

Burrard Inlet

BURNABY

Broadway

POINT GREY

Street

Street

Cambie

Granville

NEW WESTMINSTER

0   3   6 km

RICHMOND

SURREY

$43 000 or more

$33 000 -$43 000

$28 000 -$33 000

$23 000 -$28 000

Less than $23 000

Excluded

Source: Census of Canada, 1981.

Many researchers have concluded that the problems of city life often stem from the natural tendency of similar groups to cluster together. This has been shown to take place in both inner cities and outer suburbs. Inner city areas are often inhabited over the years by immigrants who buy or rent properties vacated by those who have moved outwards. Some people consider the segregation of cities into separate social and ethnic groupings undesirable. However, this attitude overlooks the fact that some ethnic areas within cities have a positive attraction for immigrants and have maintained their distinctiveness for many generations. Vancouver's Chinatown is a good example of this.

Industry in Cities

Many towns and cities have developed on the basis of manufacturing industry. You have seen that this is true of British coalfield towns of the Industrial Revolution. It is also true of many cities in the eastern United States and Canada: Cleveland, Ohio, and Detroit, Michigan, and Windsor and Hamilton in Ontario are just a few. Older manufacturing industries are often situated within the city, often on railway routes.

Railways are closely linked with Winnipeg's early growth as a commercial centre.

FIGURE 7.10   *Industrial Location in Cities. What disadvantages might the central zone have as an industrial site?*

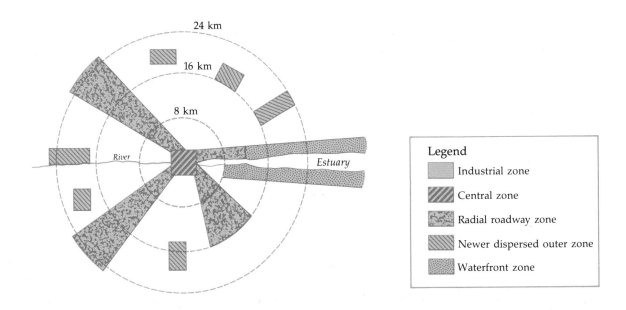

Newer industries more frequently locate in industrial parks on the outskirts, where land is cheaper. Figure 7.10 summarizes the main types of industrial location in cities, including waterfront industries in sea or river ports.

Recreational and Institutional Land Use in Cities

City dwellers greatly value the presence of parks and other open spaces within the built-up area. Such places are a refuge in which to escape from the pressures of life. Some cities are particularly well endowed with green space, few of them more so than Vancouver, with spacious Stanley Park close to the populous West End. Areas devoted to institutions such as museums, theatres, and other indoor places of interest to sight-seers also add to the attractions of cities. The recreational and sight-seeing opportunities offered by cities play a large role in attracting tourism—an important part of the economic base of many cities, including both Vancouver and Victoria.

QUESTIONS

1. What is an "economic base"?

2. What is meant by saying that the central business district is the "nerve centre of the city"?

3. Why do land values generally drop with increasing distance from the city centre?

An aerial view of Vancouver illustrates the importance this city has placed on providing parkland for its people.

Problems and Solutions in Cities

Cities constantly grow outward, but they frequently decay toward the centre, as you have seen. Physical weathering and air pollution also cause towns and cities to wear out their buildings, just as people wear out their clothes. These processes always create problems, since a city's structure and layout must accommodate more people and changing patterns of living. Thus there is a constant need for renewal in inner city areas, especially in some of the older cities of the western world. Urban renewal is a complex and expensive process requiring careful planning.

The Role of the Planner

Today planners sometimes take the blame for the problems which have arisen in our cities. However, they are seldom at fault. First of all, many cities were not "planned" as such. More to the point, planners must

FIGURE 7.11   *The Planner as Referee. Why can planners sometimes be viewed as referees between demand for land and availability of land?*

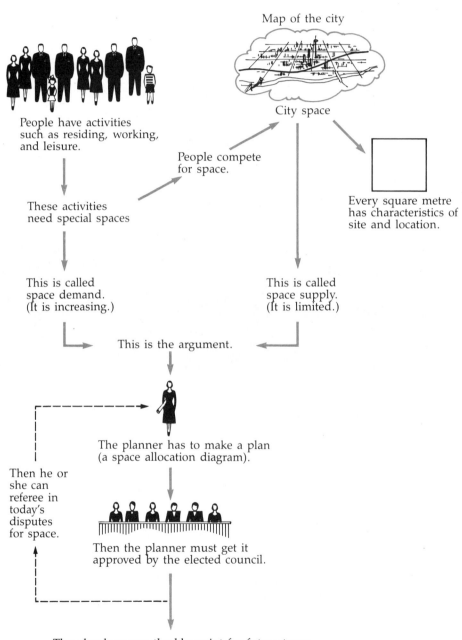

Map of the city

City space

People have activities such as residing, working, and leisure.

People compete for space.

Every square metre has characteristics of site and location.

These activities need special spaces

This is called space demand. (It is increasing.)

This is called space supply. (It is limited.)

This is the argument.

The planner has to make a plan (a space allocation diagram).

Then he or she can referee in today's disputes for space.

Then the planner must get it approved by the elected council.

The plan becomes the blueprint for future town development (and for refereeing in future disputes).

often act as referees in the ongoing struggle between the users of land and its limited supply (Figure 7.11). The aim is to try to plan land use in ways which will benefit as many people as possible. Land preserved for one particular type of use is said to be **zoned.** Planning must be a flexible process, able to adapt to changing circumstances. The modern emphasis in planning has therefore moved from **end-state planning,** in which details of the plan are fixed from the start, to **structure planning,** which allows for continual modification as the plans are carried out. Planners know they cannot please everybody, and they also know that they themselves have no power to ensure that their plans are ever put into action. This decision belongs not to the planners, but to elected representatives on municipal councils. They are the real decision-makers.

Normally, municipal councils have to operate under less than ideal conditions. Money may be scarce. Urgent situations, such as the need to rehouse people quickly, may lead to substandard houses. Most importantly, pressure groups may influence decisions—especially at election time! For example, in British Columbia much agricultural land around cities is protected by being part of the Agricultural Land Reserve. But the provincial government can overturn this protective legislation in individual instances if a land developer makes a strong case in favour of building on a particular parcel of land. Planners have seldom been able to withstand pressures to expand the city outward.

Cities and Traffic

The widespread sprawl of the modern western city has been made possible by the automobile. The automobile has also helped to segregate the city into zones. Many people reside in one zone, work in another, enjoy recreation in a third, shop in a fourth, and so on. Streets were once places where people could meet and talk, but today they are dominated by traffic. However, this situation shows signs of changing. Traffic-free zones have been created in some cities, and restrictions on traffic have been imposed in certain residential areas.

Different cities have attempted to solve the traffic problem in different ways. In Los Angeles, California, the solution adopted was to build freeways to allow rapid movement by automobile from one part of the city to another. The result has been the expansion of the built-up area to its present enormous size. Nor is the solution particularly successful, as the famous Los Angeles traffic jams would suggest. Some other cities have invested heavily in public rather than private transport. The subways in Toronto and Montreal and the Sky Train in Vancouver are attempts to avoid the building of extra highways, which adds to, rather than solves, the problem of traffic congestion in the city centres.

Freeways in Los Angeles.

Urban Renewal

Many of the older cities in Europe and North America have had to face the problem of overcrowded inner residential areas. For example, a survey done in the 1950's in Glasgow, Scotland revealed that 750 000 people lived in an area of 10 km² surrounding the central business district. Only one house in five had a flush toilet, and very few had a bath. Most homes consisted of one or two rooms, with many people living at a density of three or more persons per room. New housing was urgently needed, but it was impossible to rehouse the existing numbers of people on the same land area.

These buildings are about to be demolished for urban renewal.

An example of the renewal of old tenement buildings. What features appear to have been added during this process?

Several strategies have been adopted for urban renewal. One is to build low-rent municipal housing on the margins of the city. This has been tried in Glasgow, and in many other cities, usually without much success. Many of the early housing developments were built without such social amenities as shops or recreational facilities. Crime and vandalism usually increased, with the result that the new developments of the 1950's have often become the slums of the 1980's.

Another strategy was to build **comprehensive development areas** in place of the old slums. It involved tearing down old buildings and constructing a completely planned urban unit, with housing (often high-rise to accommodate more people), shops, and social facilities. The success of this approach has varied from city to city, but all comprehensive redevelopment has proved to be very expensive. In addition, high-rise housing has also become unpopular in many cities, since people find that vertical living has the effect of isolating them from their neighbours.

More recently, a third approach has been adopted with some success, especially in European cities. Instead of tearing down old buildings, developers are completely refurbishing them to modern standards to allow occupants to remain in familiar and comfortable surroundings. In Glasgow, the renovation of old buildings has been underway since the 1970's. Clean-air legislation has made the cleaning of stone and brick a worthwhile investment, and the visual appearance of the city has been transformed as a result. The Strathcona region of Vancouver is another example.

Planners have been looking more actively at ways of trying to rejuvenate the life of the inner city. They talk of **infill** (the development of vacant space in the city core) and **gentrification** (the buying up and refurbishing of formerly rundown areas, usually by young professional people who want to live near the centre of the city). Several districts of Toronto, Montreal, and New York City have become fashionable as a result of this trend (Figure 7.12). Most planners involved in recreating the inner city agree to some extent on the following points:

- More emphasis should be placed on public transit and on cycling paths and walkways, while the use of automobiles should be reduced.

- The separation of urban functions should be replaced, wherever possible, by an intermingling of activities. Businesses, professional offices, shops, and homes should all be located in certain small areas or neighbourhoods.

- Again where possible, streets and squares should be made into areas where people can meet and relax. Unfortunately, the climatic conditions prevailing for much of the year in many Canadian cities do not encourage this innovation. Nevertheless, in some parts of North America it is already being put into practice.

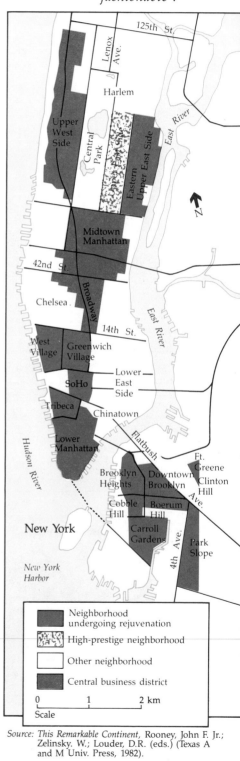

FIGURE 7.12 *Fashionable New Districts in New York. What factors might cause an area to become "fashionable"?*

Source: *This Remarkable Continent*, Rooney, John F. Jr.; Zelinsky. W.; Louder, D.R. (eds.) (Texas A and M Univ. Press, 1982).

CLOSE-UP

False Creek (South), Vancouver

Many cases of urban renewal schemes are much closer to home than Europe. An excellent example is the creation of a new residential community on the southern shore of False Creek in Vancouver, directly across from the site of EXPO 86. Early in Vancouver's history, False Creek was devoted to sawmills and port activities. After World War II, as trucking took over from rail transport, the industries around the Creek became less prosperous and, in some cases, run down.

In 1974, Vancouver City Council produced the first phase of a plan for the residential development of False Creek (South). The plan was based on several principles:

- medium-density housing with good areas of open space

- various forms of development, from ownership to rental, as well as cooperative housing and condominiums

- occupants with a wide range of incomes

- different types of households, including the elderly, mature couples, young families, and single persons

FIGURE 7.13 *False Creek Development. What factors made False Creek a desirable place for urban renewal?*

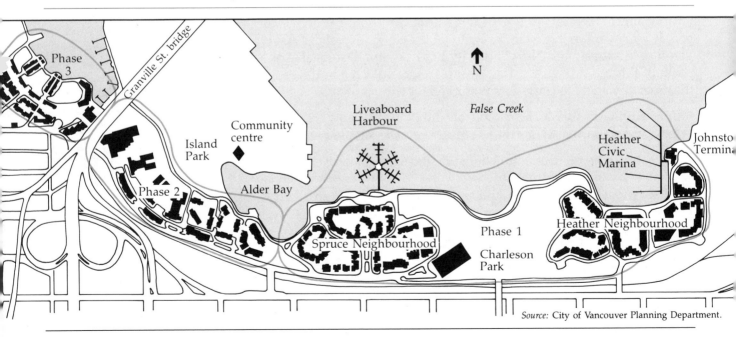

Source: City of Vancouver Planning Department.

False Creek is an example of a successful urban renewal project.

The intention was to make False Creek comparable to the pattern of the City of Vancouver overall. The plan was also designed to provide affordable housing close to downtown Vancouver, so that some people at least would not have to commute long distances from the suburbs.

False Creek is being built in three stages, as you can see from Figure 7.13. Provision was made for playgrounds, day care, and local shopping. A walking and cycling path on the shoreline was a prominent feature. The shoreline itself was redrawn to create bays and sites for marinas. The planned reduction of local industry improved the water quality to the point where swimming is now possible in several locations.

One problem has emerged, however. In the original plan, inadequate space was allocated for streets and car parking. There has been some concern about how safe it is for children to play in the streets, which the plan had originally encouraged.

Overall, False Creek is a fine example of urban renewal. It has clearly been helped by the natural advantages of its site, which faces downtown Vancouver and the mountains beyond. The waterfront location has proved attractive, and there has been little turnover of population. Indeed, residents have expressed high levels of satisfaction with False Creek as a place to live.

QUESTIONS

1. State two causes of inner city decay.

2. What is the difference between end-state planning and structure planning?

3. Make a list of some of the limitations faced by planners in trying to control the growth of cities.

4. What is a comprehensive redevelopment area? Why are such areas more expensive than the renovating of older properties?

5. List the similarities and differences in the urban renewal policies of Glasgow and Vancouver (False Creek).

6. What are some of the advantages and disadvantages of living in a community like False Creek?

7. What are two of the obstacles to large-scale urban renewal projects such as False Creek?

Social and Economic Contrasts in Cities

Contrast the lifestyles suggested by this picture with the picture on page 239.

One of the most important aspects of life in cities today lies in the sharp contrasts in living standards to be found there. In Chapter 3 you examined the concept of living standards, and looked at contrasts on a global scale. There are also contrasts within countries, making necessary the kind of regional policies seen in Chapter 6. To complete the picture, the contrasts within Canadian cities should be examined, even

though the extremes of wealth and poverty here are not as great as in Mexico City.

The data for Canadian cities are available from the national census. All large cities are divided into census tracts, each consisting of an average of 5000 to 6000 people. The census tract, as you read earlier, is the basic unit for which census information is published. Each census tract is made up of perhaps twenty **enumeration districts.** Each district consists of a group of households for which one census enumerator is responsible at the time of the census.

The following are some possible indicators of living standards which can easily be obtained from census tract data:

- density of population per square kilometre

- number of persons per room (over 1.5 is regarded as crowded)

- number of houses in need of major repairs

- proportion of persons with less than grade 9 schooling

- proportion of single person households

- average market value of housing

- unemployment rate

- proportion in managerial and scientific occupations

- average income of families

- proportion of low-income families

Many elements, including these, work together to form the overall picture of urban living standards. Three maps of Vancouver were presented earlier (Figures 7.7–9). Two more are added here. They show levels of education (Figure 7.14) and the proportion of people who hold managerial or scientific jobs (Figure 7.15). Table 7.5 provides selected statistical information for four specially chosen census tracts in the urban area. Information like this throws light on contrasts in social conditions within cities. In Vancouver's case, the contrasts are certainly not as great as those seen in many Third World cities. Nevertheless there is a clear east-west divide, with higher income groups located mainly west of Cambie Street, and again north of the Burrard Inlet.

FIGURE 7.14 *Education Levels in Vancouver (1981).*

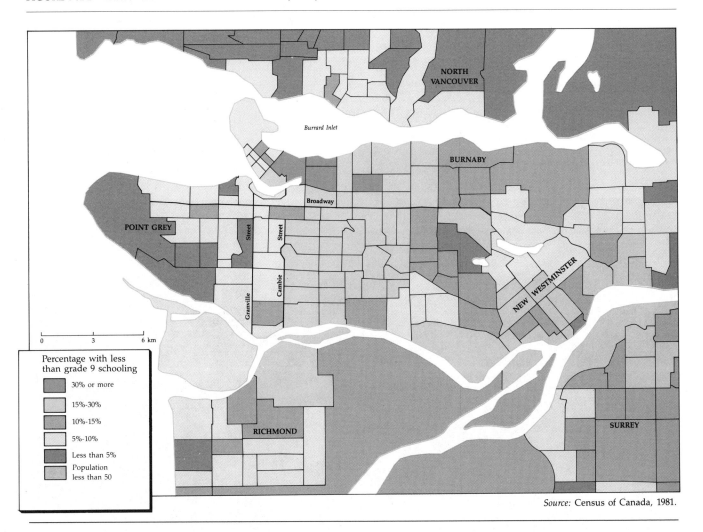

Source: Census of Canada, 1981.

TABLE 7.5 *Data for Four Census Tracts. Use the figures in this table to compare the standard of living in Vancouver's West End with Burnaby, and that of East Vancouver with Marine Drive.*

	West End	East Van.	Burnaby	Marine Drive(s)
Census tract	065	050.01	052.01	007
Population density (per km²)	24 839	4 287	3 702	1 704
Rooms per dwelling	2.8	3.2	5.4	7.1
Av. value of dwelling ($000)	119	92	136	310
Median family income ($)	17 782	18 799	21 437	42 823
Low income families %	19.4	22.6	25.5	5.5
Single parent families %	15.1	19.6	17.4	10.1
% in managerial jobs (males)	11.3	9.2	3.5	25.8
% in construction trades (males)	7.0	9.2	14.3	5.4

Source: Census of Canada, 1981.

FIGURE 7.15 *High Status Jobs in Vancouver (1981). How does this map relate to Figure 7.14?*

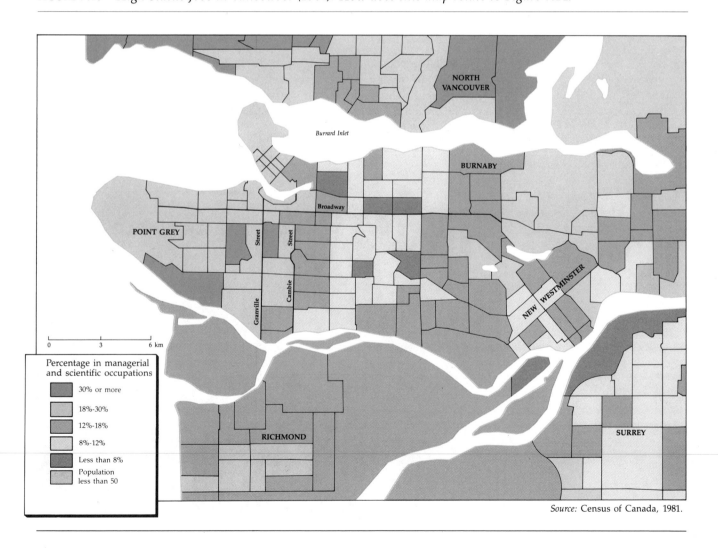

Source: Census of Canada, 1981.

One problem remains to be considered. If most social indicators have similar patterns, which ones should be given priority treatment as a cure for urban ills? You have seen that multi-million dollar housing schemes are not necessarily a cure, and can create new slums out of old. The residents of rundown urban areas need not only extra resources, but also employment opportunities, and perhaps a better image of their own part of the city. How to achieve these goals is one of the greatest problems facing those who design and manage cities.

QUESTIONS

1. What is a census tract?

2. Name two indicators of urban living standards which have to do with housing facilities, and two which have to do with social and economic characteristics of people.

3. How does the distribution of people holding managerial or scientific jobs (Figure 7.15) relate to education levels (Figure 7.14) in Vancouver?

4. Match each of the census tracts in Table 7.5 with one of the following:
   (a) high-quality suburban residential area
   (b) apartment-dominated inner urban residential area
   (c) mixed industrial/residential district
   (d) older middle-class suburb

The availability of a variety of entertainment is one reason why people choose to live in urban centres.

Living in Cities

While people may often indulge in criticism of cities, they should never lose sight of the fact that by choice human beings are increasingly a race of urban dwellers. This is clearly true for the world as a whole. But even those North Americans who escape to the outer suburbs or beyond are still, in essence, urban. The reason is that the city is not only a place to live, but also a state of mind not easily abandoned the moment one crosses a city boundary.

Perhaps no one is in total agreement about what makes urban life so attractive. However, most historic events and political movements have originated in cities. Works of literature have been written, great music composed, and fortunes made—and lost—in cities. All this is because cities are centres of ideas and information. It is therefore not surprising that their residents are prepared to put up with many of their faults in order to share in the benefits and excitement of urban living.

How People See Their Community

Not all citizens share equally in the benefits of urban life. Many find the city a place of solitude and fear. The point was made earlier that cities can be places in which people feel alone, even when surrounded by other people. This is usually the experience of those without a

How people view their community can be influenced by their personal experiences.

network of relatives or friends. Human beings are by nature social creatures, and people's feelings about a place generally depend on how well they are integrated into its social structure.

This is where the concept of **neighbourhood** comes in. By this is meant the area around a person's home, where friends or at least acquaintances live. Psychologists have done research into how people perceive their neighbourhoods, using the "mental map" technique. They have concluded that a person's image of a city is important both for using the city's facilities and also for emotional well-being. In some cities, such as Dallas, Texas, and San Francisco, California, residents' mental images of the city are actually used in designing new developments.

Figure 7.16 shows how one resident of Northridge, a northern suburb of Los Angeles, views the entire city. Local features loom large in his mental map, while more distant features receive little attention. Even Disneyland—probably on *your* mental map of greater Los Angeles—does not get a mention.

FIGURE 7.16   *Mental Map of Los Angeles. (The legend indicates the relative significance of various factors of Los Angeles to a suburban resident: the greater the significance, the thicker the line.) Name two factors that might have determined the image of the person who drew this map.*

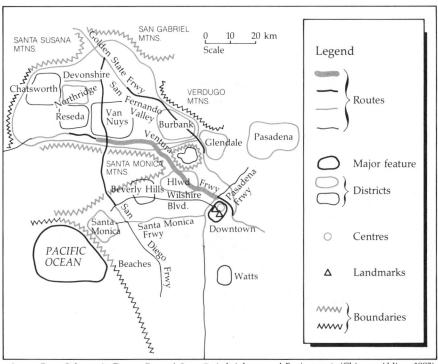

Source: Peter Orleans, in Downs R., and Stea, D. (eds.) *Image and Environment*, (Chicago, Aldine, 1983).

Another, rather novel, way of mapping a city is illustrated by Figure 7.17, the "Map of Fear" in New York. This map was compiled by asking New Yorkers in general which areas of the city they would feel least secure in. Harlem comes out on top of the "fear scale", with the Bronx and the Lower East Side coming in second together. The Map of Fear reflects a mainly suburban perception of some of New York's under-privileged areas. It is quite possible, of course, that some residents of Harlem might feel equally insecure in parts of the outer suburbs, away from their normal social contacts.

FIGURE 7.17   *Fear in New York. (The darker the shading, the more widespread the fear among New Yorkers of that particular part of town. The numbered locations list, in ranked order, the 20 most feared neighbourhoods in the city.) What conclusions can you draw about life in New York City, based on the information on this map?*

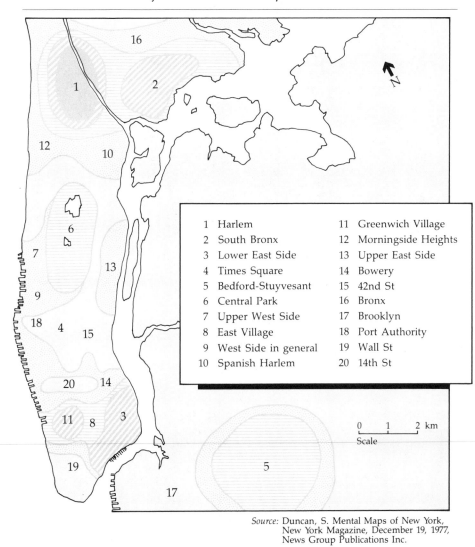

1 Harlem	11 Greenwich Village
2 South Bronx	12 Morningside Heights
3 Lower East Side	13 Upper East Side
4 Times Square	14 Bowery
5 Bedford-Stuyvesant	15 42nd St
6 Central Park	16 Bronx
7 Upper West Side	17 Brooklyn
8 East Village	18 Port Authority
9 West Side in general	19 Wall St
10 Spanish Harlem	20 14th St

Source: Duncan, S. Mental Maps of New York, New York Magazine, December 19, 1977, News Group Publications Inc.

The Cities of Canada—A CMHC Study

In 1979 the Canada Mortgage and Housing Corporation (CMHC), the largest issuer of mortgages for housing in Canada, launched a project to find out how satisfied Canadians were with their own cities. The cities surveyed were the 23 Census Metropolitan Areas of Canada, with Charlottetown substituted for Oshawa to provide a better provincial balance.

Several hundred respondents in each city, drawn from inner zones as well as from various parts of the suburbs, were asked to rate 17 aspects of their city. These included physical appearance, cultural facilities, levels of education, public transport, economic conditions, medical facilities, crime levels, and the natural environment.

TABLE 7.6 *Satisfaction Index—Canada's Cities. Based on these figures, do you think the crime rate affects people's sense of satisfaction with their city?*

	Satisfaction with city	Crime index
Calgary	14	4
Charlottetown	7	23 (best)
Chicoutimi-Jonquiere	13	22
Edmonton	17	2
Halifax	10	3
Hamilton	19	5
Kitchener	6	18
London	4	12
Montreal	20	6
Ottawa-Hull	3	14
Quebec	8	13
Regina	22	1 (worst)
Saint John	23 (worst)	10
Saskatoon	5	7
St. Catharines	2	20
St. John's	12	21
Sudbury	18	17
Thunder Bay	15	9
Toronto	9	19
Vancouver	11	8
Victoria	1 (best)	16
Windsor	21	15
Winnipeg	16	11

Source: Canada Mortgage and Housing Corporation.

TABLE 7.7   *Problems of Canada's Cities. Identify the features which give you a favourable or unfavourable impression of cities.*

Indicators	Cities mentioned	
	Favourably	Unfavourably
Natural environment	Victoria, Vancouver	
Social environment	Saint John, Saskatoon	Regina, Toronto
Cultural facilities	Montreal, Toronto	Thunder Bay, Saint John
Parks & recreation	London, Ottawa	Hamilton, Windsor
Pollution	Kitchener, London	Hamilton, Saint John
Traffic problems		Calgary, Edmonton
Public transport	Montreal, Toronto	Vancouver, Saint John
Crime	Charlottetown, St. John's	Regina, Edmonton

Source: Canada Mortgage and Housing Corporation.

Four indices were calculated on the basis of different combinations of the 17 aspects about which information was collected. Samples of the results appear in Tables 7.6 and 7.7. Some, though not all, of the results are fairly predictable; others may come as a surprise. It is one thing to form ideas about what a city is like, and quite another thing to live there. An encouraging feature of the study was the fact that even in the case of the city with the lowest score on the satisfaction index, over 60 percent of those surveyed were more satisfied than dissatisfied with life there.

QUESTIONS

1. Give examples to show that cities are centres of ideas and information.

2. What evidence is there that the person who drew the mental map of Los Angeles (Figure 7.16) lives in the northwestern suburbs of the city?

3. List Canada's cities in your order of preference, and compare the results with the Satisfaction Index (Table 7.6).

Chapter Summary

Technology, particularly in the fields of transportation and communications, has helped to shape the cities of the western world. People flocked to urban centres from the time of the Industrial Revolution onwards. Today the trend is mainly outward, though a small proportion of urban dwellers are moving in toward the city centres.

In the Third World, cities continue to have attractions for people living in rural poverty. The rapidity of urbanization in developing nations is a source of many complex problems, including a housing shortage and a lack of employment.

As the final section of this chapter suggests, all of us have a subjective view of our own community, whether small and rural or large and urban. Experience shows that in spite of the problems of cities, which are numerous, most people prefer some form of urban living.

IN REVIEW

1. (a) What is "urban renewal?"
   (b) Describe three strategies for urban renewal.

2. (a) What is decentralization?
   (b) Why has it become a trend in American cities?
   (c) Why is it less common in Canada?

3. Why is urbanization increasing in the Third World?

4. (a) Explain the term "decentalization".
   (b) What factors contribute to this trend?

5. (a) How does land use in a city reflect the city's economic base?
   (b) What is the role of the urban planner in assuring effective use of land?

6. Describe the effects of widespread automobile ownership on North American cities.

APPLYING YOUR KNOWLEDGE

1. (a) What factors have led to rural-urban migration in this century?
   (b) What are the effects of this migration on rural areas?

2. If you live in a town or city, draw a simplified map of its commercial, industrial, and residential zones. Do they form a pattern? If so, can you explain the pattern?

3. How can census data help city planners set priorities for such services as publicly funded transportation and housing?

FURTHER INVESTIGATION

1. Visit or write your city or municipality planning office. Determine what future development or redevelopment is planned in your neighbourhood. What public involvement will there be in this process?

2. Determine which part of your town or city has the greatest population density. Which area has the greatest growth potential?

3. Do a survey of the students in Grade 11 at your school to determine their shopping patterns. Do they use neighbourhood, district, or regional centres? What factors influence their decision?

CHAPTER 8

Global Solutions

This book began by looking at Marshall McLuhan's idea of the global village. It was argued that the world must be regarded as one interrelated system. This would imply that the solutions to world problems must also be considered on a global scale, whether the problems involve population growth, food supply, resources, or urban living. In this final chapter you will be examining the important theme of aid, and looking at some of the international agencies that try to solve social and economic problems throughout the world. International aid has played a major role in relieving the miseries caused by famine. Equally important are the efforts of such agencies as the World Health Organization in helping to eradicate—or contain—numerous diseases throughout the world. A less well-known problem is the financial crisis which has placed enormous burdens of debt on many Third World nations. In all of these areas, efforts are being made, on both a large and a small scale, to help the world's less developed nations improve their economies and quality of life.

- *What are the benefits—and problems—of food aid?*
- *What progress is being made in eradicating the major diseases of the Third World?*
- *Why has the Third World been hit by an acute financial crisis?*
- *Why is international aid so necessary?*
- *What is Canada's role in international aid?*

International Aid

The foremost international agency is the United Nations. Since its founding in 1945 the UN has been concerned with human rights and the welfare of less developed countries. The UN has individual branches dealing specifically with agriculture, health, and education.

To the work of the UN are added the efforts of individual governments working through their various agencies. A Canadian example is the **Canadian International Development Agency (CIDA)**, which is funded by the federal government. Finally, there are numerous private relief agencies, sometimes called **non-governmental organizations** (NGO's), committed to lightening the burden of human misery throughout the world.

There are at least three forms of international aid. Aid is described as **multilateral** when various governments contribute to a joint organization, such as the World Food Program (WFP) or the World Bank, which then administers the aid program. This form of assistance is not to be confused with **bilateral aid,** in which one government gives aid directly to another. Finally, there is **non-governmental aid,** raised mainly by relief organizations such as OXFAM. This type of aid may be distributed by the agencies themselves, or may be fed into multilateral programs.

Food Aid

Food Agencies of the United Nations

One of the main branches of the UN, also founded in 1945, is the Food and Agriculture Organization, which has its headquarters in Rome, Italy. The FAO is charged with developing all aspects of agriculture throughout the world, including the production, processing, distribution, and marketing of food. Another UN food agency is the World Food Program. Its work is coordinating all kinds of food aid. A third agency, the World Food Council (WFC), is a smaller body, set up as a

Why is it necessary for the United Nations to provide food aid for Third World countries?

FIGURE 8.1 *Structure of the United Nations. This shows how the organization responds to the needs of hungry people.*

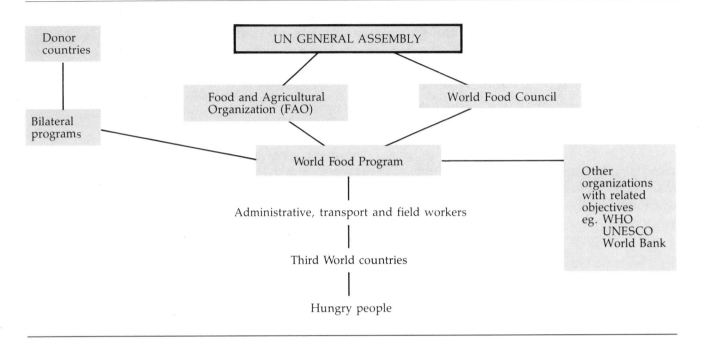

kind of "think-tank" in 1974. A simplified plan of UN organizations relating to food and agriculture is shown in Figure 8.1.

Long-term Development Aid *vs*. Short-term Food Aid

You saw in Chapter 4 that media coverage given to the African famine in 1984–1985 led to a sharp increase in emergency food aid to the countries affected, especially Ethiopia. There is, however, a great deal of misunderstanding and controversy over food aid, as distinct from long-term development aid. On the one hand, large surpluses of grain, milk, and butter exist in western Europe, and particularly in North America. On the other hand, at least one-quarter of the world is suffering from malnutrition. It would appear to be a simple matter of matching western surpluses to Third World needs. This is far from being the case. Simple food handouts can have various adverse long-term effects. Clearly, they can damage the regular trade in farm products throughout the world. Perhaps less obviously, they can also harm the very people they are intended to help. Consider the following quotation from the 1982 OXFAM publication *Against the Grain*:

> "The Third World is seen as a vast refugee camp with hungry people lining up for food from the global food aid soup kitchen. This view is

false. Some disasters aside (and these *are* important areas for food aid) the basic problem is not one of food, but poverty. Free handouts of food do not address this problem, they aggravate it."

It must be emphasized that this quotation does not criticize the giving of food aid in emergency situations where people are in immediate danger of starving to death. Food aid is vital in these cases. In addition, this view of food aid refers only to handouts of free food, not to long-term sales of food at subsidized prices from one government to another.

Giving emergency food aid to people who are starving is a humanitarian act with which everyone can agree. However, it does not solve the problem of why they are starving, nor will it prevent famine from occurring again. The poverty which produces famine is deep-rooted. Usually, changes in an entire way of life, including traditional farming methods, are necessary before the problem of famine can be resolved.

Why are long-term development plans, such as improved farming methods, so important in solving the problem of hunger?

For this reason, many relief agencies now view food aid handouts as a strategy for short-term emergencies, rather than as a means of achieving their long-term objectives: raising food output and standards of living in poor countries. It must be emphasized that food aid does not have to be an alternative to development aid. Both can be given simultaneously. Nevertheless, some agencies expressed concern that the Ethiopian emergency had the effect of diverting public support away from long-term development towards short-term food aid. Some African governments also began to express concern about their increasing dependence on food aid. In the words of Thomas Sankara, the late president of Burkina Faso, "I swear that contrary to appearances a little of us dies with each grain of millet we receive." Food aid has the unfortunate effect of encouraging people in developing countries to become dependent upon grain from western donor countries, rather than upon foods which can be grown locally.

Non-emergency food aid projects also have certain problems. If they cut the consumption of local food by reducing the number of buyers for it, prices might fall. This would discourage local farmers from growing food for sale. Most food agencies recognize this, and therefore attempt to give food aid on the "additionality principle". This means that food should be given only to those who are unable to purchase it in the ordinary way, so local food production is not interfered with. Unfortunately, this principle is hard to put into practice. Targetting those in the greatest need is difficult. Thus, food aid is frequently consumed by those whose needs are less. Indeed, it is estimated that three-quarters of regular bilateral food aid is sold commercially in the receiving countries, often without touching those in greatest need.

It may be hard to acknowledge that there can be any drawbacks to food aid, but Third World countries are increasingly trying to achieve long-term food self-sufficiency. The value of long-term aid is that it can help to increase the agricultural output and overall standard of living in Third World countries. Some methods of achieving these goals are

How can forestry management (left) and domestic water programs (right) improve a community's standard of living?

better soil management, reforestation, irrigation, and domestic water supply and sanitation programs. As well as helping agriculture, aid can also lead to marked improvements in the health of people in less developed countries. This is a most important area to which world aid can be directed, and one which you will be examining later in this chapter. The simple fact is that healthy people are better able to produce their own food supply.

QUESTIONS

1. What is the responsibility of the FAO?

2. What is bilateral aid?

3. Under what circumstances is food aid vital?

4. What negative effects can be caused by non-emergency food aid?

5. Give examples of long-term development aid.

6. How can improved health increase food supply?

"Grassroots" Aid

In many instances, aid channelled through governments operates on the "trickle down" process. Much of this aid is diverted into urban projects before it can reach the lowest levels of society, where the need is greatest. Various forms of aid therefore try to deal directly with projects at the community level. This "grassroots" approach is increasingly popular with non-governmental organizations. One particularly effective organization, which delivers its aid in the form of information about farming techniques, is the Developing Countries Farm Radio Network (DCFRN).

The Developing Countries Farm Radio Network

Radio has been used for many years to spread information about farming techniques in the less developed world. However, in 1975, while on assignment in Africa, CBC Senior Farm Commentator George Atkins noted that much of this information was not relevant to most of the farmers for whom it was intended. As a result, in 1979 the Developing Countries Farm Radio Network was established under the sponsorship of Massey-Ferguson Limited (now Varity Corporation). In 1980, Ontario's University of Guelph added its sponsorship, and CIDA contributed funds. Today, the DCFRN has an estimated radio audience of over 100 million in more than 100 countries.

The purpose of the DCFRN is to spread simple, low-cost techniques, designed to improve food supplies, nutrition, and health, from one part of the less developed world to another. Local broadcasters receive items in script form in English, French, or Spanish. They interpret this information in the local language for the farmers they serve. The broadcasters are also required to fill in feedback forms, and are invited to share farming techniques which have been proved successful locally. Topics are wide ranging. Here are some examples of program titles: "Growing disease-free seed", "Nitrogen fertilizer that doesn't cost any money", "Gully erosion—How gullies form, and their prevention".

The following is an extract from a DCFRN program entitled "Two Basic Needs of Cattle":

> GEORGE ATKINS: Everybody knows that people and animals must have water to drink. You know that people must have clean water—but have you ever thought much about the water your animals and poultry drink?
>
> In Islamabad, in Pakistan, I talked with the Assistant Animal Husbandry Commissioner, Dr Muhammad Zafarullah. Here's what he tells his farmers about water for their cattle.
>
> ZAFARULLAH: If there is fresh water available to them all the time, not dirty water but clean water, then they will give greater production; even up to 50 percent increase can be obtained.
>
> ATKINS: So, if you have a cow and it doesn't get enough water, or the water is bad and it gives only two litres of milk a day, that same cow can give you three litres if there's good water for her to drink whenever she wants it.

Why would the DCFRN appeal to farmers who, like this Egyptian, follow traditional farming methods?

There's another thing they should have too—and that is salt. They don't need much, but they need it. There may be a natural salty spot in the ground nearby that your animals lick—if not you should get salt for them...

ZAFARULLAH: You can bring the bucket of salt water and put it before the animals so once in a while they can come and take it as they like. It should be left up to the animals—they will take as much as is needed by them.

ATKINS: You see, he said "needed by them". Your animals do need a little salt, whether it's salt water, a natural place in the ground where they lick, or salt you get for them in some other way. They will do much better for you if you make sure that they have salt when they want it. However, don't expect them to drink salt water instead of fresh water, because that will make them sick.

We've been talking about two things your animals must have, good clean water and some salt.

All radio scripts are carefully written to convey the complete message via the spoken word. In most cases, this information reaches the broadcasters in their second language, in which many are less than fluent. Graphics are therefore included where appropriate to help them translate the scripts into the farmers' local

FIGURE 8.2 *New Uses for Old Tires (DCFRN). Why are old tires and tubes so valuable to the Third World farmer?*

USES FOR OLD TIRES AND INNER TUBES

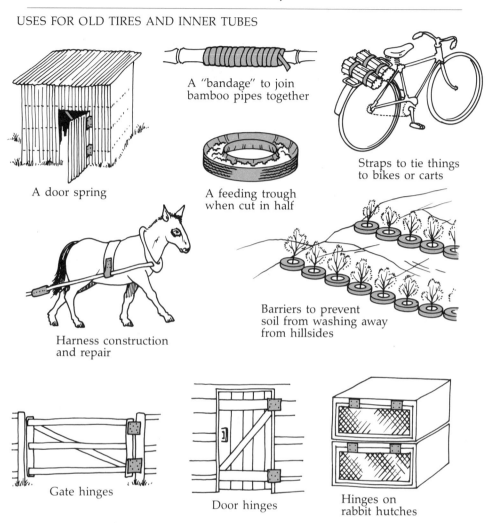

A door spring

A "bandage" to join bamboo pipes together

Straps to tie things to bikes or carts

A feeding trough when cut in half

Barriers to prevent soil from washing away from hillsides

Harness construction and repair

Gate hinges

Door hinges

Hinges on rabbit hutches

Source: Developing Countries Farm Radio Network

language or dialect. Figure 8.2 gives an example of down-to-earth advice from the DCFRN on how to use old tires.

There are obvious differences in scale between the help offered by the DCFRN and major multilateral or bilateral aid projects. The DCFRN does not require expensive or highly technological resources. Nevertheless, it succeeds in encouraging people to work hard and use their own initiative in order to become self-sufficient. Above all, the DCFRN has established a network of personal relationships at the level of self-help.

QUESTIONS

1. What is grassroots aid?

2. Why do you think radio may be better as a way of spreading farm information than pamphlets and books might be?

3. Why do you think the DCFRN tends to avoid giving advice involving high-tech equipment?

4. Why do you think farmers are likely to adopt the methods of caring for cattle described on pages 255-256?

World Health

Health is clearly a very important aspect of any nation's standard of living. Yet few people in western countries have to cope with the array of diseases which affect the less developed world, especially the hot, wet tropics.

The World Health Organization (WHO)

The World Health Organization is a branch of the United Nations dedicated to improving the health of people throughout the world. Its headquarters are in Geneva, Switzerland. The WHO has achieved much success since its founding. People of different national or political backgrounds tend to lay aside their differences when it comes to health. Even in times of war, each side will often cease fighting to allow Red Cross stretcher bearers to attend to the wounded and dying. As mentioned earlier, the civil war in El Salvador was stopped for three days in 1985 to allow the children of the country to be immunized. Some health projects have therefore achieved a remarkably high level of cooperation throughout the world.

In 1974 the WHO, in cooperation with the UN Development Program and the World Bank, initiated a major attack on tropical diseases. The program was called Tropical Disease Research (TDR), and was directed against malaria, leprosy, bilharzia (schistosomiasis), sleeping sickness (trypanosomiasis), and river blindness (onchocerciasis). Doctors and researchers from many countries, with different languages and cultural backgrounds, are continuing to cooperate in order to find cures for all these diseases.

In the course of their work, the researchers found that in some instances technological progress has actually increased the incidence of tropical diseases. For example, the construction of dams and irrigation schemes has increased the number of water snails by providing ideal environments for them. These snails are an important factor in the spread of bilharzia. The fast-flowing water below dam spillways also

Acquired Immune Deficiency Syndrome (AIDS)

In Figure 2.1 the possibility of an increasing number of deaths from incurable disease was raised. This has become a reality with the rapid spread of AIDS (acquired immune deficiency syndrome). The AIDS virus destroys elements of the body's immune system, which is the normal means of protection against disease. The virus is spread mainly by sexual contact and drug use. The AIDS virus may lie dormant for a while, but will eventually lead to a series of severe and ultimately fatal infections. The likelihood of a woman infected by the virus passing it on to her unborn child is between 25 and 50 percent.

AIDS is most common in parts of Africa, but it has spread rapidly around the world. In New York and San Francisco it is the leading cause of early death among single men between the ages of 25 and 44. The treatment of AIDS costs enormous sums of money; in 1986, the average in-hospital treatment of an AIDS patient was $U.S. 40 000.

At the time of writing there was no known cure for AIDS. It is also obviously possible that other diseases, equally hard to cure, may attack the human race. Clearly, diseases such as AIDS will have a bearing on death rates and therefore on the trends of total population numbers in the future. (From an article by Jonathan Mann in World Health, November 1986)

forms ideal breeding grounds for the black flies which spread river blindness.

TDR has achieved a great deal since it was set up. New drugs such as mefloquine have been introduced into the fight against malaria. Vaccines are being developed which, it is hoped, will prove effective against malaria and leprosy. Another method of controlling disease is by attacking the vectors of a disease, such as the mosquito for malaria and the black fly for river blindness. Above all, TDR has shown that international cooperation is possible across the barriers of race, language, and politics.

Bilharzia

This section offers a detailed look at one of the tropical diseases which the TDR is battling—bilharzia, named after its discoverer, Theodore Bilharz. The disease affects over 200 million people throughout the tropical and subtropical world (Figure 8.3). Bilharzia is caused by parasites. These organisms develop in water snails, and enter the human body as people wash, fish, or swim in lakes or canals. You read above that dams are breeding areas for these snails. Irrigation, which is increasingly used in developing countries, also provides an ideal environment for them. As people go barefoot about their farming tasks, they often walk on land flooded by irrigation water. The parasites in the snails enter the body through the feet, and breed in or near the liver or bladder. They may puncture the bladder, causing blood to enter the urine. The eggs contained in the blood are then excreted, to start the cycle over again. People with this disease may suffer from damage to the liver or spleen. They are also listless and anaemic, and can easily fall prey to other infections which often cause death.

The four methods of attack used in the fight against bilharzia are illustrated in Figure 8.3. They are:

- environmental sanitation, the provision of drinking water and toilets

- health education, to change the habits of people and thus reduce the risk of infection

- water snail control by means of improved water control techniques and, where necessary, pesticides

- drugs which control the disease in humans

Many countries run school programs to test children for bilharzia infection. The tests have found infection rates of over 80 percent in places like the Nile Delta and the Philippines, where irrigation is widespread. Infection can be easily detected by filtering urine samples for eggs. The afflicted children are given tablets of drugs such as praziquantel. Most are cured after one or two treatments. Reinfection occurs easily, however, unless effective health education programs are

What role do human activities such as washing clothes in a local water supply play in the spread of bilharzia?

FIGURE 8.3 *Bilharzia: Its Causes and Cures. In what general areas is bilharzia still a health hazard? List ways shown in this diagram which suggest how bilharzia may be controlled.*

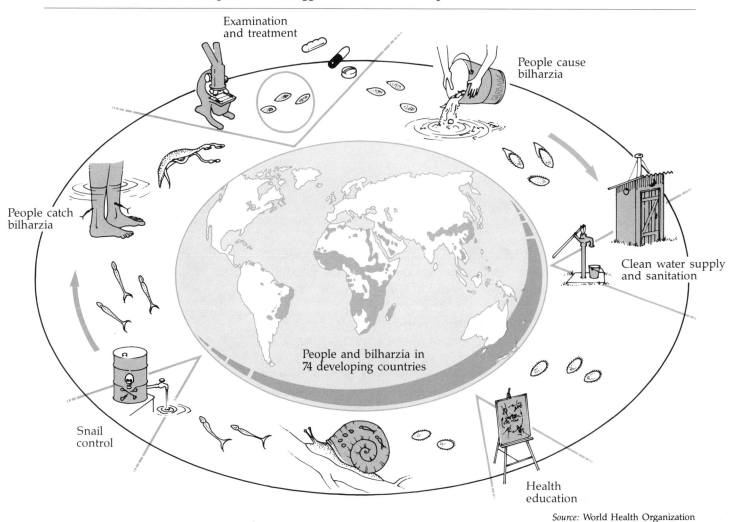

Examination and treatment

People cause bilharzia

People catch bilharzia

Clean water supply and sanitation

People and bilharzia in 74 developing countries

Snail control

Health education

Source: World Health Organization

introduced. Even more important is the provision of clean drinking water from wells, and the use of latrines, instead of ponds and rivers, for human excrement. These basic hygiene measures are preferable to killing water snails with pesticides. When chemicals are added to open water, other forms of life, including fish, are killed too.

Smallpox: A Complete Success Story

Smallpox is a very different kind of disease. It was carried by a virus rather than a parasite, and was not confined to tropical and sub-tropical regions, but was feared from the Arctic to Africa. Happily, smallpox now appears to be a thing of the past. No cases have been recorded since 1977.

At one time, smallpox was one of the scourges of the human race. Sudden epidemics could annihilate entire communities. The first inoculation against smallpox, invented by Dr. Edward Jenner in England in 1796, proved successful in reducing the spread of the disease. Systematic vaccination programs enabled the developed countries to become virtually free of smallpox early in this century. However, vaccination certificates were required for travellers until the 1970's.

From 1976 to 1977, the WHO spent $300 million (U.S.) to eradicate the disease in the parts of the world where it was still found. This is a relatively small sum, since the U.S. alone saves $500 million per year in not having to vaccinate foreign travellers. In 1977, a Global Commission for the Certification of Smallpox Eradication was formed to monitor areas with histories of smallpox. On May 8th, 1980, the WHO Assembly issued the following statement:

> "...the world and all its peoples have won freedom from smallpox, which was a most devastating disease sweeping in epidemic form through many countries since earliest times, leaving death, blindness and disfigurement in its wake and which only a decade ago was rampant in Africa, Asia and South America."

It was indeed a historic moment.

Water Supply and Sanitation

A story is told that an African woman was asked whether she understood the importance of having her children wash their hands after defecating, especially before eating. "I have to carry our water seven miles [11 km] every day," she replied. "If I caught anyone wasting water by washing his hands, I would kill him."

Why is sanitation a problem in many Third World communities?

How might the installation of this pump change the lives of the people who live in the community?

At least one-quarter of the world's population lack clean water and sanitation facilities. As you saw in the discussion of bilharzia, disease is much more easily transmitted when these facilities are lacking. The United Nations declared the 1980's to be the "UN International Drinking Water and Sanitation Decade"—not a glamorous priority, but immensely worthwhile in Third World development. Experts estimate that diarrhea could be cut by half, cholera cut by 90 percent, and all other tropical diseases significantly reduced, if clean drinking water could be made widely available.

Wells and latrines can be dug using relatively simple technology. However, care must be taken to ensure that the groundwater supply is not contaminated by the human waste from latrines. The World Bank has estimated a cost of $800 thousand million to install complete indoor water and sanitation systems throughout the less developed world. These systems would be much less luxurious than those in typical North American homes. Unfortunately, even though water and sanitation are vital to health and well-being, in less developed countries they are not always seen as such. Many areas do not yet have outdoor facilities such as latrines. Food, housing, and fuel are often seen as more urgent needs. Worldwide, the top priority for expenditure appears to be defence and weapons systems.

QUESTIONS

1. (a) How do people catch bilharzia?
   (b) How can dam construction lead to an increase in bilharzia?
   (c) Why do you think that it is so hard to control a disease such as bilharzia?

2. Which international disease has been eradicated by a program led by the WHO?

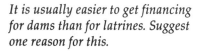

It is usually easier to get financing for dams than for latrines. Suggest one reason for this.

3. (a) List the tropical diseases mentioned in this chapter.
   (b) How does water help to spread certain of these diseases?

The Financial Crisis in Less Developed Nations

Famine and disease make dramatic television coverage, but there is another crisis taking place in less developed nations. This crisis is financial in nature. Since the 1960's these nations have been borrowing from the west to finance development projects such as dam construction and the building of roads and port facilities.

The rate of borrowing increased in the 1970's. Poor countries were hit even harder than rich countries by the twelve-fold increase in world oil prices in 1973–1980. Africa's foreign debt rose from $17 thousand million (U.S.) to $80 thousand million in the 1970's. By 1985, it was $100 thousand million.

Normally, borrowed money is paid back out of income over a period of time. Many less developed countries have found repayment difficult, for three main reasons. First, their population growth has been so rapid that their resources have been stretched to the limit. The provision of even basic services in health and education has quickly used up available funds. Second, you may recall from Chapter 5 that the prices of the commodities sold by less developed countries have dropped in comparison to the prices they must pay for necessary imports. For example, one tonne of exported coffee bought 37 t of imported fertilizer in 1960, but only 16 t in 1982. In 1960, one tonne of sugar bought 6.3 t of oil, while in 1982 it paid for only 0.7 t (Figure 8.4). The final factor making repayment difficult has to do with interest rates, which rose sharply in 1978–1982. Debts became more expensive to repay for all borrowers, but were an especially heavy burden for Third World nations.

FIGURE 8.4   *Unfavourable Terms of Trade. The graph shows the prices of non-oil commodities expressed in terms of what manufactured goods can be bought with them. Poor countries can buy much less with their commodity exports nowadays. Commodity prices in 1982 were lower, in terms of the goods they could pay for, than in any year since World War II.*

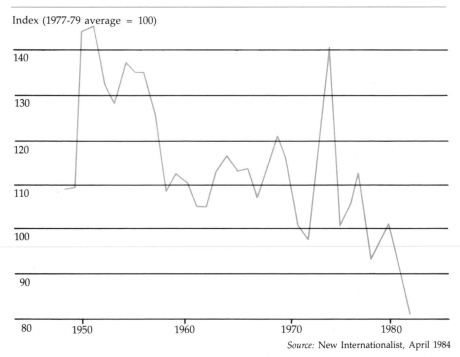

Index (1977-79 average = 100)

Source: New Internationalist, April 1984

Explain how Mexico, a major oil producing nation, can still be burdened with a high national debt.

Contrary to what you might expect, the debt problems of oil-producing Third World countries have been made worse, not better, by the falling oil prices of the 1980's. During the 1970's, loans were made to Mexico in the expectation that Mexico would repay the money out of the increasing income from its oil exports. But oil revenues have not been rising as expected. In August, 1982, Mexico announced that it could not make the repayments which were due on its international debts. Brazil and Argentina soon followed suit. The banks of western nations were obliged to extend the terms of the loan repayments to avoid a world financial crisis.

The problems of hunger and disease in the Third World are very much linked to its debt problems. For example, much land which could have been used for food has been diverted to the growing of cash crops for export, especially in Africa. You have seen that this is done to gain the necessary foreign exchange to pay interest on debts and buy imports. Nevertheless, there is a shortage of foreign exchange. Fuel, fertilizer, farm equipment, spare parts, drugs, medical supplies, and other essentials are therefore in short supply. Over time, the lack of these necessities causes transportation systems to deteriorate, food production to become less efficient, and health care to decline. These are just a few of the many ways in which the financial crisis has lowered the standard of living of people in poor countries.

The vast sums of money tied up in loans to the Third World continue to loom over the world's financial system. There may have to be further rescheduling of loans, as in the cases mentioned above. The same has been necessary in western countries, too, for large companies such as Dome Petroleum and Chrysler. Many debtor nations have, in fact, passed the point where they would have been declared bankrupt had they been private businesses. But in these countries millions of lives are at stake. Continued help to Third World nations is both desirable and inevitable.

QUESTIONS

1. What three reasons help to explain why less developed countries find it difficult to repay their external loans?

2. Cash crops are those agricultural products grown mainly for export. Why do the governments of most less developed countries encourage the growth of cash crops?

3. A shortage of foreign exchange for buying imports has caused problems for many Third World countries. What has caused the decline of foreign exchange within these nations?

4. Explain why broken-down vehicles and equipment are a greater problem in the Third World than in Canada.

How Necessary Is International Aid?

As you examined the circumstances in which food aid should be given, some questions may well have occurred to you. How necessary is any form of international aid? Would it not be better to rely on normal commercial trade to better the conditions of poor countries?

It is on the latter point that U.S. President Ronald Reagan spoke at a North-South summit conference held in the resort of Cancun, Mexico in 1981. He insisted that the "vigour of private enterprise" would provide the only solution to the world's ills, and urged nations to pull themselves up by their own bootstraps. The Prime Minister of India, Indira Gandhi, remarked that most people were fortunate if they had boots! Before trying to decide on the usefulness of aid, you should first look at some facts about amounts and conditions of aid.

Some Facts About Aid

Aid can be defined as the flow of resources from one country to another in the form of gifts or sales at lower than commercial prices. Total world aid in 1981 was $37.6 thousand million (U.S.), a tiny sum compared with the $900 thousand million spent on arms throughout the world. The sources of this aid are set out in the following table.

TABLE 8.1   *World Sources of Aid*

Source of Aid	Amount (in $ thousand millions)	Percentage of total
The West and Japan	25.6	68
OPEC countries	9.7	26
Centrally planned economies*	2.3	6

*Centrally planned economies are the U.S.S.R. and associated socialist states.
(SOURCE: World Bank Development Report, 1983)

The amount of aid given by different countries varies greatly. In 1981, the United States came first, with $7 thousand million. Canada came tenth, behind Kuwait and the United Arab Emirates. It does, however, make sense to measure a country's aid as a percentage of a country's gross national product instead of in absolute terms.

Over 20 years ago, Canada's Prime Minister, Lester Pearson, obtained agreement in the United Nations that western nations should set a target of 0.7 percent of GNP to be given in the form of aid. Less developed nations, not surprisingly, have campaigned for the higher figure of 1 percent of GNP. In the early 1980's, only the Scandinavian

FIGURE 8.5 *Donors of Aid. In what way is a chart like this misleading and unfair to nations such as Canada and Norway? Why is the percentage of GNP a fairer way of measuring aid than total dollar value?*

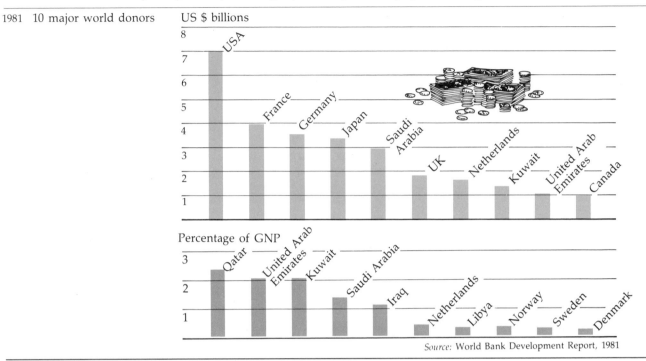

1981 10 major world donors

Source: World Bank Development Report, 1981

FIGURE 8.6 *Donors and Receivers of Aid. Make two generalizations about donors and recipients based on this map.*

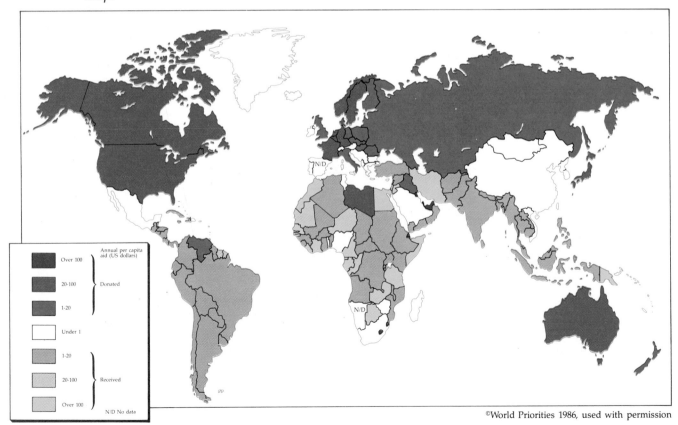

©World Priorities 1986, used with permission

countries, the Netherlands, and several OPEC countries (Qatar, the United Arab Emirates, Kuwait, Saudi Arabia, and Iraq) had attained the level of 1 percent of GNP (Figure 8.5). Canada's aid slipped since 1975 to stand at only 0.46 percent in 1985–1986. The U.S.S.R. comes last on the list, with 0.04 percent of GNP. All these figures exclude aid from non-governmental agencies.

In Figure 8.6 you can see how much has been donated and received by countries throughout the world on a dollars *per capita* basis. Note that these amounts are quite small. Aid given by Canada in 1985–1986 came to about $87 per Canadian.

Are There Strings Attached to Aid?

Aid is seldom given without some conditions being attached. Many countries insist that aid be used to buy goods from the donor country. About three-quarters of British aid is used to buy British goods— indeed, about 50 000 jobs in Britain depend on this aid spending. Canada's aid is increasingly tied to the purchase of Canadian goods and materials. In this sense, aid is "good business"; it helps domestic manufacturing industries.

Aid can also have political and cultural implications. It can be viewed as a means of gaining influence in a receiving nation, and eventually opening it to the export of goods from donor nations. Aid can help strengthen cultural ties, as when students from less developed countries attend western universities. Both this practice and the export of books and other educational materials to developing countries can create a kind of "cultural imperialism". That is, western nations or socialist states can transfer their views and values to less developed countries through these channels.

How have these women combined traditional skills with new skills to improve their community?

FIGURE 8.7   *From 1960-72, 3 000 000 skilled people emigrated from Third World to developed countries. 75% of them went to the U.S., the United Kingdom and Canada. This diagram is a comparison of the value they brought, with the aid given.*

Country

Total $50.9 billion

USA $33.9 billion

Canada $11.5 billion
UK $ 5.5 billion

Total $46.3 billion

$39.6 billion

$ 2.3 billion
$ 4.4 billion

Estimated value of skilled immigrant labour coming in . . .   Value of Development Aid going out . . .

Source: OECD

Who Gives Aid to Whom?

Aid is the transfer of resources from richer to poorer countries. But resources of various types flow in the other direction as well. Figure 8.7 suggests that the value of the skilled immigrants such as doctors, scientists, and engineers leaving poorer countries for the west may exceed the value of the aid going to these same countries.

A second and even larger flow of resources from less to more developed countries takes the form of profits made by multinational companies. Most of these are based in the west, with subsidiaries in less developed countries. It is true that multinationals have made large capital investments in less developed countries. However, the profits sent from the subsidiaries to the parent companies represent an out-flow of funds from developing nations which offsets the inflow of aid.

Multinational companies generally pursue legitimate commercial interests and keep within the law. But they have great power. They can switch operations between countries, playing off one nation against the other to obtain economic advantage. Multinationals can use several sources of raw material supply, so that they do not become too dependent on any one country. They also have enormous sums of money at their disposal, with bank credit several times larger than that of international banking agencies such as the World Bank. Indeed, the largest multinationals, Exxon and General Motors, each have sales greater than the entire GNP of Austria, Denmark, or Argentina. The role of multinationals can be positive. For example, silvicultural techniques developed in the west have been used to assist Brazilian reforestation. But multinationals tend to be secretive about their technology, for commercial reasons. Ways of encouraging more transfer of technology from richer to poorer countries must be found.

What, then, is the answer to the question which headed this section? Though it may surprise you, there is a net transfer of resources from poor to rich countries, despite international aid. Thus, the gap in living standards, already enormous, continues to widen.

The Need for International Aid

In deciding how necessary international aid really is, consider the following points. First, without aid, the net transfer of wealth from poorer to richer would proceed unchecked. Even now, for every $1 by which average incomes are raised in the less developed countries, the more developed nations are estimated to gain an average of $20.

Aid is also necessary on grounds of equity or fairness. You read in Chapter 5 that the Third World helps the west to maintain its affluent lifestyle by exporting cheap food and goods produced by low-cost labour. On the other side of the coin, the west has been able to pass on its rising labour costs by charging more for its exports of manufactured goods. The point has already been made that the developing nations

Given that current levels of foreign aid have not eliminated starvation, should western nations increase the amount they contribute to foreign aid?

need to export increasing amounts of goods just to maintain a constant level of imports. On these grounds a case can be made for aid in the name of justice.

A less obvious aspect of the situation is that appropriate types of aid help to make a less developed country less vulnerable to interference from a powerful one. Giving aid should therefore help increase the security of the world. Poverty often lurks behind revolution and terrorism. All nations gain by an improvement in the living standards of less developed countries.

We should not, however, think that aid is the only source of investment which less developed countries have. To put the matter in perspective, international aid accounts for only about 12 percent of all investment in these countries.

Aid always raises the question of motivation. Donor countries, as you have seen, often give aid for political or commercial reasons. Some individuals give aid because it makes them feel better. There is nothing wrong with this, so long as it does not lead the givers to think that their responsibility ends there. Such an attitude would be contrary to the idea of being global citizens. Aid should be the means of developing concern for fellow world citizens, not a substitute for it.

It has been claimed that the giving of aid has been too much in the direction of providing materials, whereas what poor people really suffer from is a lack of power. Most people in western nations have a great deal of power: spending power based on income; social power based on education, family, and friends; and legal and political power based on constitutional rights. If people are in need, an impressive array of social and welfare assistance is available. The world's poor lack most of these privileges. They lack spending power to buy the food they need, and bargaining power to obtain a reasonable price for what they produce. They do not have the social services which are taken for granted in western countries. In certain cases, they even lack legal and political power, having no constitutional rights.

Foreign aid does not reach everyone. These children must depend on their own skills to survive.

QUESTIONS

1. Refer to Figure 8.6. Which countries give more than $20 *per capita* in aid? Which give more than $100 *per capita*?

2. When an aid project includes the provision of equipment and machinery, CIDA encourages the receiving country to purchase Canadian-made goods. How does this practice make it easier for Canadian business people to be in favour of international aid?

3. Suggest three reasons why multinational companies are so powerful.

Canada and International Aid

The Canadian International Development Agency (CIDA)

Canada has a history of involvement in international aid, most of which is channelled through CIDA. This agency, which was created in 1968, had a budget of $2.2 thousand million in 1985–1986, and a field staff of 700 plus 300 support staff.

CIDA is equally involved in multilateral and bilateral aid (Figure 8.8). It also assists many non-governmental organizations, often by matching the amounts raised by these agencies. CIDA's largest single contribution is to the World Bank and other international financial institutions. However, new trends in CIDA's policies have resulted from the recession of the 1970's. First, public opinion has been moving CIDA away from multilateral aid and toward bilateral aid. In addition, the financial pressures on the Canadian government, which carries an enormous deficit, have led to a reduction in planned spending on international aid. There has also been an increase in the extent to which aid is tied to the purchase of Canadian goods.

As a result of these pressures, it is possible that CIDA could find itself more interested in directing aid toward the middle-income Third World countries rather than toward the LLDC's, where the need is greatest.

FIGURE 8.8   *Pie Graph of CIDA's Aid. What kinds of programs do you think Canadian aid should be directed towards?*

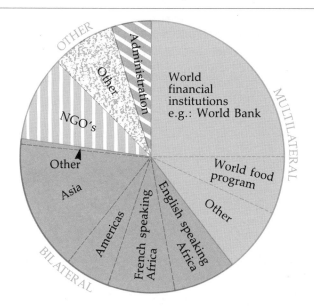

Total aid in 1985-86 = 2174 ($ million)
(0.46 of GNP)

Source: CIDA

The reason for such a policy change is that the relatively better-off Third World countries have more to offer Canada as commercial partners.

Some Examples of CIDA's Aid

Asian countries receive 41 percent of CIDA's bilateral aid. Bangladesh, one of Asia's poorest countries, receives the largest amount of CIDA aid. In 1984–1985 Bangladesh received $103.3 million, including $61.5 million in food aid. It now appears that Bangladesh is in fact approaching self-sufficiency in food supply. The remainder of the aid to Bangladesh goes to support rural development activities, such as storage facilities, fertilizer supply, and assistance to irrigation works and transportation networks.

Non-Governmental Aid in Canada

Much aid in Canada is raised privately by churches and charitable organizations of all kinds. Some of these donations are supplemented by grants from CIDA. One organization which has taken advantage of this scheme is Operation Eyesight Universal.

Changes to Bangladesh's transportation system are being supported by CIDA.

An Operation Eyesight Universal team in action.

Operation Eyesight Universal

This organization was founded in India in 1963 by a missionary surgeon, Dr. Ben Gullison. He inspired a group of Calgary businessmen to support the work of curing certain types of blindness. Tens of thousands of children go blind every year because of the lack of retinol (vitamin A) in their diet. An even greater number of people, including children, suffer from curable eye conditions such as trachoma and cataracts. Simple operations and the use of relatively inexpensive drugs can restore sight to many sufferers. OEU treated 1 203 372 people in 1985, not just in India but in 16 other countries as well. Sight was restored to 92 184 blind or nearly blind people. The photograph shows an Operation Eyesight team at work in India.

From an eye camp on the east coast of India, A.T. Jenkyns of Calgary, the past president of OEU, reports: "I saw a mother with a two-year-old who had just had a double cataract operation. He cried when a nurse took off the bandages. And he hollered blue murder when he was passed to the surgeon. The doctor flashed a penlight in his eyes, confirming that they were healing properly, and handed the boy back to his mother. Now he was quiet. Slowly he opened one eye, then the other, and *looked at his mother.* He *looked* at her."

OEU raises money from the public on the basis that $25 will restore sight to one individual. Each donor receives the name and location of an individual who has had sight restored because of the donation. Additional grants are provided by the federal government (CIDA), and the governments of Alberta and British Columbia.

QUESTIONS

1. What is the purpose of Operation Eyesight Universal?

2. What is the main cause of blindness in children in the Third World?

IN REVIEW

1. Why do you think OXFAM has suggested that food aid should be confined to emergency situations and be given for short periods only?

2. **(a)** Distinguish among multilateral, bilateral, and non-governmental aid.
   (b) What are the advantages and disadvantages of channelling aid through governments?

3. Explain how a fresh water supply and sanitation facilities can reduce the amount of disease in the Third World.

4. Do you consider that the disparities between rich and poor nations constitute a threat to world security? Give reasons for your answer.

5. From the information in this chapter, what are two other factors, apart from the net transfer of resources from poor to rich countries, that you think are helping to widen the gap in living standards?

6. President Reagan was quoted as saying that private enterprise (*i.e.*, the business world) would provide the solution to the world's ills. What problems might make businesses unlikely to invest in poor countries?

7. Why is proper sanitation a priority for the United Nations Development Program during the 1980's?

8. Why does the amount of money spent on aid tend to drop during recessions in western countries? Why is this drop harmful to less developed countries dependent on the export of minerals or on visits by tourists?

9. Why has the debt load of poor nations lowered the standard of living of the population of these countries?

APPLYING YOUR KNOWLEDGE

1. **(a)** In what ways do you think aid can be counterproductive?
   (b) Make a list of areas of need for which you think aid should be expanded.

2. What connection do you think exists between the control of serious tropical diseases and food production?

3. Do you agree that continued help, particularly to the poorest countries in the world, is both inevitable and desirable?

4. Many doctors, scientists, and engineers have emigrated from poorer to richer countries. If you were a doctor in a poor country, what do you think would be an important reason for staying? What sort of reason do you think you might have for leaving?

5. (a) Since 1975, Canada's aid has slipped from 0.7 percent to 0.46 percent of its GNP. Why do you think this happened?
   (b) If Canada increases aid to 1 percent of its GNP, what will be the effect on the average Canadian?

6. Canada's aid to poorer nations is increasingly tied to the purchase of Canadian goods and materials. Discuss the advantages and disadvantages of these restrictions from the perspective of
   (a) the aid receiver;
   (b) a Canadian business;
   (c) a Canadian politician.

FURTHER INVESTIGATION

1. In what sense can technology be both a part of the world's problems and a part of the solution to them?

2. The text states that what poor people really suffer from is a lack of power. Do research to discover to what extent this is true of the poor in Canada.

3. If your class decided to participate in an aid project, how would you determine which country or group would receive assistance? Which organization would best utilize your contributions?

4. What attitudes and actions can you adopt as a citizen, not only of Canada, but also of the world?

Conclusions

It is always easier to identify problems than to find workable solutions to them. Perhaps more human energy should be devoted to finding these solutions than to apportioning blame for the serious problems which exist around the world. Throughout this book, it has been suggested that there are some conditions to be met before successful solutions to social and economic problems may be formulated. It seems fitting to close with a summary of these conditions.

1. *Problems need to be defined clearly so that the limited resources available will not be directed to the wrong ends. A negative example is the large amounts of money spent on destroying shantytowns and constructing high-rises which failed to solve the problems of the cities.*

2. *Solutions must be examined to ensure that they do not lead to even greater problems. A negative example would be if the Green Revolution were to lead to a reduction in the world's plant gene pools, thereby restricting the breeding of new varieties in the future.*

3. *Where possible, solutions to problems should motivate individuals, as in China's recent agricultural reform. Yet millions of people throughout the world do not yet have a personal stake in what they labour at. Those who are liable to be exploited by others cannot be expected to work hard to raise their productivity.*

4. *Technology must be adapted to local circumstances, and where possible should use local materials and labour: "Think globally, act locally." Intermediate technology has been used in countless positive examples where production has been increased without the need to import expensive technology or oil.*

5. *People should realize that it requires political will to carry out reforms. Many governments may have to give up entrenched positions and change their priorities.*

6. *Personal knowledge and good will are essential. All people need to have an understanding of the great inequalities which exist in the world, and a desire to see them reduced.*

7. *Above all, global solutions require flexibility. Many of the formulas used in the past will not work in the more densely populated and interdependent world of the future. As the 21st century approaches, people will find many challenges to face. Humankind will have to adapt quickly to change in a rapidly changing world. Today's solutions will not necessarily solve tomorrow's problems.*

G L O S S A R Y

acid rain Rain which contains dilute acids, particularly sulfuric acid, as a result of emissions of sulfur dioxide and other gases from factory chimneys, power stations, and car exhausts.

aquaculture The fishing equivalent of agriculture.

additionality principle The giving of food only to those who are normally unable to purchase it, thus causing the minimum interference with demand for agricultural products.

age-specific death rate The number of deaths per thousand of total population in a specific age group.

A.I.D.S. (acquired immune deficiency syndrome) A disorder that breaks down the body's defences against disease.

appropriate technology The level of technology considered appropriate for a less developed country which has an abundance of labour but little capital to purchase and maintain expensive machinery; also referred to as *intermediate technology*.

arable land Land which is ploughed in order to grow crops.

automated Refers to mechanically controlled systems of manufacturing.

bid-rent graph A graph which represents the value of land to potential bidders at different distances from the centre of a city.

bilateral aid Aid given by one government to another.

bilharzia A tropical or sub-tropical disease in which parasites breed in the liver or spleen of humans. Their eggs are excreted, and the larvae spend the early part of their life cycles in the bodies of water snails, eventually entering the human body through the feet. Also known as *schistosomiasis*.

biotechnology Scientific efforts to improve plant and animal species.

birth rate The number of live births (i.e., excluding still-births) per thousand of total population in one year.

break-of-bulk point Point where goods are transferred from ship to train or the reverse (also called the trans-shipment point).

Canadian International Development Agency (CIDA) The agency through which most Canadian overseas aid is channelled. It is funded by, and is responsible to, the federal government through the Minister for External Relations.

capital goods Either manufactured goods that require further processing or the machinery used by factories to manufacture goods.

cash crop A crop grown for commercial sale.

census A national count of population, usually done every five or ten years.

census tract A division of a large Canadian city (or census metropolitan area) for which census data are collected and published.

central business district (CBD) The central zone of a city, recognized by its dependence on business activities, shopping, and entertainment facilities.

cohort An age group (or age-sex group) of a population, for example, females aged 25 to 29.

comprehensive development area An area, usually in an older part of a city, in which the previous buildings and other forms of land use are replaced by an entirely new plan.

computer-assisted design (CAD) The use of computers in technical processes, for example, the drawing of blueprints or the manufacture of engineered products.

consumer goods Either manufactured goods that require further processing or the machinery used by factories to manufacture goods.

culture The way of life of a group of people or a society, including their view of their environment.

death rate The number of deaths per thousand of total population in one year.

decentralization The tendency of people to move away from the centre of cities to the suburbs or to the surrounding rural areas.

demographic transition model A simplified version of the stages through which the birth and death rates (and therefore the rates of population growth) have passed in some countries, and through which they may come to pass in others.

demography The study of population trends, particularly births and deaths, population structure (by age and sex), and population growth.

Department of Regional Industrial Expansion (DRIE) A federal government department responsible for stimulating economic development in the less prosperous regions of Canada.

dependency ratio The number of people below 15 and above 65 years of age in a population, expressed as a percentage of those aged 15 to 64.

desertification The expansion of deserts as a result of mismanagement of the land, for example, overcropping or overgrazing.

district centre A medium-sized shopping centre serving a district within a city.

economic base The jobs performed within a city for a market elsewhere, which therefore bring money into the city.

economies of scale The reduction of the costs per unit of production which can be obtained when an article is produced in large numbers.

emigration   The process in which people leave a country (or other unit such as a province or city) to reside elsewhere.

end-state planning   Town or city planning in which the final details are planned from the start.

enumeration district   The area which can be covered by one census enumerator during a census.

European Economic Community (E.E.C.)   An association of western European nations formed to develop a unified economic policy. Members, as of 1987, are: Belgium, France, Italy, Luxembourg, The Netherlands, West Germany, The United Kingdom, The Irish Republic, Denmark, Greece, Spain and Portugal.

fertility   The rate at which a population reproduces.

fodder crop   A crop grown for consumption by animals.

foreign exchange   Money in the form of other currencies, required in order to buy goods or services from other countries.

fossil fuels   Carbon-based materials which have been stored by nature for millions of years, including coal, oil (also oil sands), and natural gas.

gene pool   The total number of genes within any group of plants or animals.

general fertility rate   The number of live births per thousand of women in the 15 to 44 age group in one year.

gentrification   The process by which formerly run-down urban areas are brought up and refurbished to become fashionable districts.

Green Revolution   The use of scientific plant breeding to achieve high-yielding varieties of crops, particularly in the Third World.

Gross National Product (GNP)   The sum total of the value of all goods and services produced in a country in one year.

groundwater   Water stored naturally in porous rocks and cracks in the ground, and useful for both domestic supply and irrigation. Groundwater accounts for about one-quarter of all the fresh water on Earth.

high-yielding varieties (HYV's)   Varieties of food crops produced by scientific plant breeding which yield considerably more than traditional varieties.

hybrid   The result of the crossing of different species of plants or animals.

immigration   The process in which people enter a country (or province or city) to take up residence.

indicator (of living standard)   An element of the standard of living which can be used to measure contrasts between societies: examples are the infant mortality rate, or the number of cars per thousand of population.

industrial crop   A crop such as cotton or tobacco which is processed to make a non-edible product.

industrial robot   A machine which performs repeated operations under electronic control.

infant mortality rate   The number of deaths of infants (under one year old) per thousand live births.

infill   The construction of buildings on vacant or empty sites within cities.

inflation   The rate at which money loses its value over time; or the rate at which prices for goods and services rise.

integrated circuits (ICs)   Miniature electrical circuits on "chips" of silicon; used in the micro-electronics industry for both performing calculations and storing data.

intermediate technology   See *appropriate technology.*

irrigation   The supplying of supplementary water to crops where precipitation is lacking or unreliable.

Just in time inventory control   Computer system developed to reduce warehouse cost.

kwashiorkor   A disease caused by severe lack of carbohydrates and proteins; often recognized in children by their bloated stomachs and wasted limbs.

labour intensive   Refers to jobs using a large amount of human labour and little capital investment.

land reform   The redistribution of landholdings, usually achieved by the takeover of large estates and their division into small units suitable for individual farmers.

landless labourer   A person who works on a farm but owns no land.

least developed countries (LLDCs)   A group of 36 countries within the less developed world, identified as least developed by a 1984 Report of the U.N.

less developed countries (LDCs)   All countries which have a high dependence on agriculture and a low *per capita* income.

life expectancy   The number of years a person may be expected to live, measured from birth.

literacy rate   The percentage of the adult population having at least a minimal ability to read and write.

malnutrition   Bad or poor nutrition, usually the result of a lack of carbohydrates or proteins.

marasmus   A severe form of malnutrition in which the victim looks like skin and bones; has a high fatality rate.

material technology   The use of new materials to accomplish traditional functions, for example, fiber optics.

mature industrial economies   Economies with an established industrial base; for example, the economies of North American and Western European nations, Australia, and Japan.

migrant   A person who moves his/her place of permanent residence.

monsoons   A prevailing wind that seasonally reverses direction, responding to a change in air pressure caused by the heating and cooling of a large land mass.

mortality   The rate at which people within a society die.

multilateral aid   Aid given to less developed countries which is distributed by central organizations, for example, the World Food Program.

multinational company   A company which operates in more than one country.

neighbourhood   The immediate locality around a person's home; the area which is perceived to be familiar and friendly.

neighbourhood centre   A small shopping centre serving only a limited part of a residential zone within a town or city.

net migration   The number of immigrants to a country (or other unit of area) minus the number of emigrants.

Newly Industrialized Countries (NICs)   Countries which have experienced rapid industrialization since about 1970; for example, Brazil, Singapore, and the Republic of Korea.

non-government organization   An organization involved in aid-giving which is independent of government.

non-governmental aid Aid given by a non-government organization.

non-renewable resources Resources, such as ores and fossil fuels, which can be used only once.

nuclear fission The splitting of the nucleus of the uranium—235 atom.

nuclear fusion The joining together of atomic nuclei.

oral rehydration therapy The use of a solution of salts, sugar (or starch), and water which has been found very successful in treating the dehydration caused by diarrhea.

Organization of Petroleum Exporting Countries (OPEC) A group of 13 petroleum exporting countries which seek to act together to obtain the maximum advantage from exporting oil. (See Figure 5.2).

per capita income All income earned from the production of goods and services in a country divided by the population of that country.

physical quality of life index An index devised by economist Morris D. Morris to measure quality of life in different parts of the world. The index uses three indicators: life expectancy (from age 1), infant mortality, and literacy rate.

population density The number of people per unit of area.

population pyramid A diagram of the age-sex structure of a population, usually compiled by five-year age groups, with the youngest at the bottom.

poverty line An arbitrary income level, usually determined by the government, below which a family or individual may be considered poor.

primary The sector of the economy related to the production of materials from natural sources, for example, timber, fish, minerals, or farm products.

probable reserves The volume of minerals likely to be present, based on estimates by geologists.

protectionist Refers to measures designed to reduce the amount of imports into a country, mainly by means of tariffs and quotas.

proved reserves The volume of minerals, as indicated by drilling and other tests.

quarternary The sector of the economy related to research and development activities.

quota A limitation of the amount of a particular type of goods which may be imported into a country.

R & D (research and development) The efforts made or money spent by companies and governments to develop new products and technologies.

R/P ratio A measure of the lifespan of resources, found by dividing the known reserves by annual production; usually applied to oil and natural gas.

regional centre A large shopping centre or mall which attracts people from a wide area of a city.

regional policy The measures taken by a government to try to reduce the inequalities between richer and poorer regions of the country. Typical measures are tax concessions and subsidies.

renewable resources Resources, such as timber, fish, and the products of the soil, which have the capacity to continue to produce indefinitely, if properly managed.

Richter scale A logarithmic scale used to measure the intensity of an earthquake.

savanna A belt of tropical grassland lying between the equatorial forests and the hot deserts.

schistosomiasis See *bilharzia*.

secondary The sector of the economy related to the production of goods; based on manufacturing and construction.

shantytown An area of makeshift housing, usually found in Third World cities, and occupied by migrants.

sharecropper A farmer who pays for rented land by giving a portion of the crops grown on that land to the landowner.

strip mining The extraction of minerals from the surface rather than by means of shafts and tunnels.

structure planning A flexible town or city plan in which details can be filled in or modified in the light of events which take place during implementation.

subsistence farming A type of farming in which most of the produce is consumed by the farmer and his/her family.

sustained yield harvesting A system of production of renewable resources such that the volume of the product harvested does not exceed the amount replaced by natural growth. This principle is a stated objective of Canada's forest industries.

system A set of inter-related elements in which changes in any one element will affect the others; often applied to parts of the physical world, such as vegetation regions or river basins.

tariff A tax paid on imported goods, designed to raise the price of imports and thus protect goods produced within the country.

tax concessions A strategy often used by governments as part of regional policy to encourage companies to locate in less prosperous parts of countries.

tenant farmer A farmer who rents, rather than owns, land.

tertiary The sector of the economy which relates to the production of services rather than goods, including transport, trade, financial, professional, and government services.

total fertility rate The average number of children which a woman in a particular country has in her lifetime.

total population change The total change in population in a country (or other unit of area) in one year; the sum of natural increase (or decrease) and net migration.

trans-shipment point See break-of-bulk point.

urbanization The processes by which cities originate and expand.

vector The carrier of a disease, for example, the anopheles mosquito for malaria.

vital statistics The recording of births, marriages, and deaths on a continual basis.

zoning The designation of a part of a town or city by its government for one particular type of use, for example, residential or industrial.

INDEX